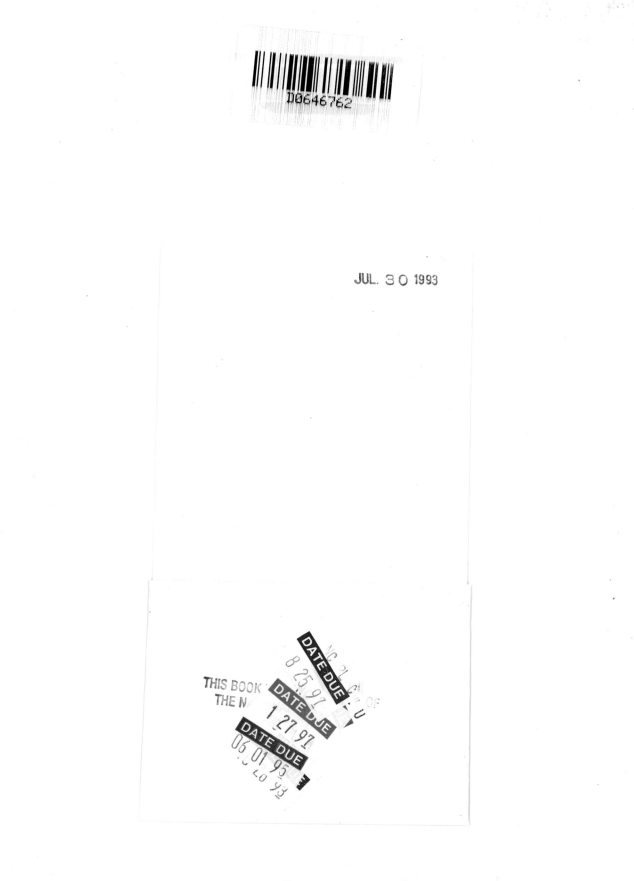

MARTY STOUFFER'S
WILD AMERICA

MARTY STOUFFER'S
WILD AMERICA

by
Marty Stouffer

Times
BOOKS

All photograph credits to be found on page 376.

Library of Congress Cataloging-in-Publication Data

Stouffer, Marty.
[Wild America]
Marty Stouffer's wild America / by Marty Stouffer.
p.   cm.
Includes index.
ISBN 0-8129-1610-7 : $24.95 (est.)
1. Zoology—North America.   I. Title.   II. Title: Wild America.
QL151.S76 1988
591.97—dc19

Interior Design by Robert Bull Design
Manufactured in the United States of America
98765432

ACKNOWLEDGMENTS

This book, the *Wild America* series, and indeed, the life of wonderful opportunities I have enjoyed thus far, would not have been possible without the help and support of a great many people along the way. Though it's impossible to mention them all by name, I would especially like to thank the following:

First of all, I owe a deep debt of gratitude to my family: my parents, Agnes and Martin Stouffer, who continue to be as supportive today as they were when I was growing up; my brothers, Mark and Marshall, veterans of many a filming expedition; my sister, Mari; my cousin Steve; my wife and helpmate, Diane; my daughter, Hannah, and though he's still too young to know how much it helps to have him around, my son, Luke.

Almost as close as family, and certainly as helpful in their own way, are my friends David Huie, Gred Konrad, and C. C. Lockwood.

As I've remarked elsewhere, I have a lot of help putting the *Wild America* programs together, and I'd like to take this opportunity to thank my staff: my assistant, Susan Johnson; editors John King and Cynthia Gamble; and writers Karen Chamberlain, Michele Brandt-Morton, and Paula Smith, each of whom helped with this book.

Special thanks also go to cinematographers Jim Balog, George and Kathy Dodge, Greg Hensley, Steve Kroshel, Steve Maslowski, Ken Middleham, Bruce Reitherman, Neil Rettig, and Earl and Nadine Senn; to veterinary consultants Dr. Greg Hayes and his wife, Becky; to film conformer Carl Hunsaker; to sound recordist Greg Simone; to composers Neil Argo, Patty Carlson, Peter Kater, and John Murtaugh; and to all the technicians at our film lab, Western Cine, and at our video facility, Wickerworks.

Most of all I'd like to thank the program managers at hundreds of PBS stations across America for giving me the opportunity to do something that I love so much.

I would also like to credit and thank Leitz Binoculars;

ACKNOWLEDGMENTS

Arriflex, Photosonics, and Leica Cameras; Moviola Editing Consoles; Eastman Kodak Film; Angenieux, Canon, Century, and Zeiss Lenses; Lowell Lights; Sennheiser Microphones; Nagra Recorders; Sachtler Tripods; Chevrolet Trucks; and Zero Haliburton Cases—none of which pay me to endorse their products.

To the many others who have helped, my sincere thanks. I hope you take as much pride as I do in what we have accomplished together.

CONTENTS

CONTENTS

MARTY STOUFFER'S
WILD AMERICA

*The "friends" I returned to find. Early snows in mid-October
caused this herd of bighorns to descend into the Swiftcurrent Valley
of Glacier National Park at the start of the rutting season.*

P R O L O G U E

I was returning to Glacier National Park to check up on some old friends.

A raw November wind chilled my face as I parked the truck off an out-of-the-way dirt road, loaded my backpack frame with camera gear, and began a mile-long hike into the secluded valley where I had last seen them. Cloven tracks in patches of wind-packed snow told me they might still be around, and I stopped often to scan the rocky slopes with my binoculars.

Sure enough, as I rounded a massive rocky outcrop, there they were, less than a quarter-mile away—the band of big-horns I had spent the better part of two years living with and getting to know. But the sheep I now spotted were mostly ewes, with a few yearling males. Where were the great rams, with their magnificent curling horns? November was the rut-ting season, and I had come back to Glacier on the slim chance that I might film the event that had obsessed and eluded me for years—the spectacular head-butting clashes of the Rocky Mountain bighorn.

I scanned the landscape, hearing for a few moments nothing but the wind. Suddenly, as if on cue, from the hillside above me came a single hollow crack that echoed over the valley, sounding as if two chunks of the mountain itself had been struck together. Looking up, I couldn't believe my eyes. Less than a hundred yards away, two superb rams were back-ing away from each other, preparing for another clash, as several other rams looked on. Crouching, using boulders for cover, I ran up and across the hillside and flattened myself against the ground within yards of them, knowing full well that my sudden presence might halt the whole contest. To my amazement, neither the battling rams nor the onlookers paid the slightest attention to me as I slipped off the pack to get at my camera, and then tried to steady it in my not-so-steady hands.

The two rams had backed away from each other to get a good running start, and as I began filming, each rose on his

Finally being able to film the clash of two bighorn rams was a dream come true. Ever since I was a child, I had hoped to see this dramatic moment in the wild. Bighorn rams butt heads with such explosive force, you'd think they would quit after the first clash. But their skulls and necks are uniquely constructed to absorb the strain of repeated blows.

hind legs and charged toward his rival, head up at first, then cocked down and to one side just before their heavy horns collided with tremendous power and force. Again a great hollow crack sent echoes ringing across the valley. Stunned by the impact, each ram froze for a moment on the spot where he had landed.

As they sized up each other's horns, I caught my breath. The months of patience, of living with the sheep and getting them accustomed to my presence, had finally paid off. Here I was with my elbows in the frozen alpine gravel, filming the event I had wanted to film for years. And yet it had come as such a complete surprise, I felt in a state of shock. As I looked up at the rams, puffs of vapor steamed from their nostrils as they prepared for another charge. Suddenly something else, something deeper, flashed through my memory.

I remembered being six years old, perched on the edge of my seat in a darkened movie theater, staring up from this same angle and this same distance, as two bighorn rams

*Changing film magazines on the Arriflex BL under blizzard
conditions became a matter of course while I was filming bighorn in
Montana's Glacier National Park.*

reared up and lunged toward each other on the screen in front
of me. The name of the film was Walt Disney's *Vanishing
Prairie*, and it had affected me powerfully at the time. Then,
the screen illusion was so strong that it didn't occur to me to
want to *film* those magnificent rams. Instead, I felt I *was* one

5

of them. Now, I realized that the effect of watching that scene so many years ago had been a driving force propelling me to this moment.

Lying there staring through the camera's eyepiece, smelling the musky odor of the rams and bracing my boots in traces of their manure, I realized that although I would never be a bighorn, this was the next best thing. Right here in front of me, almost close enough to touch, were truly wild animals engaged in one of the most impressive of all natural rituals. No movie screen, no smell of popcorn or crowded-together humans, nothing between me and them but a few feet of frosty mountain air.

There was no more time for reflection as the two rams reared up and began their next lunge. I pressed the camera button and lost myself in capturing their every move. But as I think about it today, those two scenes—the real one and the earlier one on the screen—seem to take on a polarity, as if all the vital currents of my life had flowed from one toward the other, from stimulating make-believe to accomplished reality. In between lies the story, not only of my life so far, but to a certain extent of Wild America itself, and the films I've made to reflect and share my love for our land and its wild creatures.

FROM ARKANSAS TO ALASKA

Most of my boyhood in Arkansas was spent
in the rural outdoors. Here I am at age nine bringing
a respectable-sized catfish home for dinner.

For as long as I can remember, wild animals have been an essential element of my life. My moments of greatest joy and satisfaction have come from being around them, and I've developed a special interest in those that make their home where I do, in North America. Like most people, I'm fascinated by any creature that lives in total independence from people, but I've always wanted to get closer, to understand what makes it truly "wild."

Careful observation is one way to do that. I love to watch the free natural grace and beauty of wild creatures, how a breeze ruffles their fur or feathers, how an eagle tilts its wings to catch an updraft or a falcon folds its wings to plummet, how a powerful cougar manages to stalk with such stealth, and how a delicate mule deer bounds away on legs like sprung steel. But beauty isn't everything. I also want to understand every aspect of wild behavior—what makes different creatures alert or afraid, relaxed or restless. What signals indicate the exact moment when a hidden cougar is about to spring, and how does a deer suddenly become aware of this before the cougar pounces? So I think that another way of getting close is to try to put myself inside an animal's head, to imagine how it feels and discover what makes it pay attention.

I remember trying to teach myself at an early age to use all my senses to think like a wild animal. And according to my mother, my fascination with wild creatures began even before that. She tells a story about me when I was two or three concerning the little plastic animals that kids play with at that age. I wouldn't play with the domestic ones, like cows and horses and pigs and chickens. Instead, I always picked out the wild ones—rhinos and elephants and lions and giraffes, bears and deer and elk and bighorn. *Those* were the ones that excited me, and I would play with them for hours in the sand and among the rocks and shrubbery of our backyard.

Our backyard was part of six acres of land ten miles out of Fort Smith, Arkansas, where I grew up with my parents, my two brothers, Mark and Marshall, and my sister, Mari. Today it's part of a sprawling city suburb, but back then it was still

My whole life has been spent learning to think like a wild animal—learning to sense, for instance, the exact moment when a bobcat will lunge from cover toward its prey. Invaluable lessons, especially considering my career path.

very much the country. Luckily, my parents encouraged us to explore, so my playground wasn't limited to the backyard. When we were quite young, my brothers and I and our cousins Butch, Steve, and Danny often headed into "the woods" with BB guns to "live off the land." At that age, this meant more pretending and stalking than it did actually killing and eating anything, and we were usually home in time for supper. But those early experiments in self-reliance brought my senses alive and taught me the value of watching and waiting. And even though what we called "the woods" was hardly a wilderness, for young boys it was wild enough.

The woods began down at the end of a dirt and gravel country lane, where an old moss-covered bridge spanned a narrow rocky stream. Turtles crawled over the bridge and swallows nested under it. Upstream were low hills from which water seeped to form the stream, and downstream it was bounded in some places by mossy banks, in others by grassy meadows. All around were the woods through which the stream meandered, collecting here and there in shallow pools.

The bridge and stream were the lifeline of the woods, not only for us youngsters but for much of the wildlife of the area

Everything that enriched my Arkansas childhood revolved around the animals we cared for, both wild and tame. Clockwise around our white donkey Misty are me at age eleven, my sister, Mari, and my brothers, Mark and Marshall.

as well. The turtles that crawled over the bridge came there to bask on logs and rocks, and the swallows that nested under it veered and swooped over the water to catch insects. Mourning doves flitted down to the edge of the steam to drink, then sat in a dead tree nearby, cooing gently in the stillness of the summer woods.

And just as wild animals were naturally drawn to this artery of life, so were we. The stream was central to our idea of "living off the land." We caught bluegills with our fishing poles, and snakes and frogs with our bare hands. We poked around with sticks in the rocky pools and plucked out crayfish, or "crawdads," when they clasped the end of the stick with their claws. Any southern boy knows what good eating crawdads make, but we also played with them and used them for "backwards races." Crayfish, when their stalked, swiveled eyes see danger, suddenly snap shut their fan-shaped tails and shoot backwards through the water. When we jabbed our sticks down through the water in front of them, the race was won by whichever of these lobsterlike creatures propelled itself backwards farthest and fastest.

Even now, I often find myself thinking of our little stream and the carefree days we spent there. I'd love to go back, but it's gone now, along with the bridge and the woods. You could say that water still flows there, but it doesn't flow freely. Instead, it's carefully controlled and regulated, enclosed in a concrete conduit. And our family's six-acre corner of the world has since been whittled down to two-and-a-half acres, with the rest paved over for an interstate highway bypass. It's a story that has become too familiar all over America.

Where will this all-too-predictable development ultimately lead us? No one knows for sure. But you'll know what it means to wildlife if you take that one little bridge and stream and multiply it all across America. You'll discover that the answer to the equation is at best a massive minus. Gone, and gone forever, are millions of swallows and doves, turtles and crayfish and bluegills. And gone are the plants and animals *they* fed upon, and the ones that fed upon them. They simply have no place left to live. To me, the number one problem facing all wildlife today, in America and elsewhere, is this continuous and irreversible destruction of their habitat.

That points to another loss: the firsthand personal experiences of children who might have seen those creatures up close, learned from them, and experienced the freedom and wonder of the wild places where they lived. Every time I return home to find civilization choking out more and more of my former little corner of the earth, that loss is made very real to me. It's true that adults are forever trying to recapture childhood pleasures and finding that it can't be done. But at least we might try to preserve for our own children those childhood places we've loved. When I travel around America and see what we've lost—wildlife habitat turned into sprawling suburban wastelands of shopping centers and speeding cars—I'm truly saddened. Where is our wisdom? Those feelings have much to do with my campaign to preserve wildlife habitat.

My mother always took an interest in teaching us kids the down-to-earth essentials of life, and I agree with her that one effective way to instill a sense of responsibility in children, and to teach them about sex, reproduction, birth, and death, is to give them a pet to care for. My parents, especially my mother, encouraged us to have a variety of pets, including wild ones.

Now let me say at the outset that I don't want to prompt anybody to go out in the woods and adopt an "abandoned" baby animal. All too frequently, people with the best intentions come across babies alone in the wild, and thinking that the mother has been killed or has otherwise abandoned them, take them home. Seldom is this the case, and the babies often die, either from shock or because they aren't cared for properly.

My family never intentionally set out to acquire a wild pet; they simply came into our lives in the course of growing up in a rural area. Over the years, my brothers and cousins and I found an interesting variety of animals. I remember, for instance, the time Marshall came across an intact nest of baby woodpeckers lying on the ground beneath a dead tree whose limbs had been broken off in a heavy wind. One of the little nestlings died soon after he brought them home, another was killed by a cat before it could fly, but the third one lived to fly away—so at least the odds in favor of the woodpeckers were better after bringing them home than if the nest had been left there on the ground. In another instance, my cousin Butch discovered a young barred owl with an injured wing down by our favorite stream. We named her Leona and splinted her wing, and as it healed, she hovered around the house and later the backyard, until one day about a year later she flew away for good. Many years later I paid homage to her in a program in the *Wild America* series, called "Owls—Lords of Darkness."

And I do have to admit that I'm not entirely guiltless: when I was too young to know better, I literally stole Foxy the fox from a den that I discovered. Again, I have to say that this was not the right thing to do. But I loved that little silky kit, with its wide blue eyes and perky black ears, as he grew and took on the keen, alert appearance that gave him his name. We took good, conscientious care of Foxy, and he became a kind of second family dog. Both the wild and domestic versions would eat out of the same dish, tussle playfully together in the yard, and sleep in the same shade. Foxy stayed around as a pet until he also was about a year old, when his own instinctive restlessness caused him to drift on, no longer accepting our handouts of food, and to begin his life as a fox in the wild.

And then there was Stanley the beaver. Stanley came into our lives because of a trapper who had trapped a female beaver illegally, too late in the winter, after she had given birth. He told us he had heard some babies whimpering inside the den as he was removing the dead mother from his trap, and he had felt remorseful, but not enough to go back for them. We went down to the mud-bank den ourselves and found one of the babies still alive. We took him home, raising him at first on a bottle, and later on the bark of weeping willow trees. He had the run of the house, but preferred the half-filled bathtub that we kept fresh for him. Mark had a particular fondness for him and adopted him as his personal mascot. Like Leona and Foxy, he eventually grew big enough and skilled enough to survive in the wild. We were able to turn him loose in the Arkansas River, near where we had found him, and he slipped quietly into the water and swam out of our lives.

Although I was happy to see Stanley return to the wild, I was also angry that the trapper had killed his mother illegally and had left her young to die. Yes, you can accuse me of stealing a fox kit. I'll attribute that to childish exuberance. Even at that age, however, I realized that grown-ups ought to know better than to take an animal out of season, and, even worse, leave its young stranded and destined to die. It made me realize for the first time that wildlife needed to be protected from humans. And I'm sorry to say that many times since then, when I've seen hunters and trappers in action, I've not been impressed by the less-than-ethical manner of some. Such experiences have colored my view of people and wildlife over the years to the point where my sadness at seeing wildlife disappear has become tinged with a bit of cynicism. I know that there are more good hunters than bad, and that many trappers do care about life in the wild. But it's my enthusiasm for animals, not man, that has held me steady, and I've felt even more strongly since Stanley the need to speak for creatures that can't speak for themselves.

These feelings, which I'm sure are common to many, were enhanced by knowing certain wild animals intimately. I never forgot that our wild pets were wild—that was precisely what fascinated me about them. But because they were also my friends, who took food from my hands or climbed into my arms, I've never forgotten, and indeed, have actively sought out, the unique, exquisite pleasure of being close to and actually touching a wild animal. And there were other ways in which Stanley, Foxy, Leona, and the others were valuable to me, not just then, but now. Although I didn't think of it that way at the time, I studied our wild pets in the way that an artist contemplates his model. I began to understand how the smallest gesture could signify great meaning, and the ways in which an animal's form related to its function.

Stanley, for instance, plodded along on land with an awkward waddle, a low-profile character seemingly lower still in motivation. But in his natural element, water, he was anything but clumsy. In fact he was swift and graceful, using his flat tail as a rudder. As a rodent—the beaver is North America's largest—he had to gnaw on something constantly in order to keep his sharp, continuously growing front teeth at a manageable length. We kept him supplied with willow branches, which he would manipulate in his handlike front paws, rotating the branch as he gnawed them down through the bark. Using the two split nails on his webbed hind feet like combs, he would groom himself by gathering oil from the glands near the base of his tail and combing it through his coat. The oil kept the long guard hairs and dense underfur of his coat waterproof, and when I picked him up I could feel the solid layer of fat beneath his thick skin, fat that would keep him warm for hours in the water.

Orphaned Stanley the Beaver was bottle-fed in our bathtub until he was old enough to eat willow bark. We broke so many twigs from the willow in our yard that it eventually died, but Stanley lived to be released into the wild.

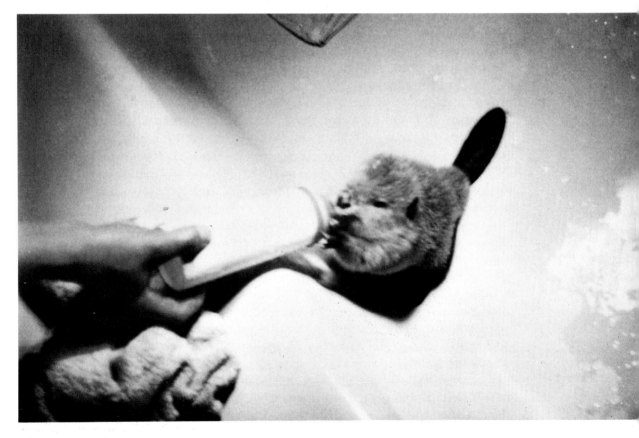

Our wild pets also taught me vital lessons about animal behavior, though even then I realized that the behavior I watched was probably distorted by closeness to people. Stanley, for instance, was basically a busy but peaceful creature. In the wild, he wouldn't need to be aggressive, because he could always swim to safety in his stick-and-mud lodge. But in his bathroom hideaway, if we startled him suddenly he would hiss through his teeth at us, or in the typical warning signal of his kind, slap his flat tail loudly against the water.

When I was older, I also had a fawn. Someone had "rescued" it and the Forest Service brought it to me. Of course, if it had been left alone the mother would have come back sooner or later. But by the time the fawn was delivered to our doorstep, it wouldn't have been a good idea to take it back to the woods, because by then the mother might have abandoned it entirely. The fawn was a female, so I named her Faline, after Bambi's fictional girlfriend. At first she refused to nurse. I had to get her interested in sucking on something, so I started her on my own nipple, such as it was. Then I had to get her to accept an artificial source of milk, so I would sneak a baby bottle in on the side. The technique ultimately worked fine, but initially it tickled so much that I squirmed half in pain until she finally learned to accept the bottle by itself. Faline was quiet and shy, and seemed always to want to lie down and hide. When I tried imitating a sound that a mother deer makes—a sheeplike bleat—she would get up and come to me. Then one day, quite by accident, I found out that when I sneezed, she immediately fell flat on the ground. A mother deer makes a warning call that is quite similar to a snort or sneeze. The effectiveness of my forced sneezes lasted only a week or so before she no longer responded to them, but during that time I was able to communicate with Faline just like her mother might have, and I was thrilled. Not only did these discoveries give me a way to relate to the fawn, but I hoped that they might in some way help her to grow through what would have been the "normal" stages of being a deer. Eventually, as an elegant yearling, Faline one fall evening drifted like a shadow from the far edge of the lawn off into the woods, out of our lives and into her own.

Faline, Stanley, and several of the other baby animals we

kept were basically cute and cuddly, Stanley being something
of an aquatic teddy bear. But now when I look back, it was
the hunters among our pets that intrigued me the most. I
studied carefully, and came to admire, the cunning intelligence of the predators. Whenever I watch a wild fox now, I'm
reminded of Foxy, and I feel as if I know all foxes—and to a
degree, coyotes and wolves, since they're also members of the
wild canid family. If you reach out too quickly toward a fox—
which as kids we often did because we loved running our
fingers through Foxy's soft, thick fur—it will immediately leap
beyond your grasp. Today, if I'm filming a wild fox sniffing a
snake and the snake strikes at the fox, I'm able to anticipate
and follow the fox's jump with the camera, without ever having
seen that particular fox before. I can tell by the way the fox
twitches its nose and pricks up its ears that it's getting ready
to leap, and I know that when it does, it's going to go four feet
straight up in the air. From watching Foxy find mice in our
backyard, I also learned how wild foxes hunted when they
couldn't see their prey. Jumping, again, is part of the technique. First, the fox dances around in a kind of wild "fox trot,"
disturbing the nest of a field mouse until the mouse scurries
out of hiding. Then the fox leaps at the prey, finally pinning it
under its paws. More catlike than other wild dogs, it may play
with a dead mouse, or even a live mouse, rushing and circling
and pouncing instead of simply running down its prey and
grabbing it.

We do have wild animals in our household now from time
to time, but the same guidelines apply as when I was a kid.
With the exception of the bear cub in "The Man Who Loved
Bears," we don't seek them out. Rather, as with the two fishers that we rescued and filmed for "Fishers in the Family," if
we see that an animal clearly needs human help, we try to
give it, in a manner least destructive to the natural habits of
the animal.

In addition to the wild pets, we had a number of domestic
ones. To a large degree, we had Mari to thank for this, with
her early love of horses and ponies, and her willingness to
take care of them while we boys were still too young for such
responsibility. But one year for Christmas, my parents gave
me a gift that began with a card under the tree with my name

on it, to which a string was attached. I followed the string out through the window and into the backyard, and discovered that it was tied to the horn of a white billy goat. I loved that animal instantly. I'd grab him by his horns and tug him around, feeling his strength and smelling his musky hair. Many years later, when I lived with Rocky Mountain bighorn sheep, I felt close to them immediately; they had a familiar look, smell, and feel. Billy, however, was frustrated because there were no other goats around, and so his normal butting behavior went unfulfilled. Well, almost unfulfilled. Wild bighorn sheep habitually smack heads with other rams, as do domestic sheep and goats, although their battles are not quite as dramatic as those of wild ones. This particular goat was usually well-behaved, but he had his instincts intact and took advantage of the chance to practice them whenever anyone bent over. Billy would get a running start from about twenty to thirty feet away and bump the unsuspecting individual in the buttocks. Probably not very safe and certainly not very kind, but it never failed to elicit laughs all around. And, of course, many a time I made the mistake of bending over within sight of the goat, and literally became the "butt" of his unintentional joke myself.

It goes to show that you don't have to have a wild fox or a beaver as a pet to enjoy and learn from animals. A large part of my childhood was spent with domestic ones—feeding and watering the horses and donkeys and goats and chickens. I have to admit that I had as much fun with Billy, or with our cat and her successive litters of kittens, as I had with Stanley the beaver or Leona the owl. Pets don't have to be wild to be interesting, and I encourage people to get to know as many different animals as they can. Any creature can provide valuable lessons in caring for living things—and in exercising every last ounce of your creativity, ingenuity, and patience in doing so.

Some of the lessons we learned were harder to come to terms with than others. Death, of course, but in some cases birth. At one point, in an effort to encourage our skills in animal husbandry and also to instill in us some kind of business sense, my mother had all four of us kids involved in various money-making projects. We raised chickens and turkeys, several dozen to several hundred at a time. For a while we also raised mice and hamsters, and had almost a thousand at once. Mass production, it's true, but I still learned a great deal about nature. We saw, for example, how a mother hamster, if disturbed, would eat her own young. The first time one of my brothers noticed a hamster having babies, he yelled for us to come and look. As we crowded together with our noses against the cage, babbling to each other and looking at her, she became confused and disturbed, and to our shocked surprise, began eating her tiny, pink, helplessly naked babies. I learned how vulnerable an animal could be to outside pressures while giving birth, and why it might be that females of many species leave even the company of their own kind to undergo the process in privacy.

Because of this early lesson, in filming for the *Wild America* series we have gone out of our way to film birth with a long lens from an unobtrusive distance, or on some occasions not at all, because it can be so stressful. A wild mother might eat her babies as our hamster did, but what's more likely is that infant young might be abandoned by the frightened mother and then die from exposure. With that in mind, I am careful to follow the rule that an animal's well-being is always more important than the success of a given film.

I think about the well-being of wild animals in a different light now than I did when I was growing up. As with most rurally raised boys, guns and hunting were part of my life from the time I was about five until I was about twenty-one. The stock of my first BB gun was hacksawed off to fit my tiny arms. Hunting was more socially acceptable during the 1950s and 1960s, especially in the southern United States, and in season I regularly shot doves, ducks, and deer for the family table. But I can't apologize for that phase of my relationship with wild animals, because it was one that had great meaning for me. As with most things in life, there is more than one way to approach the concept of hunting, and the major difference is in attitude. I've often thought the approach to hunting boils down to two camps; some hunters are lovers and some are rapists. The difference, of course, is a matter of respect.

The truth is, at times I've felt as much at one with nature when I've been hunting as when I've been filming. Hunting an

Although I now hunt with a camera, the years I spent stalking wild animals with a shotgun or rifle helped to develop the sense of timing, judgment, and other skills I now use as a wildlife cinematographer.

animal is a more immediate, primal way of relating to it: the one-on-one encounter of predator and prey. When I'm filming, on the other hand, I often feel more like a photojournalist covering a war—like him, I'm an observer, documenting the action on film, but not trying to influence the outcome. Certainly filming is a way of getting closer to wild creatures, and I'm excited about being present to observe the experience of the animal, but I'm not directly part of that experience. When I hunted, however, I felt myself to be an integral part of the cycle of life around me. Like the wolf, I would kill a deer, leave the gut pile for the scavengers to feed on, and take the meat to feed myself and my family. It was a satisfying feeling, and I don't have a problem with hunting when it's done in an ethical, perhaps almost a spiritual, manner—when the hunter respects both himself and the animal being pursued, and understands each of their places in the pattern of nature. Much of my criticism of hunting is aimed at hunters who lack that quality of respect, and who abuse the opportunity and the privilege of being part of an eternal cycle. Some even use it as an excuse to escape from family problems or to get away for a few days of drinking with the boys. I never drank when I hunted, and more often than not I hunted alone. Deep down, I still feel I'm an avid hunter who's channeled the desire to be closely connected with wild animals into an appetite for filming them.

My interest in photography evolved to some degree from these considerations, but it actually began much earlier, with my family's custom of documenting events in our lives. We had an old Kodak Brownie box camera, another that was probably one of the first Polaroid cameras ever made, and a Kodak 8-mm movie camera. My favorite was the movie camera. Our parents would film birthday parties and such, and then hand the camera to one of us kids, and we'd take turns filming each other. We didn't have much technical understanding of what we were doing, and the results usually looked like they'd been shot from the back of a bucking bronco. But we filmed our domestic pets—our white donkey Misty trotting around behind Mari while Mark and Marshall took turns jumping on and falling off—and our wild ones—Foxy and the dog chasing each other around the yard. We even filmed some of our adventures in the woods, and then invited friends over to see the invariably corny results. Even now, viewing these home movies gives me a jolt of nostalgia as well as a good laugh. Several scenes from this time, along with a couple of my early experiments with the camera, were included in the *Wild America* program, "Photographing Wildlife."

The first time I consciously combined photography and wildlife was in making several short movies of deer- and duck-hunting trips during my teens with my brother Marshall and friends C. C. Lockwood and Joe Durden. By this time, I knew that you couldn't make a very interesting movie by just turning the camera on and pointing it in any direction. I had watched a lot more movies and had gotten a bit more sophisticated about the techniques involved in making them. In putting together these little records of our hunting experiences, I grew even more critically aware of how to put short scenes together into longer sequences, how to bridge different scenes with cutaways that helped them fit together, and how to count— "one thousand one, one thousand two, one thousand three"— to get the pace of the action. Along with learning to shoot film,

I discovered that it could be edited—you didn't have to *keep* the boring parts—and soon a certain area of our family library became the proverbial cutting room floor, covered with a tangled nest of black filmstrips.

My interest in photography continued to grow over the years. Like many people, I'm fascinated by moving pictures and by the idea of being able to preserve the present into the future. It's not immortality by a long shot, but it's a better aid to memory than, say, saving a shoebox full of old prom corsages. During this period, my father nurtured our interest in mechanical and technical things as strongly as my mother did our interest in wildlife, and I'll always be grateful to him for the times that I've been able, miles from nowhere, to repair a broken-down camera or truck by myself. Because our parents had long encouraged these two parallel interests—photography and wildlife—they gradually but inevitably began to merge as I approached my late teens.

But when the time came to decide what to study in college, well, that was another matter. I wasn't acquainted with any wildlife cinematographers in Arkansas who might have served as role models to guide me in a choice of career. On the other hand, there was a man I'd always respected, my friend Pete Daily's father, who was an attorney. I admired him not only because he was friendly to me, but because even though he enjoyed his legal work, he drove around with his fishing hat on and a canoe on top of his station wagon. I knew he spent time at his office, but more often he seemed to be either going fishing or just coming back from fishing. So that was the life of an attorney, I thought. Here is a guy making a living and enjoying it, yet he has plenty of time to take off and head for the woods. Maybe that's the sort of occupation I should get into. To some people that might seem like a pretty shallow reason for wanting to be an attorney, but at age seventeen, I felt it had some logic. After all, what I loved most was being in the woods, even though I didn't quite know how to make a career out of it.

When I was accepted into the pre-law program at the University of Arkansas, I decided to major in English, which was recommended for pre-law students. I also took other required courses, such as zoology and biology, which interested me at the time, and which of course were of great benefit to me later. Unfortunately, the only filmmaking course offered by the University of Arkansas in those days was a basic introductory one that covered much of what I had already learned on my own.

One of the requirements of the fraternity I joined was to spend a certain number of hours per day studying in the library. An irksome rule, but I couldn't be more grateful for it now. While it did keep me indoors on many a sunny Saturday for four years, I spent most of those hours reading every, and I mean *every*, book in that library that was remotely related to wildlife or the out-of-doors. I may have deserved the D− I got in second-year Latin, but if I'd been tested on white-tailed deer or grizzly bears, my grade would have been A+. I also studied every book they had on photography and filmmaking. It's an appetite I haven't lost: my research on wildlife topics continues unabated, and I also try to keep up with every new development in film and cinematography by reading the latest books, magazines, and technical reports on both subjects.

One summer vacation during those college years, I drove up to Alaska with two friends, David Huie and Charlie Warner, in an old beat-up Chevy station wagon. Part of the reason we went was simply to see our forty-ninth state, with its hordes of magnificent wild creatures. Another reason was to hunt some of them. And yet another intention was to make a "big home movie," at least an hour in length, of our trip in order to have something to show for it when we got back.

Our original plan was to arrive in Anchorage by the first of August, spend the whole month traveling around and hunting a variety of animals, and then return in time for school in September. As it turned out, we ended up leaving earlier, at the beginning of June, encouraged by meeting a man in Fort Smith who worked summers as a hunting guide in Alaska. He mentioned that he owned a couple of boats and a bush plane, talked a lot about places we were already eager to see, and showed us amateur snapshots that, paradoxically, made those places seem more real and immediate than the pretty picture-book photographs that had made us want to go there originally. He would, he said, fly us all over the state during August if we would spend the months of June and July building some cabins for him to use for the hunting trips he guided.

So, based on his urging, we packed our gear, which included fifty rolls of film and a Super-8 Anscomatic movie camera I'd bought at Gibson's Discount Center, into the old Chevy and headed north to Alaska. More than a week later, we finally drove into Anchorage, weary but full of enthusiasm for what we'd already seen on the way and what still awaited us during the summer. We weren't too worried about finding the hunting guide once we arrived, because his name was on his license plates and Anchorage was not all that big. But just as we were entering the city limits, a Volkswagen van with the very license plates we were looking for went speeding past us in the other direction. Whipping the old Chevy around at an intersection, I took up the chase, and after almost an hour of holding the overloaded station wagon on the narrow rainy highway, we finally overtook the equally overloaded van, waved its driver over, and demanded to know what was going on. There we stood in the drizzle, while the guide, for reasons he refused to discuss, told us he was leaving town—permanently. Which meant that we were stuck in Alaska, two months before the hunting season began, with no work and very little money.

We made the best of the situation for as long as we could by picking up a variety of odd jobs, and doing some low-budget traveling in between. We fished for salmon along the Gulkana River, and visited islands in Prince William Sound to hunt and film black bears. We did quite a bit of hiking in Mount McKinley National Park (now renamed Denali), an area larger than the state of Massachusetts centered around 20,320-foot high Mount Denali, the highest peak in North America. Here I saw for the first time, up close, caribou and moose and other large mammals that had always seemed so magnificent to me. The reality was even more powerful than my imagination. It was here that I saw a wild grizzly for the first time in my life, on a rock right above the roadside. As we stopped the car, that huge Toklat grizzly, a beautiful straw-gold color phase of the species, rose up on his hind legs to watch us, and I thought that I had never seen anything so magnificent.

Up on the slopes of Denali, we also came across a band of pure white Dall sheep. They're the only white wild sheep in the world, and I think they're among the most beautiful animals anywhere. The whole herd turned to stare at us, and then, without moving away, resumed their grazing. I was struck by the way the almost-tame acceptance of the sheep contrasted with the spectacular wild beauty of the place where they lived. Standing on the shoulder of that huge mountain, breathing in air so fresh it seemed never to have been breathed by another living thing, and trying to take in the overwhelming grandeur of the view, I was thankful that we had chosen this incredible state for our first trip outside the continental United States, and elated that we were able to film so much of what we saw.

If a person could live on scenery alone, we would have been well off, but things being the way they are, by the end of June we were broke. We had left Arkansas with about $500 each, which was quite a bit of money back then, but there was considerable difference between the cost of living in Arkansas and that in Alaska. Gas, which was 30¢ a gallon back home,

Dall sheep, like this magnificent ram, are the only wild white sheep in the world, and the hope of seeing one was a primary reason for my first trip to Alaska.

cost $2 a gallon here; $8 motel rooms were $50; even a 50¢ hot dog was now an inflated $4.

We kept trying for jobs, even camping out in front of state government offices hoping to be hired as smoke-jumpers to fight the forest fires that were raging all over the state that summer. But as the days passed and no work became available, it was beginning to dawn on us that even if we did find jobs for the whole month of July, we still wouldn't earn the thousands of dollars necessary to hire a hunting guide by August. The only situation that might prove feasible was the one that had recently disappeared out from under us—an exchange of work for guiding services. Before we'd left Arkansas, I had, in fact, been corresponding with a guide who said he'd be willing to provide flying and guiding time in the Brooks Range in exchange for my insulating his cabin and building him an outhouse. The only hitch, and it seemed a big one, was that he had wanted one person, not three. David and Charlie had been good sports about all the disappointments, but as it turned out, they were already so discouraged that they were ready to go back home anyway. So on the last day of June, we shook hands and said reluctant good-byes at the Anchorage airport. I had no idea then that I would come close to not making it back myself.

When I contacted this second guide again, he had changed his mind (it seemed to be a trait of the trade), not about the exchange itself, fortunately, but about the form of work it would take on my part. He still needed the work done, but said that I would be more useful to him as an assistant guide. In my original letter, I had mentioned to him that back in the sixth grade I'd taken a correspondence course in taxidermy, and had since mounted everything from cat-killed birds to my own deer heads. I was capable of dressing hides and "caping out" trophy heads—preparing them properly so that the hair wouldn't fall out—so he had decided that I could help by preparing trophy heads and packing out meat for his clients. But that wouldn't be until August, and the question for now was how would I survive through the month of July.

Late on Fourth of July evening, with golden summer sun still angling into the Seward bar at 10 P.M., I was feeling lonesome and pondering this question over a beer when I met two brothers from Washington state who had come to Alaska because they'd heard there was money in the roofing business. They'd been making some of that money, and when they offered me temporary work, though I knew what a dirty, sticky business it was, I was glad to accept. Every day, we'd get covered from head to toe with hot, black, smelly goo, and at the end of every day we'd just peel off our clothes and throw them away. Once a week or so, we'd go down to the Salvation Army store and buy a half-dozen new sets of clothes. "New" is the wrong word. Actually we'd buy the oldest, baggiest, most disreputable-looking outfits on the racks—baggy pants and shirts and jackets or even suit coats, shoes that were too big or didn't match—it didn't matter, so long as they were comfortable, and disposable.

Toward the end of July, as my roofing career drew to a close, we went out to tar some roofs on Kodiak Island. Nearly constant rain kept us from accomplishing much work, but it was there that I met a halibut fisherman and arranged to go out with him on his small trawler to a place called Cape Chiniak, where I wanted to film a colony of Stellar's sea lions I had heard about. Not until later did I learn a most important piece of information about this rocky point off the southwestern side of Kodiak Island: Cape Chiniak is one of the most dangerous places in the world to be out in a boat. Unaware of this fact, while the fisherman set out his lines, I jumped into his little dinghy and rowed over to a low group of jagged rocks where, as predicted, a group of these huge sea lions was basking at the edge of the breaking swells. I lashed the dinghy's painter to one rock and climbed over to some others in order to film the animals from a good angle. I had never before seen large sea mammals up close in their natural habitat, and I got so absorbed in filming them that I forgot to pay attention to what was happening around me. When I looked up, the wind had risen, the sea had broken into an angry chop, and the rocky point I stood on was separated from the bulk of the island by a wide gulf of churning surf. I looked around for the dinghy, only to see it bouncing through the waves a hundred yards from where it should have been, dragging its loose painter. As the tide had risen, so had the boat, unhitching itself from the rock.

No boat was ever more aptly named than this Alaskan fishing trawler
that left me stranded in rising, icy seas.

Because it was Alaska, where people are used to preparing
for emergencies, I was carrying a rifle in addition to my camera equipment. Although I was aware that this could turn into
a very serious situation, I could still see the halibut fisherman's boat less than a mile away, so I wasn't ready to panic.
My little boat soon disappeared from sight among the waves,
so I started firing a repeated series of three shots. But the
universal distress signal seemed to have no effect on the direction of the fishing trawler. If anything, the boat seemed to
be moving farther away.

I sat down on a cold, slippery rock and took stock of my
situation. My camera and rifle were with me; the food I'd
brought for lunch was probably rolling around in the bottom
of the dinghy, soggy with seawater—if the dinghy was even
still afloat. I checked my pockets for matches and fire supplies, and found a little book of local tide tables. Thumbing
through it, I learned that I was even worse off than I thought.
The tides in that area of Alaska fluctuate extremely, second
only in the Northern Hemisphere to those in the Bay of Fundy.

According to the chart, a thirteen-foot high tide was due, and in three hours the rocky point I was standing on would be under water. I fired off another series of shots, but the trawler made no response. To make matters even worse, a bank of fog was rolling in, and soon I was able to see the big boat only now and then through the drifting gray. Then, as the fog shifted and parted again, the boat was gone.

I was out of ammunition, the rising tide had already forced me as high up as I could get on the rocks, the wind had gotten stronger, and waves were lapping at my feet. I had plenty of room to move around, but there was no place to go but sideways. By this time the sea lions had floated free from their rocky ledges, and though some were still milling and diving about the rocks, others were swimming away. I felt totally abandoned, and began seriously to consider doing the same thing, even though I knew I wouldn't last as long in that freezing water as it would take me to swim back to the rocky coast of Kodiak. I tucked my feet up, held my camera and my rifle close to protect them from the spray, and pulled my collar up around my ears. Call it cockiness or plain stupidity, although I didn't know what was going to happen, the thought of dying simply was not on my list of options.

Suddenly I heard the muffled sound of an engine approaching. I peered out through the thick mist, but could see nothing that even dimly resembled the outline of a boat. Still, the noise grew louder and louder and finally I realized in bewilderment that the chopping sound of a motor was coming from *above* me. I looked up to see a Coast Guard helicopter hovering through the fog, directly overhead. What an immense sense of relief! Since there was no place to land, they began to lower a rescue basket down to me, and during this process the men were leaning out of the chopper, paying out line, and frantically waving and shouting at me. As I reached for the wildly swinging basket, they gestured more vigorously and shouted even louder, but I still couldn't hear them clearly and had no idea what they were trying to tell me, except that I thought of course I should try to catch the basket and get into it. Of course. I reached once more for the basket, and the next thing I knew I was flat on my back on the rock, shaking my head and trying to figure out what had happened.

I had been stunned by a massive jolt of static electricity, built up by a combination of charged wind, churning water, and idling helicopter rotors. If I had let the basket hit the nearby exposed rock first, I would have been okay. Instead, it hit *me* first, and I personally grounded the electrical charge. The Coast Guard men had been trying to warn me. The basket was still arcing in wide circles around my head, the wind was still howling so that I could hear nothing but it and the waves, but up in the helicopter, the Coast Guard guys were laughing their heads off. I finally got hold of the basket and dragged myself in, along with my camera and rifle.

After I got back to the big island, I learned that the halibut fisherman had found his dinghy, half swamped but still afloat, in the channel, and had towed it behind the trawler back to Kodiak, reported me dead, and gone out to dinner. He'd made no effort to search for me, nothing. A different passing trawler had reported my distress signal to the Coast Guard, while the fisherman who had given me the ride out was passed out in the hold of his boat, drunk all afternoon. I gave him a hard time when I found him that night, but in all fairness to him, he really thought I was dead, and if I had been in that cold water for even fifteen minutes, I would have been. Once the literal and figurative shock had worn off, I felt very fortunate to be alive. I hadn't exactly been reckless, just careless, but Alaska is a harsh, unforgiving land, edged by an equally dangerous sea. As one of the Guardsmen said, "You're just lucky. Fisherman and crabbers die out there all the time."

A few days later, as I sat in the copilot's seat of the guide's little Cessna floatplane, droning toward the remote valleys of the Brooks Range, I resolved to be more careful in the future. Water was just not my medium, I decided, and from now on I'd leave filming anything to do with the ocean to the Cousteau family. But now I was headed for the adventure I'd planned and researched for months, and I felt eager and confident about my ability to handle whatever might lie ahead. Those were the days of youth, when little did I suspect that each situation presents its own set of circumstances.

I spent the first couple of weeks framing and insulating the little cabin next to the lake, building an outhouse, and in my spare time filming the passing herds of caribou. Among the things I learned were that you don't, no matter how warm the temperature, take off your shirt when putting up fiberglass insulation; you don't build an outhouse with its ventilated side facing the north wind; and that caribou are much more interesting than carpentry. When the guide arrived with a couple of clients, I was more than ready to get out of the base camp, take up my pack, and head out into the stern beauty of the Brooks Range.

We were going after Dall sheep. One of the clients was a seventy-year-old man who wanted only to see a band of the famous white sheep, shoot one of them, and eat it. He didn't care about bagging a trophy-sized set of horns, but he did want to enjoy the game that he shot, which made me sympathetic to him. The other client was just the opposite. A taxidermy specialist from Seattle, all he could think about was getting

I paid for part of my summer in Alaska by insulating the "Merry Hilton," a primitive hunting cabin in the Brooks Range. It turned out that the insulation may have saved my life.

his name in the record book, and when, after more than a week of hunting he finally shot a ram with 39-inch horns—one inch below the minimum he had set for himself—he spent hours with a tape measure, trying to figure a way to make them come out longer. If horns would stretch, he would have made them do so.

By the terms of the guide's permit, as an assistant I was not really allowed to hunt. But on the other hand, I was a paying customer, since I was working in exchange for the guide's services. What this boiled down to was that I was low man on the totem pole, and after the other clients had each taken their sheep, and I had done all the work of cleaning, skinning, and caping out their animals—not to mention cooking and keeping the camp clean—I was allowed a chance to go after my own animal. I had been watching from the sidelines while the others had made five attempts in two weeks to outwit one particular old ram with a very large set of unusually tightly curled horns, more like those of a Rocky Mountain bighorn than the normal wide sweep of a Dall's. Through binoculars we had seen that the ram's horns were also "broomed" —bluntly broken off at the tips from years of rubbing them on rocks and clashing with other rams. That was one way we knew he was old, and because he was far past his breeding prime, he was the ram I wanted.

As it happened, it was nearing the end of August by then, and an early snowstorm was moving in. Everyone was in a hurry to get packed up and fly out of the backcountry before it hit. Gray clouds were rolling in like cold fog along the ridges, and I knew I would have only one chance to find this ram, who had never been where anyone expected he should be. To camouflage myself, I stapled pieces of white plastic garbage bags around my dark clothing so that it would blend with the white snow. While the others stayed in the cabin, I set out with my rifle, heading through new-falling snow for a little cirque where I'd seen the old ram by himself a couple of times when I was out exploring on my own. But I never got all the way there. While I was carefully following a faint sheep trail across a barren, fog-shrouded hillside, I looked up to see the old ram staring back at me from no more than 50 yards away. I swear he saw me before I saw him, but I think he was confused by the camouflage, so he didn't move immediately. Before he did, I raised my rifle.

When I walked through the door of the cabin and placed the old ram's head on the table, no one wanted to believe it. Still less were they pleased when their tape showed that each of his magnificent horns measured 41 inches—which meant that had they not been severely "broomed," they would surely have neared the 48 inches required to equal the world's record. Not that the value of this experience had anything to do with tape measures and record books. In fact, I found myself wishing that the horns didn't look so massive and beautiful compared to the much thinner 39-inch set. The taxidermist obviously wished the same thing for different reasons, as he sputtered and tried not to lose his temper. And the guide, understandably, was highly disgruntled that I had bested and displeased one of his clients. Jealousy emanated from everyone in the cramped little cabin except the old man, who for the first time in two weeks looked me in the eye and gave a little nod.

But for me it seemed not so much a triumph as, in some mysterious sense, an appointed meeting. I had known that this great-grandfather of a ram was old, no longer a breeding member of the herd, and now I could see that his teeth were all worn down or gone. It was astonishing that he'd survived this long, and he would have starved during the approaching winter. In hindsight, of course, I know that this is a hunter's rationalization; nevertheless it's true. But while I might be able to justify shooting the old ram, I could not justify that I had deprived the wolves in the area of *their* natural food by killing him before they could get to him.

Nevertheless, we feasted on sheep meat that evening, no one saying much of anything. In the morning, we loaded the gear, trophies, and ourselves into the tiny Cessna, which was tethered at a makeshift dock on the lake next to the cabin. Nighttime temperatures had dropped below freezing for the past several nights, and a thin rime of ice had begun to form around the margins of the shallow lake. With pontoons on the plane, it was essential that we fly out before any more ice interfered with its ability to take off. But there were already other problems with taking off—specifically, the weight of us and all our gear, including the uneaten meat. Three times we skimmed down the lake for takeoff, and three times the plane just wouldn't lift. Finally the guide said that we'd have to lighten the load, and informed me that I could stay behind with the meat and some of the gear while he flew his two clients to the nearest airport at Bettles. Then he said he'd return for me the next day.

I watched the Cessna lift off with no trouble this time, and with not even a farewell tilt of its wings, disappear between the lowering clouds and the nearest ridge of mountains. I turned toward the cabin with a sense of isolation, stashed the gear inside, and took out my camera to use up what was left of my last roll of film on the little arctic ground squirrels that I had attracted to the cabin weeks before with scraps of bread and crackers. As the storm clouds grew more threatening and thin snow began to blow through the air, I was glad for their company. Little did I suspect that they would be all the company I'd have for quite a while.

By the next afternoon, a full-scale blizzard was raging outside the cabin, and I found myself unexpectedly thankful for the time I'd spent insulating it, itchy fiberglass and all. A small kerosene stove provided enough heat, and I had a few days' worth of dry provisions in addition to what was left of the Dall

Access to the remote Brooks Range cabin was by float plane only. But before I could leave at the end of summer, I had to wait for the lake to freeze solid so that the plane could return and land on skis.

sheep meat. I was sure the guide would be back as soon as the storm broke, so I settled in and tried to make myself at home as best I could. But it took three days for the storm to subside, and then it backed around and came through again for a couple more days. I began to get worried; I had run out of cereal, flour, and other supplies, and I wasn't sure how long the kerosene might last.

To make matters worse, after the skies cleared there was no sign of the plane. Two days went by, then three. Toward the end of the storm, the temperature had dropped well below freezing, and there it stayed while ice slowly formed on the lake. I felt very uneasy. The floatplane couldn't land now even if it tried, but I would have felt a lot better if I'd seen some sign of it trying. Another day went by, then another. What had happened? I had visions of the plane crashing, still overloaded, on the way to Bettles. Did anyone in the world besides the guide and his clients know where I was? I was sure the taxidermist would never tell anyone where to rescue me, but if the guide had died, would his wife or my parents send out a search party before it was too late?

After subsisting—gratefully, I must say—on nothing but the old Dall sheep meat after my other provisions gave out, by the twelfth day that, too, was gone. I could have gone out hunting, but I was too nervous about missing the plane if it did come back. After the experience with the halibut fisherman, I wasn't sure that anyone would bother to wait around for me. I was reduced to chipping frozen bits of meat from a caribou carcass that we had pretty much used up before shooting the sheep. The nights turned even colder, the lake froze over solidly enough to hold a ski plane, one of which I knew the guide owned, but still no plane appeared.

On the afternoon of the fourteenth day, just when I was certain I'd be spending the next couple of months, if not forever, right where I was, a droning noise echoed over the ridge. A beat-up plane that I didn't recognize skidded to a halt on the frozen lake, and the next thing I knew the guide was telling me, with no apologies at all, to load up the gear so we could get back in time for him to be at a poker match that night. Needless to say, I was a little irritated. I knew he'd had to wait for the lake to freeze over, but it had done that two days ago. And I knew I wouldn't have starved. Besides hunting, I could have chopped holes in the ice and fished for ling cod and grayling in the lake. But I could have frozen, and at least he could have flown over to check on me, or dropped a few supplies, just for reassurance. When I mentioned this, he just shrugged, and I was too relieved to be getting out of there to press the issue. I believed in self-reliance as much as the next man, and practiced it, but I'd had enough of the Alaskan version of every man for himself. I loved what I'd seen of this great wild land and its wildlife, but I was glad to be going home.

At the beginning of September, I returned to Fort Smith with almost 100 rolls of Super 8-mm film, and bought a little $20 Super 8 editing unit, which consisted of a set of hand cranks to wind the film through a viewer and a splicer to cut and tape the pieces of film together. Humble equipment by today's standards, but my hopes were high. During the next semester, I worked after classes and on weekends to put together my "big home movie." Despite all the setbacks—and maybe partly because of them—Alaska had been a wonderful experience for me, and for the first time I felt the desire to share that with a broader audience than family and friends.

The scenes that went into the film were the very best I had: from the little parka squirrels I'd filmed before I'd been rescued in the Brooks Range, to moose and caribou, Dall sheep, black and grizzly bears, salmon, and even sea lions. When I finished editing it into a two-hour film, I knew that I'd succeeded in making the "big home movie" that had been my goal, and it was even better than I thought it would be. Beyond showing the highlights of "How I Spent My Summer Vacation," it presented a good overview of Alaska and its wildlife, and even without a sound track, it contained the essential elements of humor and human interest. I called it *Alaska— America's Last Frontier.*

After I showed it to my family and a number of friends, I began to get requests from people who had heard about it and wanted to see it. I even got letters from total strangers asking if I would show it to the public. So I presented it at the University of Arkansas in Fayetteville and twice at the Municipal Auditorium in Fort Smith. I would stand up with a microphone

This self-portrait with Super 8mm camera and Dall sheep horns became a publicity photo for my first successful lecture film. At this moment I was alone in the Arctic.

and narrate to the picture: "This is David and me loading our packs. We're ready to hike up the slopes of Mount McKinley." The memories were wonderful, and I never got tired of relating them, but the audience was even more wonderful. Each showing sold out completely, with about 1,800 people a showing. Tickets were $1 in advance and $1.50 at the door, and when I counted the proceeds, I felt like a millionaire. I'd spent more than a thousand dollars traveling around Alaska, including the price of the camera and film, but my investment was returned many times.

The experience was definitely a turning point for me. I said to myself, "Wait a second, if you can make money doing something fun, isn't that what it's all about?" I wasn't greedy —I've never cared much about being rich, which is a good thing, because wildlife filming is *not* a good way to make money—but I realized I could earn enough to support myself while doing something I loved. Not only had I been able to cover expenses for the summer in Alaska, I was also able to buy a new camera. This once again left me broke, and started a habit that continues right up to the present: whatever money I make on one project, I recycle immediately into a future project. In a more practical way, I've found that film footage can also be recycled, and material on a given subject used more than once. For example, a Dall sheep sequence and some fishing scenes from the Alaskan film both made their way into the *Wild America* series in the program, "Photographing Wildlife."

The experience with the Alaskan film was a revelation, and left me restless to do more traveling and filming. I could no longer face the idea of law school, perhaps for good reason: my original impulse for becoming an attorney was not grounded in an overwhelming fascination with matters of law, but merely in wanting to buy time to do what I most loved. And now I had found another way. I was pleased with the Alaskan film; it was well-done, but it wasn't really professional. What next, I wondered, as I entered my last year of college. I felt the urge to travel to a new continent, to see other creatures that would appear to me as splendid in their native wilderness as those I had read about, then finally seen close up, in Alaska.

IT'S DARKEST JUST BEFORE DAWN

The trophy shed at safari company headquarters in Maun. Every three-week safari resulted in ten to fifty trophies for each of several clients, in addition to many nontrophy animals that were killed for camp food. We were only one of several safari companies in the area taking this terrible toll on wildlife.

A ll through my stifling senior year of college, I felt restless, haunted by all that I'd read about Africa. One of my favorite childhood books had been *I Married Adventure* by Osa Johnson. She and her husband Martin had organized one of the last great foot safaris in the early 1920s, and had set up a permanent camp in northern Kenya, where they lived. The couple had produced a number of books and films on Africa, including a documentary on gorillas, one on the pygmy peoples, and the first ever on lions. Osa Johnson had been quite a shot. She'd stand by with a gun while Martin rolled the film, and if an animal charged toward the camera, Osa would reportedly drop it at the last second right at her husband's feet. It sounds a bit exaggerated now, but it sure sounded exciting then.

When I picture the hefty volume with its zebra-striped cover, I can still remember the thrill I felt reading and rereading their adventures in Africa. Her stories about those faraway places made a lasting impression on my young mind. As I grew up, I continued to read about Africa, and the more I learned, the more fascinated I became with the idea of a safari. For a person in love with wildlife, what better place to go to than the richest of all continents in terms of animals?

As a college English major, I had read my share of action adventures by Robert Ruark and Ernest Hemingway, and by Christmas of my senior year, I knew what I wanted to do. That winter I wrote to at least a hundred safari companies, asking if they would like a promotional film made of their operation. I used my experience with the Alaska movie as a background reference, making it sound very professional, and I admit that I exaggerated my talents a bit more by assuring the safari company that I was thoroughly familiar with the 16-mm format, though in reality my forays so far had only taken me to Super 8-mm. Sixteen-mm film was still too expensive unless a person was getting paid a professional's salary.

I must have sounded convincing to somebody, because finally one company wrote back saying they'd take me on. If I could pay my own way there and back and supply film and processing, they said they'd cover all other expenses. I was so excited to get the letter, I rushed out the next day and emptied my bank account and borrowed money from my parents to buy a Beaulieu 16-mm camera and some professional quality sound-recording equipment. Then I set out to learn to use it, which was no small task, considering that the Beaulieu was much more complex than the Super 8-mm camera, and I had never before recorded sound for any of my home movies.

The day after I finished my last college exams, without even waiting for graduation ceremonies, I flew to Johannesburg, South Africa, and from there to the capital city of Gaborones in the republic of Botswana, where the safari company was based. Even after a summer in the remote wilds of Alaska, the trip from Johannesburg to Gaborones was something of a culture shock to a boy who had spent most of his life in rural Arkansas. And what I saw on safari in the country of Botswana would change my life forever.

We spent much of our time in the southern part of Botswana, on the vast, unbroken stretches of the Kalahari Desert. Most of the Kalahari is more an arid steppe than a true desert, greener than the drifting dunes of the Sahara, and more populated than most desert areas in our own country. Somewhat like the sand hills of Nebraska in appearance, the sandy rolling landscape of the Kalahari is dotted with thornbush and shrubby trees, and in many areas is fairly well covered with grass—tall and green in the rainy season, dry straw-blond during the drought months, and occasionally blackened for hundreds of square miles by fires that rage for weeks, playing an essential part in desert grassland ecology by destroying old growth to make way for the new.

We also spent a good deal of time in the delta country of the Okavango River. Flowing south out of Angola, the Okavango enters Botswana as a broad avenue of crystal-clear water, lined with wide beds of floating papyrus and flanked by palm trees. But as it stretches toward the desert, it spreads like the fingers of an outstretched hand into a huge lush delta, teeming with wildlife, before finally soaking into the sands of the Kalahari. The luxuriance of the Okavango contrasts sharply with what Rudyard Kipling described as the "great, gray-green, greasy" Limpopo River, which struggles to flow for a few months of the year not far south in the Kalahari itself. In these two areas of delta and desert, there was suitable habitat for virtually every species of wild creature native to southern and eastern Africa—and that's saying a lot!

I had arrived in the last great wilderness area left on the African continent. During the dry season, we traveled into the Okavango delta a number of times—by Land Rover, by native dugout canoe, or on foot, depending on the wishes of the current two-week client. On the way north, we would pass through a large settled area on the edge of the Okavango, the center of which was the town of Maun. Located there was Riley's Hotel, with its infamous bar—the hangout for as motley an assortment of characters as one could imagine, including a number of has-been professional hunters and ex-mercenaries from the wars in the Congo.

I listened to their bloody and blood-curdling stories in wide-eyed amazement, as we paid for drinks by plunking rifle cartridges down on the bar. The .375 H&H magnum cartridge, the most commonly used for big-game hunting, was the standard unit of measure: one cartridge equaled one unit of Botswana's currency, the South African rand, worth about $1.40 at the time. Squabbles broke out when someone tried to substitute a less well-known caliber cartridge.

Riley's bar was also about the only opportunity for female company, who included the wives and daughters of geologists, explorers, and professional hunters who were out in the bush, or young vagabonds from neighboring South Africa or even from England. All of them seemed to be searching for adventure, just like I was, and my observation was that most of them found all the excitement they could handle. It was much like I imagined the Old West in our country to have been, with mining town saloons full of heavy drinkers and loud talkers blowing off steam at all hours of the day or night.

At the time I was there, Maun's population consisted of more than 5,000 blacks, but fewer than 100 whites who permanently resided there. What the whites lacked in numbers, they also lacked in social graces. They were not well-regarded by the various black officials and policemen who had run the town since Botswana gained its independence in 1966. So, more than once, I felt a bit misunderstood and out of place. I was even thrown in jail several times for such minor offenses such as not having my visa stamped at the consulate every thirty days.

Between the powers-that-were and the occasional angry gunplay and romantic rivalry at Riley's, it soon became clear that my place was in the bush, and I tried to spend as much time out under the stars as possible. Some of the time I traveled with one of the other safari employees, or with a black assistant, but more often I was on my own. I carried all of my possessions and equipment with me at all times, including two 55-gallon drums of water and two of gasoline. Each of these liquids saved my life at least a couple of times during the six months I spent in Africa.

The safari company had semipermanent camps set up in a half-dozen locations out in the bush. A camp would sometimes be occupied by as many as twenty clients, hunters, and assistants, sometimes by only a maintenance crew of two or three, and sometimes left deserted for weeks at a time. As often as I could, I would slip away between assignments to one of the unused camps. It was there that I could escape the usually rich and often spoiled clients. And it was there that I could best immerse myself in the wildlife I had come to Africa to see in the first place.

Just as the vast prairies of our American West once supported huge herds of bison, antelope, deer, elk, and the predators that followed them, so the African grasslands provided food and shelter for an even wider variety of herbivores, carnivores, and scavengers. The density of large mammals on some of Africa's savannahs was, and still is, unequaled anywhere, but Botswana and the Serengeti Plains are the only two major areas that remain. In getting to know the wildlife of the Kalahari, I felt both in awe and at home, amazed at the ways in which they corresponded to, yet differed from, those of my own country. Migrating herds of wildebeest and hartebeest reminded me of the caribou I had seen in Alaska, and also of the once-great herds of bison that I would never see roam our Plains. Our bison seemed a more docile version of that aggressive harem-master, the Cape buffalo. The various horned antelope and bushbucks—six-foot-tall giant eland; majestic, spiral-horned kudu; odd-looking oryx; dainty, twenty-pound steinbok; and swift and graceful impala—were much more diversified than their antlered equivalents in America—elk, whitetail, blacktail, and mule deer. I already knew that the American pronghorn, though similar in appearance to several African antelopes, is not related to any of them; in fact, it is not even considered a true antelope. Yet the common springbok reminded me so much of the pronghorn that I felt right at home.

The graceful springbok antelope of the Kalahari Desert looks and acts much like our American pronghorn. But the springbok is a true antelope, while the pronghorn is in a family all by itself.

Among Africa's carnivores, the feline species seemed to outnumber the canine. But I noticed that lions, which hunt in prides, corresponded somewhat in their hunting behavior to America's wolves, which also hunt in packs; and that the legendary speed of the cheetah gave tremendous advantage to its rather doglike hunting technique of simply running down its victim. Of all the felines, only the leopard seemed to match our mountain lion in catlike stealth and stalking ability. Opportunistic hyenas were common, filling an ecological niche similar to that of coyotes in this country, and we have versions of their bat-eared fox, honey badger, warthog, and white-headed fish eagle. Occasionally I saw pangolins (primitive, proto-mammalian edentates similar to American armadillos) wandering through open grassland, and some warm rivers and saline lakes were inhabited by crocodiles, just as alligators prowl our southern swamplands.

But not since before the last ice age has America claimed any counterpart to the largest of Africa's mammals. I was fascinated by the hugeness of elephants, rhinos, hippos, and giraffes, and felt fortunate to be able to see hundreds of them up close. In that sense, being on safari was a wonderful filming opportunity. In addition to the chance to see creatures that I had only read about, I had at my disposal thousands of dollars' worth of trucks, tents, water, gasoline, and support services —a luxury of logistical backup that I never could have afforded by myself. But in another way the safari experience turned out to be horrible, because safari groups, including mine, were bringing great numbers of people into the Kalahari for the primary purpose of hunting and killing as many animals as was legally permissible in as short a time as possible. And in addition to my self-imposed task of filming the safari's activities, and despite my attempts to get out in the bush to film on my own, I found myself more and more often using a rifle instead of a camera and caught in the role of "assistant professional hunter." I'd become a good shot during my teens, and when the safari people saw my marksmanship, I was regularly elected to risk my life for the glory of others.

What this meant was that clients who fancied themselves great white hunters, and who had arrived on safari with visions of dropping a charging lion with one shot, failed far more often than not to live up to that image. Here were people spending up to a thousand dollars a day for thirty days of hunting, during which they would shoot approximately 100 animals each. The sheer numbers were bad enough. But what actually happened was even worse: with miserable regularity, these visiting "sportsmen" would only wound an animal, which would then run off and hide. Many such game animals, especially Cape buffalo or lions, are extremely dangerous when wounded. And if a professional hunter ever lost a client—if even *one* of his paying guests were ever killed by an animal— he lost his license permanently. That was it. So the client was simply not allowed to go after wounded dangerous game. Instead, the professional hunter would just say, "That's too bad, you blew it," and invite the client to go back to sit in the parked Land Rover and relax with a gin and tonic, have lunch, or whatever.

Meanwhile, it was not only ethical but essential that the wounded animal be found and finished off, since some of our closest calls happened when we were charged by an animal previously wounded by some other party. Sometimes the professional hunter would accept the responsibility of this sad task, but more often the job fell to his assistants. Along with a guy named Lars, another assistant, I frequently had to track down and kill whatever had been wounded, and then collect its head or skin or horns or tusks, or whatever the client in the Land Rover wanted as his "trophy." Or else the client would pose to have his picture taken after the dirty killing work was done and before the dirty butchering work began. That was what we did, and even now what bothers me is not the risk to my own life, but that all of that clumsy slaughter was committed in the name of false glory.

In the course of this work, we met with all kinds of hair-raising ambushes and last-ditch attacks. Once we were charged by an elephant suffering from an old muzzle-loaded musket wound at the base of its tusk. In this instance the damage wasn't caused by a client but probably by a poacher. In any case, the wound had become badly infected, and the elephant was enraged and obviously in a great deal of pain. We had been walking most of the day and were hot, dusty, and totally absorbed in slapping away the horde of tse-tse flies

My Bushman tracker and I share a moment of nervous relief after finishing off an enraged young male lion that had been wounded by a safari client. On hunting safaris, this pattern was repeated all too often.

that swarmed around our heads and shoulders and bit the instant we stopped slapping. Though we had been vaccinated against sleeping sickness, the flies were still a great annoyance. So, leafy branches in hand, we slashed away at our own bodies, stopping only long enough to replace one tattered branch with a fresh one. There were five of us in the group, and our slapping and slashing drowned out the noise of the charging elephant until it broke out of a dense stand of palm trees not fifty feet away.

After we had put this once-magnificent animal out of its misery, I remember thinking that my childhood anger at the trapper who took a beaver out of season seemed like a minor storm in a small teacup. There were other times that I was attacked by animals that someone else had wounded—a hippo, a crocodile, several Cape buffalo, and a few lions. But there's no glory in doing whatever it takes to release a creature from its suffering—and none in retelling the incident, either.

On the other hand, I'm not saying "Oh well, it was just a job, and somebody had to do it." I'd certainly done my share of hunting by then, and in that sense I'm hardly blameless.

We shot this bull elephant after it suddenly charged us from a grove of palm trees. Examination revealed a poacher's bullet festering in the nerve canal of its tusk, creating maddening pain for the elephant.

But I was more than a bit naive in thinking that safari hunts in Africa were just a glamorous, exotic version of duck hunting back home. After the first month or two of observing the superficial attitude of most clients toward their victims, and of being drafted to handle these kinds of incidents, I began to realize how difficult it was going to be to make a promotional film on what seemed to me less a form of hunting than a form of butchery.

The difference was brought home to me during several encounters I had with some Bushmen in the Kalahari. These tribal people have, out of intimate knowledge of and respect for the land and its animals, evolved elaborate methods of hunting, and they hunt only for food. I went out with them several times to watch and film them going after ostrich and two types of antelope—gemsbok and springbok—all of which can easily outrun even a Bushman. I marveled at the stamina and persistence of these natives, and though I had always thought myself fairly competent at reading animal tracks and signs, their skills in this regard left me in awe.

Alone, or accompanied at most by one other hunter, armed only with a lightweight bow and tiny poison-tipped arrows and perhaps one spear or knife, a Bushman travels on foot out into the brushy grassland. Like a marathon runner, he trots along for hours until he locates an animal that can be approached closely enough to attempt a shot. While I was in the Kalahari, most game animals were still relatively unafraid of people and could be approached quite closely. Their flight distance—the number of feet within which you could approach before they ran away—was sometimes as little as 75 to 100 feet. By contrast, the flight distance of elk in Colorado is at least 1,000 yards, because they're well aware of high-powered rifles. In Botswana, the safari companies had not been active for very long, and the native Tswana people had never possessed enough guns to affect the animals' behavior.

Bow and arrow poised, a Bushman would trot slowly up to a springbok or gemsbok until the animal was ready to turn and flee. At that moment the man would stop, slinging his bow forward and at the same time shooting the arrow upward into a high arc, like a shot-put or javelin thrower. Even with this added inertia, the arrow would still only prick deep enough to leave its poisoned steel tip beneath the skin, the wooden shaft dropping to the ground as the animal plunged away. The poison used by the Bushmen is made from a small grublike caterpillar ground in a pestle and then cooked and dried to concentrate and preserve its potency. It is very slow-acting, but eventually effective.

Because his quarry does not die immediately, the hunter also has to rely on his tracking ability. Now, there are advantages and disadvantages to tracking in the Kalahari relative to other types of terrain. The main advantages are that imprints are easily made in the soft or sometimes crusty desert sand, and the brush is thick enough to protect them from being easily erased by the wind. Rain is rare, so there is little danger of them being washed out. On the other hand, the disadvantages are the other side of the same coin. The tracks remain for a long time, but in such a dry climate it's extremely difficult to tell *when* they might have been made. To use a counterexample, in snow you can date a track by looking at the crust and studying textures that reveal the extent of recent freezing or thawing. In mud, you look to see whether it has dried and crusted over, or whether it is still moist on the bottom, perhaps with water seeping into the depression of the print.

But when the track is in sand, it's much more difficult to tell its age, and to compound that difficulty, in many places on the Kalahari every square yard is covered with months-old animal tracks coming and going in all directions. It seems impossible to determine which animal is the one you're tracking, and yet the Bushman I followed was able to jog over a crisscrossed maze of tracks with hardly a sign of hesitation, always on the trail of his particular quarry. If the animal joined up with a herd of fifty others, the Bushman still knew which one was his. In the case of one springbok, we followed it for several days, camping on the trail, and when the animal got weak enough, my companion closed in with his spear.

A primitive, prolonged method, perhaps, and to many it may seem little different than wounding the same animal with a gun and then having to finish it off later. But take into consideration a few other factors, among which are that the Bushmen developed their skills over centuries in a natural predator-prey relationship with their game, and to them it is not just a sport, but an essential life-and-death contest in which food, and not simply ego gratification, is the prize. To the Bushman, hunting involves not just one quick moment of killing, but the skill of impeccable attention, the virtue of patient persistence. His life's work is to accumulate and to exercise the knowledge that will feed him and his family, and if he fails, it's not a matter of sitting in the Land Rover with a martini, but of starvation.

When his quarry was finally dead, the Bushman would remain with it to guard it from hyenas, vultures, lions, and other scavengers—which in Africa gather immediately, attract others of their kind, and can reduce a carcass to less than skin and bone in a matter of hours. In my memory I have a distinct picture of that Bushman standing like an unconcerned sentinel over his gemsbok as the brilliant African light cast his dark shadow across the animal's body. In the poise of his detachment, in his complete and unquestioning possession of the animal, I sensed a victory so ordinary that it was eternal.

Unfortunately for the Bushmen, an alternative to hunting by ancient skills was already developing while I was there. Although most Bushmen took great pride in their skills and normally refused handouts, they would accept them if the need arose. On one occasion, after more than a week of unsuccessful hunting—and in all fairness to them, out of my concern for their hungry children rather than at any request from them—several tribesmen and I hopped into my Land Rover and drove out into the bush. Within fifteen or twenty minutes, we had spotted a hartebeest, driven up within easy rifle range, and shot the animal. As one of the larger species of bushbuck, the hartebeest would provide camp meat for several days. It was the African version of welfare, and although it didn't seem that the occasional windfall, when needed, could seriously affect the Bushmen's way of life, in the long run it had to. If, after spending a week or more away from their camp on an unsuccessful hunt, they saw me go for a short drive with my proverbial white man's thunderstick and bring down a bushbuck in minutes, it couldn't help but have an effect on the way they looked at their own lives. I saw the same kind of thing happening in Africa that had happened on our continent with the American Indian and Eskimo.

And I couldn't help but find other analogies, very few of them positive, to what had already happened in my own country. One easy comparison was Africa in 1970 to the American West of a hundred years earlier, with Botswana's railroads and people pushing further and further across, and permanently into, the wide open expanses of semidesert and savannah. This country the size of Texas had only one paved road, but it was crisscrossed with dirt tracks where farms and ranches were springing up around government "bore holes," and settlements and towns were spreading across what had recently been uninterrupted plains, empty except for wildlife.

The bore holes, or watering wells and troughs for stock, are pumping stations set up in areas without natural water holes as an incentive for non-native people to settle and farm in that area. Unfortunately, not only do the bore holes draw off critically important underground water instead of conserving it, they also facilitate the replacement of the wild herds of wildebeest, zebra, springbok, hartebeest, and all the rest with domestic herds of cattle and goats. Unlike the wild herds, the domestic ones do not migrate between water holes, or between areas where recent rainfall has sprouted fresh new grass, but instead are restricted by herders to areas around one particular bore hole, where they graze the grasses down to nothing and trample and destroy the soil. And all too often the method of restriction takes the form of a fence, which prevents free migration by the few wild populations that remain.

Of course, predatory species which once kept those wild populations of herbivores in balance are no longer welcome. I met a family of whites who had recently emigrated from South Africa to farm in an area along the southern edge of the Kalahari. The father boasted of having killed a whole pride of lions —a male, two females, and three or four of their young. Their only explanation was that the lions had lived in an area where they were running cattle. No, they hadn't suffered any stock losses, they said, but they might someday, so they killed them all in order not to have to worry about lions. Or at least *those* lions, I thought to myself, and I mentioned aloud that maybe

Contrary to what you might think, the expression on the face of this young male lion in the Okavango Delta is not a snarl. It's his way of testing the breeze for the scent of prey.

they should have kept that particular pride around in order to keep another, perhaps not-so-amiable pride, from moving into the territory. My suggestion met with total confusion; they couldn't comprehend it; and of course their solution was that they would just shoot those lions, too, and any others that came into the area. Imagine their reaction if I had said what I was really thinking: that a cow or two might be a small price to pay just to have a few lions around to look at, and to hear them roaring to each other in the starlit blackness of a desert night.

The parallels with what had happened in the American West were astonishing, and very disturbing. The Bushmen were moving deeper into the desert to escape the spreading towns, while the settlers were saying what we had once said: "Let's get rid of the wild animals so we can have the land to ourselves." Meanwhile, in America people had already started saying, "Where has all the wildlife gone?" and "Wouldn't it be nice if we preserved a little ecological diversity, along with some slices of our own history?" But the wolves and cougars that once stalked Pennsylvania are gone forever, if not for anyone's good, and so, even in 1970, were many of Kalahari's beautiful black-maned lions.

Since 1970, a number of game reserves have been set aside in the swamps, deserts, and salt pans of Botswana, and they provide sanctuary for a cross section of animals, including predators. But they do not take into account the ancient instincts of the herds that migrate in search of watering holes. During a drought period in the early 1980s, thousands and thousands of wildebeests died when, in the last stages of their long journey toward water, with many animals already dying of thirst, the great herds came up against a fence that separated them from domestic cattle—and from the life-giving river toward which their age-old instinct had driven them.

Africa has been called the "dark continent," a mysterious land of brilliant light and deep shadow, full of contrasts as sharp as the patterns on a zebra's hide. For centuries, it was a continent teeming with life, but in our own time it has teemed with death. And so it was in the Okavango and on the

Kalahari when I was there. While working on the film for the safari company, I saw more animals shot and killed than I could have seen in twenty lifetimes anywhere else. There was death everywhere, all the time. The air in camp smelled of blood, and out of camp, like something dead or dying. We were up at 4:30 every morning, had tea, and left to hunt, and it was a very unusual day when something was not killed before we returned a few hours later for breakfast. The mighty hunters then shot springboks, impalas, and warthogs before lunch, not to mention lions, cheetahs, and elephants in the afternoon. And I witnessed human carnage, also, in surprise encounters with terrorists down from Angola, but even more in the everyday conditions of unsolved hunger and untreated disease that I saw on every side. In fact, I found when I later returned to the States that I had contracted tuberculosis myself, almost certainly from sharing an ostrich-egg "canteen" with my Bushmen friends.

I had thought of myself as a hunter, for food and even for sport in its true sense, though I had never been particularly interested in trophy hunting. In Africa, maybe it was just me, but I certainly couldn't see any sense, much less any glory, in shooting warthogs and measuring their tusks for trophies. Even that absurdity didn't matter, however, so much as the incredible *volume* of the killing I saw, during just half a year with one small safari company. I knew that people could not continue like that, mindlessly killing with no thought for the next day, much less the next year and the next generation, without encountering some dire consequences.

The dark side of Africa is not its primitiveness, but our own—our own greed and unexplored motives—and this darkness affected me deeply, leaving me disillusioned about many things. Long before it was time to go home, I was sick at heart and wanted no more part of the slaughter. When I turned twenty-one there, it was the lowest point in my life. After what I'd witnessed, I never wanted to touch another gun and I never wanted to see another animal die. Three months after my birthday, I had completed filming for what I had been contracted to do, and I was more than ready to go home. I loved the land and its wildlife, and I would rather have seen it during those days of drastic change than not to have seen it at all.

When this photo was taken at the trophy shed on my twenty-first birthday,
I was already sickened by the slaughter and more than ready
to leave Africa, my life changed.

But I didn't want to stay, and I've never wanted to go back. My killing days were over. It was ironic, in fact, that my only rifle was stolen shortly after my return to Arkansas. I felt no need to replace it.

I still had to put together the promised film, which I did, and I sent the "promotional" version to the company. At the same time, I had enough film to edit another version of my own, which I called *Botswana: Where a River Dies*. This program is still in worldwide syndication, but its beginnings were anything but auspicious. Inspired by the previous success of my Alaskan film, I went all-out with my African project, combining the more professional quality 16-mm format with sound tracks of bird calls, animal voices, music, and narration. With its wildlife action scenes, it surpassed the travelogue status of the Alaskan effort, and ended up being a much better film.

I promoted it in the same way I had the Alaska movie— put up posters, rented auditoriums in my home town of Fort Smith and in neighboring Oklahoma, where I had had successful showings before, and even edited a short television commercial and bought the airtime to show it. While preparing to entertain everyone else, I entertained myself with the fanciful notion that people were just waiting for me to finish the film so that they could stand in long lines that stretched for blocks, eager to give me money so I could go traveling and film even more. But when the doors were opened, nobody else seemed to share my fantasy, and the turnout was thin at best. I never have been able to figure out whether the lack of interest stemmed from the subject matter or from some other factor, such as offering a film about hot, dusty Africa in Arkansas —a state with sweltering summers. Since then, I've had a theory that people would rather watch a film about Alaska than one about Africa simply because someday they might realistically be able to load the kids into the family station wagon and go see Alaska for themselves, but not Africa. Of course, the only hard evidence I've gathered in support of that theory is the success, ten years later, of the *Wild America* series.

I was still feeling down in the dumps from my bitter experiences in Africa, and the failure of the Botswana film to attract an audience did little to help. But my mother had always encouraged us to look on the bright side, and in my experience the old adage that "it's darkest just before dawn" had often proved true. Already I was doing research on a new idea for a film. It had come to me during the long flight back to the United States, when I happened to pick up an issue of *Life* magazine and read about a man named Jim Morgan, who was studying and trying to save the declining populations of bighorn sheep in Idaho. His story, and the brave, idealistic approach he had taken, really moved me and helped direct me toward the meaning I was searching for in my life.

I must have read that article three or four times during the long trip home, and on the plane I decided that I was going to do a film about bighorn, one which would show my admiration for these majestic creatures and which would also contribute to the attempts to save the species. I had seen much too clearly what carelessness and callousness toward native wildlife could bring. After the slaughter and bloodshed of Africa, I was going to turn my camera and my talent toward doing something worthwhile and meaningful in my own country. In Africa I had filmed death. I returned to America to film life.

T H R E E

B I G H O R N !

*For almost as long as I can remember, the magnificent Rocky
Mountain bighorn has been a kind of personal totem, the wild creature
I thought I would be if I were reincarnated as an animal.*

W hen I think of myself as any one animal—as the animal I'm most like—it's the bighorn sheep. If I had been given the chance to be born with four legs instead of two, not only would I have *wanted* to be a bighorn, I know I *would* have been a bighorn. Of all wild animals, it's the one with which I feel the most affinity, and share the most characteristics. Like a bighorn, I'm stocky and sturdy in build, and I even feel that I move like they do, straight-legged and stepping firmly on the ground. I prefer the same type of cool, seasonal climate and rugged mountain habitat that most bighorns live in. And finally, when people tell me I'm hardheaded, I must admit that I've seldom backed away from locking horns with anyone.

My earliest memory of bighorns was watching them butt heads in Walt Disney's film *The Vanishing Prairie*, when I was about six. Right then and there, I fell in love with them. The way the rams stood proudly on the high mountain crags, their thick, heavy horns curled in big circles, like some kind of wild crowns on either side of their heads, and the way all the sheep, young and old, males and females alike, could leap up and down rocky cliffs with ease, looking as if they couldn't trip if they tried. Whenever I looked at a picture of or saw a movie about bighorn sheep, I would feel a tugging desire to see them someday in the wild.

The first time that happened was almost fifteen years later, in the summer of 1968, when I went to Colorado with my friend David Speer. We worked on construction in Aspen, and on our days off, hiked around in the mountains. On one occasion we were lucky enough to spot a small band of bighorn, but they were several hundred yards away, and almost immediately disappeared over a rocky ridge. That brief glimpse only whetted my appetite to know more of them, to get closer to them.

Later, as I read and reread Jim Morgan's article on the plane trip back from Africa, that appetite resurfaced as a gnawing hunger. By then my motives had matured along with the rest of me. No longer did I want merely to satisfy a childhood dream of getting close to bighorn. I wanted to film them in all their modes of behavior, and above all I wanted to capture their head-butting ritual. What was more, I wanted to record them on film for their own sake as well as for mine, in order to help keep them from vanishing permanently. Perhaps I'd grown up in another way, too; I now found myself dissatisfied with Disney's romanticized portrayal of the sheep, with its crashing "Anvil Chorus" background music. I wanted to know what bighorns were *really* like, in all the inherent dignity of their everyday lives, rather than some exaggerated perspective conferred upon them by Hollywood.

But where would I start? While I was doing my disheartened best to edit and then promote the African film, I found myself rereading with growing excitement everything I could find on bighorns. I knew that the four species of North American wild sheep were, according to fossil records, descended from giant ox-sized ancestors that roamed Europe and Asia during the alternately ice-encrusted, then warm and arid Pleistocene Age. More than two million years ago, this era of mammalian evolution fostered some of the most bizarre headgear to appear since the time of the armored dinosaurs. Mammoths with coiled tusks, elaborately antlered deer, and great-horned bison and giraffes were, along with the giant sheep, among the more conspicuous species to evolve.

While gradually becoming smaller in size (for reasons no one is sure of), wild sheep survived repeated periods of glaciation, developing into many different, successful, and widespread species, among them some of the first to be domesticated. Four types of wild sheep eventually crossed the ancient Asian land bridge to North America: the pure white Dall sheep of Alaska, the closely related gray stone sheep of the Yukon and British Columbia, which are known as "thinhorns," the more massively crowned Rocky Mountain bighorn of the Rockies, and the desert bighorn of our arid southwestern mountains. I had already filmed Dall and stone sheep on my trip to Alaska. Now I wanted to concentrate on the Rocky Mountain and desert bighorns—the two most endangered species of sheep—with the idea of eventually putting together a full-blown, hour-long special that might even include Asian and European varieties and would be entitled "The World of the Wild Sheep."

I was especially fascinated by how well-adapted the bighorn had become to its life on steep mountainsides. It has a double-layered hoof, the hard outer shell of which spreads out over craggy rocks, helping to give the soft inner layer traction on near-vertical surfaces. Agile and sinewy, these sheep blithely traverse narrow mountain ledges and bounce down twenty-foot cliffs with ease. For food, they depend to a great extent on bunchgrasses, and also browse upon sedges, heather, willows, and where available, the buds and leaves of various trees. In summer they climb to the highest vegetated cirques of the peaks, while in winter they retreat lower to south-facing windblown slopes and valley bottoms where they can more easily paw through the snow for food. Although herds will travel miles to salt and mineral licks, they remain basically attached to their upper and lower home ranges, moving between them year after year, a habit of the species which can make it difficult to transplant them into other areas.

The more research I did, the more I realized how urgent it was to do something to help the bighorn. For thousands of years bighorn sheep had thrived over a wide range of our high plains and were one of the most abundant animals reported by early explorers in the western mountains. But within a hundred years of the white man's arrival in the Rockies, the estimated original population of more than 2,500,000 bighorn had been worse than decimated, with the survivors forced into the most inaccessible areas of the mountains. No more than 25,000 bighorns—just 1 percent of their once-plentiful numbers—are thought to remain, and those are limited to fragmented remnants of their original range, mostly in the Rockies into Canada. Here, they are more vulnerable than ever to factors which continue to reduce their numbers.

Tough and hardy as they are, wild sheep have proved no match for conditions imposed by man, such as fences, overgrazing, disease, and indiscriminate hunting. Since bighorn are especially dependent in winter upon the bunchgrass and browse available on sunny, windswept slopes, if they are confined by fences to areas of deep snow, or if the edible vegetation has already been removed from those sunny slopes, they will starve. Also, parasitic diseases to which the bighorn has little resistance, especially lungworm and scabies mites, were

The entire story of a bighorn's life—his age, diet, and position in the hierarchy of the herd—can be read in the way his horns swell, curl, and taper.

introduced suddenly, in evolutionary terms, by domestic sheep. And finally, not only have bighorn been hunted for the preferred flavor of their flesh, but the horns of the rams have long made them among the most sought-after big-game animals of the world.

Wildlife management for the most part refused to concern itself with the bighorn until sportsmen began to complain that they couldn't find any more of them to shoot. Since then, unfortunately, the bighorn has been managed primarily to continue to provide hunters with what they consider a worthy target—an animal with horns which, when viewed in profile, form at least three-quarters of a full circle, a "three-quarter curl." This sort of trophy-biased management removes prime breeding rams from herds whose isolation and reduced numbers have already depleted their gene pools. But legal hunting, which at least can be controlled to generate both income and information to support—one hopes—better management policies, is only part of the problem. Even more insidious is poaching. The motive for poaching bighorn is without exception to obtain a trophy, as in the reported case of a hunter who, unable to decide which of three rams had the largest horns, shot all three, removed only one set of horns, and left all the animals to rot.

Trophy-hunting, of course, is nothing new. A century ago Indians knocked two solid logs together as a challenge to attract head-butting rams, the horns of which would then be sold for a good price to white "sportsmen" too lazy to meet the difficult demands of hunting in the high country. But poaching is on the upswing, and ironically seems to increase in direct proportion to the protection granted the bighorn. This upswing began back in the 1940s, after an eastern sportswriter encouraged good hunters to go for a "grand slam"—a head from each of the four North American wild sheep. One of the most coveted acquisitions in the shadowy world of trophy hunting, a "grand slam" doesn't come cheap. Hunting any wild sheep is expensive hard work, if one can even obtain a permit. An unscrupulous few prefer to pay others to do it for them, but the price is hardly less: a set of Rocky Mountain bighorn horns fetches $20,000, while the trophy-sized head of a desert bighorn, the rarest of the "grand slam" four, brings as much as $50,000. The dishonest buyers are as despicable as the dishonest killers, many of whom are highly organized criminals. And both deprive the legitimate sportsman of opportunities to hunt.

I once used my correspondence-school taxidermy skills to mount the head of a 10-point whitetail buck I had shot. The head hung proudly over the fireplace in my parents' home for a few years until I gave it away, and so I can understand the primitive satisfaction that comes when the mighty hunter displays the proof of his prowess for all to see. But when someone else does all the work, and hundreds of thousands of dollars are spent to acquire animal heads as status symbols, something is terribly wrong. To my mind, the situation will change only when all sheep hunting is outlawed, or at least when all trophies become socially unacceptable symbols of the lowest motives in sportsmanship. This seems unlikely in the near future, since laws and courts in most western states traditionally have refused to take poaching seriously, either as individual whim or organized conspiracy.

Of course the primary victim is the bighorn itself—the only one who really has any right to the horns. These great spirals may measure up to 50 inches, and weigh more than 30 pounds —as much as all the bones in the ram's body. His head and horns together make up at least a fifth of his total body weight of 250 to 300 pounds, and his body is well structured to support both horns and head. The double-walled skull is strengthened with bone struts, and a wide tendon bands the skull to the spine, thus allowing the head a sort of spring-loaded recoil from blows. Behind the ears, a mass of cartilage also helps cushion the shock.

The entire story of a ram's life can be read in his horns. During his first year, the sheath begins growing from the base over a bony core. At about two years of age the horns begin to bend backward, then gradually spiral down and around to reach their greatest length and form a full curl by age eight or nine. The horn tissue does most of its growing in spring and summer, when food is plentiful, and stops growing in early fall, resulting in a deeply indented ring. Successively shorter segments are added each year of the ram's life, and his age can be determined by counting the rings. In most mature rams, the thin tips of the horns are broken off and blunted, or "broomed," from battles with rivals. The horns of older rams are often heavily scarred and severely broomed. Females have much smaller horns, which reach their maximum length by age three and, because of a difference in tissue nourishment, have rings that are less defined.

As I researched these details, my goal came to include filming not only head-butting behavior, but the rings and scars and broomed ends of a ram's horns that would give a vivid picture of his life. I wanted to present the whole story of bighorns, from birth to old age, in the hope that people who saw the film would come to care as much as I did about the future of this splendid animal.

With this in mind, I contacted Jim Morgan, asking for his help and offering mine in a joint project that might make the plight of the Rocky Mountain bighorn more widely known. The next May, Jim and I finally sat down at a picnic table in a campground in Idaho and wrote up our working agreement. He would supply his expertise with wild sheep, and I would supply my expertise in filming.

Jim had been a biologist with the Idaho Game Department, until circumstances made him realize that he was more of an animal-lover than a bureaucrat. The two aren't always compatible. Morgan had lived with, studied, and photographed bighorns since 1966, and in the course of his career, he was beaten up, shot at, and officially muzzled because of his outspoken efforts to reduce the overgrazing of our public lands by getting domestic livestock off what remained of the bighorn's range. In addition, it was his research that had proved beyond a doubt that the law that allowed hunters to take any ram with a three-quarter curl was based on a mistaken initial assumption: that such rams would be over the age of twelve, and thus no longer breeding stock. What Morgan discovered was that 90 percent of these three-quarter curl rams were well *under* that age, and he insisted that they should be protected in order to maintain and perpetuate the vigor of the herd. He also argued that even the oldest rams should be given the opportunity to pass on their accumulated knowledge of such things as feeding locations, weather changes, predator detection, and escape routes to the herd's younger members.

Jim had tried to work for the bighorn's benefit within the system, and when that failed, he quit. Unfortunately, he and I also didn't remain in working cooperation for very long. Though I too saw major flaws in the bureaucracy, I knew that on this project at least, I would have to work within it, even if that meant working without Jim, which as it turned out, I did. I admired Morgan and his stance, and still do, and I owe him a debt of thanks for all that he did to help me get started filming bighorns, as well as for all he's done to help them on his own.

And so began almost three years of traveling back and forth to film mountain sheep in Montana, Wyoming, and Canada, and desert bighorn in Nevada, Arizona, and California. Often I enjoyed the companionship and assistance of my friends David Huie and C. C. Lockwood, both of whom had also gone on to careers in wildlife photography. I remember many a long night around a campfire, in campgrounds or in the wilderness, telling stories and playing pranks on one another, and despite some difficult times, I always looked forward to their company. Much of the time, though, I traveled by myself because I wanted to film everything the bighorn did, and this often meant staying out to film sheep for weeks on end in downright uncomfortable weather of all sorts.

At first we traveled by truck, camping out most of the time under the stars. But after being caught in an early autumn snowstorm in Wyoming, C.C. and I realized that it would be foolish to think that we could get away with keeping ourselves and the camera gear in any kind of reasonable shape without a better form of shelter. So we took time out to return to Arkansas and buy an Airstream trailer, and then headed out again for the bighorn breeding season in Yellowstone National Park. By the time we got there, most roads in the park were already closed for the winter. But from the rangers we learned about a herd in the Mammoth Hot Springs area, and found a band of females with their weanling lambs, plus some young males. We stayed and filmed their activities for several days, waiting for the rams to work their way down from the high country, which they usually do soon after the ewes and the younger animals come down. But the weather turned mild, and the rams stayed put wherever they were.

We knew that bighorns were more accessible in Glacier National Park in Montana, and we reasoned that if we went north where it was colder, the rams might already have arrived in the lower valleys. So we pushed on to Glacier, and after questioning rangers, hiking around, and constantly scanning the mountains with binoculars and spotting scopes, we finally located a band of twenty mature rams. They were in superb condition—coats thick and shining, bodies firm with a layer of fat that would help them get through the rutting season and the coming winter. Rams are generally calm and at ease with each other through most of the year, grazing side by side as placidly as the ewes. But these rams seemed tense and high-strung, and they weren't eating. Instead of walking casually from place to place, they would trot stiffly or run, grouping and regrouping, then huddling together in twos and threes and pushing and shoving each other.

We approached the herd very cautiously from downwind and got within good filming distance. When one ram approached another, both would lower their heads to a stretched, threatening position, then extend their necks straight out and twist their heads from side to side to show off the full size of their horns. To assert his dominance, one ram would stand near the shoulder of another and push him with his front feet, while the smaller ram stayed rigidly planted, as if trying to ignore the bully. These prefighting actions got more assertive by the day, until I finally saw signs that indicated they might really be ready to fight. Within the little groups of two and three, the more aggressive rams started kicking the more submissive rams on their forelegs, stomachs, and testicles, at first lightly, then more forcefully, as if to say that they were ready to fight. I was certain at least a dozen times while observing this kicking behavior that a fight would break out any moment, but it never did.

Instead, sometimes a younger ram would try to join in. But it wasn't welcome, and the two more evenly matched rams, usually four- to eight-year-olds, would nudge him away. The very young and the very old rams hung back and just looked on. Whenever a smaller ram confronted a larger one, there was no contest. Conflicts came about only between two rams of approximately equal size, and these matches all seemed to

Only the largest and strongest rams actually come to blows. Lesser rams rarely dare challenge the established hierarchy; many conflicts are settled with kicks or light head-butting, as shown here.

be settled nonviolently in the bluffing and kicking stages. All aspects of the rutting contests, including head-butting, serve more to establish dominance within the male hierarchy than to influence mating privileges per se. I later learned that, at least in some cases, this dominance means only that the winning ram gets to mate with a female *first*, before the loser. Rams do not keep harems of ewes, and it may be that when a ewe becomes receptive, she is most fertile with the ram that first mounts her.

To my disappointment as a filmmaker, I saw firsthand that only very rarely does a disagreement in the hierarchical structure lead to a full-scale head-butting contest. The largest rams have their dominance ranking, which closely parallels horn size, fairly well worked out from year to year. If a smaller ram is foolish enough to press a larger one into a fight, one smacking head-butt is usually enough to let him know that he'd better not try it again anytime soon. The larger rams get to rest on their laurels, for the most part, until a younger male develops the size, weight, and horn-heft to present a serious challenge. In each herd one ram normally dominates all the others with his advantages of size, strength, and age. He drives the other rams either into submission or away from the herd, and any younger challenger must fight his way up one by one through the ranks before earning the right to battle this "herd ram." Strange males from other bands, or exiled loners, will occasionally challenge the "herd ram" directly, but most of the time all he has to do is keep order within his own band.

Another interesting thing that I learned about bighorn social structure is that the rams with the biggest horns and the highest rank do not always enjoy the longest lives. The paradox works like this: when an animal is successful at gathering food, his system has enough energy left over from basic bodily needs to "spend" on luxury items, or status symbols, like large horns. It's kind of analogous to the man who can afford a Cadillac. But rams with "Cadillacs"—or massive horns—need to work while they're young, the same way the man does who owns the Cadillac, but who may pay for it by working himself to death at an early age from a heart attack. He somehow convinces himself that he can't afford to slow down—and neither, it seems, can a big ram.

The rams with the biggest horns are usually the most virile and aggressive animals, and risk wearing themselves out prematurely in the push and shove of fighting, courting, and mating. Of course, these are the animals that get to breed first with the most females, and therefore pass on their traits to the most offspring, which makes sense for the survival of the species. But it may be the less successful rams that get to live longer. In any case, it's only in old age, if he's lucky to attain it, that a big ram can relax and retire—scars, broomed horns, and all. I found myself hoping that I wouldn't have to wait that long myself before I was able to film a head-butting contest.

My second bighorn filming trip was made in June of the following year. I wanted to film bighorns in spring with the grass greening and ewes giving birth and baby lambs frolicking and learning where their legs could take them. Because Glacier National Park had more scenic mountain vistas than

Yellowstone, and because the farther north, the larger the sheep, I decided to return to Glacier. The reason for their larger size is that basically, the larger an animal's body size, the less surface area is exposed in proportion to its interior mass, and therefore the less body heat it will lose to the cold. A smaller, skinnier animal has proportionately more of its heat-producing body mass exposed at the surface, and so is more vulnerable to the cold. In evolutionary terms, the colder the climate, the more the bigger animal is favored.

Although C. C. Lockwood and I had seen only a few ewes the previous fall while we were filming the rams in Glacier, I knew there were plenty of them within the park's boundaries.

The Rocky Mountain Goat has adapted even more successfully than the bighorn to steep terrain and harsh climate. Here a female with twin kids relaxes in the brief summer sun.

Naively, I imagined that all I had to do was show up on a sunny June day, and there would be a bighorn ewe giving birth to a cute little lamb. Things don't quite happen that way, as I found out. While scrambling around some rocks in the Swift-current Valley, I came upon a ewe that looked so close to her delivery time that her swollen belly seemed almost to touch the ground. I tried to move in, close enough to film but not close enough to have her notice me, but she wandered off to the other side of the mountain. I followed at a discreet distance, thinking that any moment she would lie down and have her lamb, but she didn't, and six hours and what seemed like sixteen miles later, she still hadn't. By that time the sun had set, and I was stuck miles from the Airstream trailer, realizing with a sinking feeling that I was going to have to spend the night in the cold, without having gotten the footage I was after. It was my first inkling that many such nights might lie ahead.

The closest I did come to filming a birth occurred a couple of weeks later. In the meantime, I had decided that instead of following the pregnant ewes all over the mountainsides and up and down the cliffs, I'd stay hidden in one spot—a small open meadow gently sloping up to a shallow cave at the base of a rocky cliff. There were a number of ewes in the meadow, and it seemed logical that eventually one of them might choose to give birth in that private, sheltered area. From this natural blind behind some rocks, I set my camera on its tripod, trained it on the cave, and sat down to wait.

After a week of waiting all day, every day, at the cliff location and returning to the trailer on most nights for a warm rest, I hiked back early one morning to find that one of the ewes had just given birth. Although I wasn't there for the actual event, I'm certain that I arrived within thirty minutes afterward. The lamb was still half-wet, and the ewe was in the process of licking it dry. As it made its first attempt to struggle to its feet, I could see the long umbilical cord still dangling wet from its belly. I had learned a few lessons from the wandering pregnant ewe, and one of them was that maybe the mountains were trying to tell me something. Maybe this cute little newborn lamb was as close as I needed to get to that moment of privacy. So, letting discretion be the better part of my filming valor, I satisfied myself with footage of the minutes-old lamb, and after that gave up the game of trying to film the birth itself—never mind the dangerous game of hide-and-seek, following pregnant ewes along the cliffs and talus rockslides. Obviously it was a game they were much better at than I.

I stayed at Glacier for most of that summer, with side trips down to Yellowstone and up to Banff National Park in Canada, filming the growing lambs as they played with each other, leaping more and more skillfully among the cliffs. I also found the rams that belonged with those ewes, and spent quite a bit

The pika, a rabbit-like rodent that darts among high-country rockslides cutting and storing hay for the winter, amused me with its cheerful alarm "beep" during the many long days I spent filming at Glacier National Park.

of time with them. By that autumn I felt that I had gained the acceptance of both groups, and because the animals no longer paid much attention to me, I looked forward with even more eagerness than usual to the possibility of filming not only a real clash among the rams, but also perhaps the actual courtship and mating of a ram and a ewe. As things turned out, I was able to film neither of those activities on this trip, but what did happen was almost as rewarding.

I've spoken about my desire to get close to bighorns, and I feel that way about all wild animals. I'm more of a naturalist than I am a technical biologist or scientist, and since the days of Stanley the Beaver, I'd rather stroke an animal or hold and cuddle it than inject it or tag it to study some scientific detail of its behavior. That's not to say that I'm not interested in behavior. I am—I want to know how animals act and why they do the things they do, but most of all I want to get to know them in a personal sense, because I believe every animal is an individual, and I want them to accept me so that maybe I can learn a little about my own personality in the process. One of the best feelings in the world for me is being accepted by a wild animal, whether it's Foxy the Fox curled up in my lap, or a pigeon or a squirrel in a city park that finally takes a piece of bread or a peanut from my hand. I know that all the animal really wants is the bread or the nut, but like many people, I can't help feeling that it likes me personally and takes pleasure in its own way in the fact that this strange human animal has come into its life and offered it food.

The wilder the creature, the more satisfying the feeling of getting close to it, because gaining its acceptance is harder. It requires more time, more patience, more knowledge, and a lot more understanding. With the bighorn sheep in Glacier, it took three months before the animals would let me get closer than a hundred yards. And this was in a national park, where they weren't hunted and therefore had far less fear of humans. That autumn, when I could walk within fifty feet or so of some of the rams, I began carrying a small amount of salt with me. I'd sit in one place and, resting my elbow on my knee, hold out my hand with a little salt in my palm. Sometimes I'd whistle a sort of soft, mindless tune, but the whole idea was to remain totally still—nonchalant and unconcerned—no matter what the sheep did or how close they got while they were grazing among the rocks.

The day when one of the rams finally came up close enough to sniff the salt, he snorted and blew most of it away, but he still came back to lick the grains that were stuck to my palm. That moment was the high point of my life so far as animals

This ram's desire to lick a bit of salt from my hand resulted in one of the most thrilling moments of my life.

were concerned. When I felt that raspy tongue tickling the palm of my hand, sticky and scratchy with salt, it was with what I can only describe as ecstasy. That may sound strange, but anyone who's ever been licked by a kitten or a puppy can tell that there's something about an animal's tongue that says a lot about its innate vitality, and even its vulnerability. It's a gesture of trust between animal and human.

That moment was something that the world's richest man could never buy, and that most people, even ones who live near wild sheep, would never experience. Here was a beautiful wild animal, untamed and free, approaching me out of its own curiosity and interest, and actually taking what I offered in my hand. I felt like I wasn't even in this century, I could have been a Stone Age cave-boy up in those remote mountains, but I didn't feel alone. Instead, I felt linked to the sheep, part of their history and the great natural arc of their lives that had brought these sheep to this rocky slope and this particular ram to my side.

By the following summer I had filmed everything I could—spring, summer, fall, and even winter—on the Rocky Mountain bighorn, except the coveted head-butting behavior. To try once more for that I would have to wait until fall came again. Meanwhile, C.C. and I decided to head west for the deserts of Arizona and Nevada to see if we could find and film any of the diminished and imperiled desert bighorn.

This trip was a revelation of the great diversity of North America's wildlife, since Rocky Mountain bighorn and desert bighorn are so similar in many ways, and yet so very different. I saw firsthand how the desert sheep had adapted in structure, behavior, and physiology to the demands of life in dry places. Having no need for a large body mass with which to conserve heat, they are smaller and lighter than their cousins in the Rockies. During periods of drought, they can survive on a subsistence diet of dry grass and shrubs, and they can go for five days without water while withstanding temperatures that sometimes exceed 115 degrees. They're extremely sure-footed in the steepest, rockiest, most rugged terrain imaginable. They're our only native hoofed mammal, or ungulate, capable of making an efficient living in the harshest deserts, and they're a symbol of the wildness that still characterizes our southwestern desert mountains.

The desert bighorn has suffered from the same problems —overhunting, disease, and competition from livestock—that beset the Rocky Mountain bighorn. But they also have some problems of their own, including the added pressure of feral, non-native burros and other exotics which compete with them in places where cattle can't live. But their biggest difficulty is the lay of the land, an area of isolated mountain ranges separated by wide arid valleys, or, as one ecologist described it, mountain islands in a desert sea. Bighorns inhabit only the mountain islands, the intervening basins being used only to move from one "island" to another.

That didn't present much of a problem until this century, when people began to invade the West in numbers. Many herds live in mountain ranges with only one or two year-round springs. If these dry up or are appropriated by humans for other purposes, the sheep must move or perish. But what if they can't move? Highways, fences, canals, towns, and sprawling retirement surburbias now cut off most of these mountain ranges from each other, destroying many whole herds with one blow, leaving others even more vulnerable to inbreeding, epidemics, and poachers, and permanently preventing replenishment and recovery through contact with other herds. I was sad to see that, small as the groups of bighorns in Yellowstone and Glacier had been, the desert bighorn were far worse off, existing in meager bands of only six or eight, instead of twenty-five or thirty like their Rocky Mountain cousins.

C.C. and I finally located some of these small bands, one near Yuma, Arizona, and another not far from the bright lights of Las Vegas, Nevada. We spent more time at the one near Las Vegas, not because I cared much for gambling, but because it was more convenient to make biweekly trips there for the purpose of restocking the insulated coolers in which we kept our film on dry ice. I won't deny that we visited a couple of the casinos: who, after days on the dusty desert, could turn down a 69¢ breakfast? I should add that with summer temperatures reaching 110 degrees, it was essential to keep our film

—especially any film that we had exposed—consistently cold. The emulsion of any film is sensitive to heat as well as light, and a few hours of normal daytime temperature at that time of year would ruin it completely.

Why, you may ask, weren't we smart enough to plan our trip for a month other than July? A reasonable question, but the answer is that in doing our research we learned that mid-summer was the best time to find the fewest sources of water. High temperatures evaporated all the potholes and surface water and many of the temporary springs left by winter moisture and spring rains. The few main water holes that remained attracted the sheep almost daily. When a band of bighorn came to the water hole to drink, we would film them there and then follow them at a distance as they wandered back into the mountains. Occasionally they would let us get quite close, though at other times they bolted wildly up over precipitous ridges and disappeared completely, leaving us no way to follow.

On one occasion we tagged along after a pair of big rams for the course of an afternoon, and filmed some of their halfhearted head-butting behavior, which, though far less dramatic than during the fall mating season, at least is performed frequently, more in the spirit of play than of battle. We also filmed them doing something even more interesting: butting open clusters of yucca with their horns, and sinking their heads in between the stiff, sharp-pointed leaves to eat the pulpy heart of the plant. I found it intriguing that they did this *after* they had left the water hole, and wondered if there was some vitamin or nutrient they craved in addition to the moisture contained in the pulp.

While filming these desert sheep, I talked to biologists who were studying them, trying to learn all I could not only about bighorns, but also about the Endangered Species Act that had been passed by Congress in 1969. I wanted to know how it was determined that an animal was endangered, and how it got on the official list. The story that unfolded was complicated and far from encouraging. For example, both mountain and desert bighorn had been considered for the list of endangered species, but ultimately neither was included. Why? Many game departments in the states where the sheep were hunted wanted to uphold the status quo in favor of hunters whose license revenues they consider important. But as this century has shown all too well, all the revenue in the world won't bring back a species endangered beyond recovery. Bighorn should rightly be listed at the very least as threatened species, which means that they could become endangered quite easily due to their continued decline in practically every area where they remain. To this day, unhappily, they are *still* not protected from hunting, even though their numbers are steadily decreasing due to the diseases of domestic sheep and the disturbances of humans.

This large and healthy desert bighorn ram uses its flaring horns in play as well as in battle, and also for butting open spiny cactus and yucca plants to obtain their moisture.

That November saw C.C. and me still on the road, hauling the house trailer, and headed for Montana. Unfortunately, after months of living in close quarters together, we had one of our rare falling-outs, over something as stupid and inconsequential as a four-dollar bottle of propane. As a result, we decided we needed a break from each other, so I dropped him off at the airport in Kalispell, Montana, and drove north along the western boundary of Glacier. In light of what happened later, it was an especially poor time to have had an argument, since Lockwood was almost as fascinated as I was with bighorns, and over the past three years had been as patient about photographing them with his still camera as I was with my movie camera.

As I was driving along a remote logging road in Glacier, trying a shortcut that would take me into the area where I'd filmed my beloved band of bighorns the previous fall, I turned a sharp, icy corner, skidded on slick snow packed down by logging trucks, and managed to jackknife the trailer sideways across the road. The truck jammed head-first into a snow-bank, and left the trailer poking out over a cliff. It took me a full day-and-a-half, with a hand-cranked winch and shovel, to haul the rig out of the rocks and snow, and by the time I finally got to a place where I could park it safely, I was completely exhausted and about as depressed and lonesome as I had been since those bleak days in Africa.

I slept until I couldn't sleep any more, and the next morning I unhooked the truck from the damaged trailer and drove out to find my bighorn herd. Since I was temporarily without human friends, I was especially eager to renew my relationship with my animal ones. It was a somewhat forlorn hike into the valley where I had seen them a year ago. I had no idea whether they would still be frequenting the same area, and so I was heartened when I came across the band of ewes. But masculine company was what I was missing just then, and it was the rams that I really identified with. Lowering my binoculars, I walked on, and only a few frost-crunching footsteps later, I heard the great hollow crash of horns. Looking up, I saw two bighorn rams backing away from each other, powerful muscles bulging, to resume their original places as I rushed up that once-familiar hillside to film them. The rest of the band of rams at that point moved away up the mountain, leaving me alone with the quarrelsome pair.

As I look back, I was incredibly lucky—first, to finally find the rams actually fighting after two years, and second, to have stumbled upon one of those rare battles that go on and on. A contest often ends after only several blows, when one of the rams retreats and will no longer fight. But this match continued for two, then three more blows before I suddenly heard an ominous but familiar clicking sound from my softly whirring camera.

Out of film. The empty camera magazine that houses the film had to be exchanged for a full one, and exchanged quickly. But in my depressed mood of the past days, I had neglected to load film into the second of the two magazines I owned. Loading a magazine must be done blindly, with one's hands in a black cloth changing-bag that prevents the film from being ruined by exposure to light. Thankfully, I had had the presence of mind to throw the changing-bag in my pack, and I grabbed it out, sat up on the snow with the bag in my lap, and with my hands inside it shaking like a nervous schoolboy's, somehow managed to load film while the two bighorns slammed together again and again only a few yards away.

Because I had been in such a rush to film the head-butting before the rams quit, I had been holding the camera in my hands to shoot—not a stable situation under the best of conditions, much less with shaky hands. Since it looked like the two rams were getting ready to charge again, I yanked the tripod out of the pack and locked the camera down in it so that I could follow their action more smoothly. As they reared up and ran at each other, I shot a few feet of film steadied by the tripod—before its legs slipped out from under it.

At that point I gave in to filming "hand-held," which I hoped would work because the animals were so incredibly close, and because I was using a wide-angle lens rather than a shakier telephoto. Filming hand-held also gave me slightly more freedom of movement, and as the two rams kept up their bone-jarring charges, I was able, without distracting them, to crouch in one position, then move to another, filming them from several different angles. My heavy Arriflex BL camera was the quietest on the market, worth the extra weight in exchange for its inaudibility during those crucial minutes. I was close, but not so close that I couldn't dive out of the way if one of the rams recoiled in the wrong direction, and I hoped my crouching and prone positions would be interpreted as submissive if either of the rams began to pay attention to my strange antics.

But the long, long days and hours I had spent on the hillsides filming them in previous years almost miraculously paid off. Again and again they charged, for almost half an hour, while I rolled film, loaded magazines, and rolled film again. I was so elated that when the charging rams finally stopped I was still in a kind of euphoric state of shock, panting as hard as the rams from the physical exertion and mental excitement. It had started to snow by then, and with deep breaths I took in the smells of musky sheep, pine resin from the nearby trees, and new snow on the wind. The rams wandered off, and I never saw them fight again. In fact, for the two days that I followed them afterward, the rams that had battled seemed to stick together more closely than any other two, which has since made me wonder if quarrels among rams bear any similarity to quarrels among human friends.

Filming the head-butting ritual of the rams was even more exciting than I thought it would be. I took great pleasure in that, and also in the time spent close to the animals which had made it possible. And I was pleased that I had also gotten footage on almost every other aspect of the bighorns' lives. But it had been a long period of very hard work—much more difficult than filming in Alaska, or in Africa, where I had tons of logistical support, and where the animals themselves were so much more accessible. Here, I had tracked the bighorn across mountain ranges and deserts, through blinding snow and equally blinding heat, up and down cliffs and along sheer rock walls.

The three-year project included two of the most dangerous experiences of my life. One of these was being caught in a heavy wet spring avalanche near Banff, while strapped into a pack with all my camera gear. Luckily, by making swimming motions while being carried along by the tumbling snow, I was able to stay near the surface of the slide, and as it settled to a halt, I found myself buried only up to my chest. I was shaken up, but was finally able to extricate myself from that heavy, densely packed snow without injury. The other close call was being stranded on a narrow icy ledge where the slightest move would have meant a fall of at least a thousand feet. I had been following a sick, coughing ewe as she struggled up the cliffs, thinking that she might actually be going to die and that I could film it as a visual example of the way bighorn succumb to lungworm and other diseases of domestic sheep. Instead, I ended up on that terrifying ledge, palms flattened against the cliff wall, not daring to move as muscles fell asleep and the midday sun slowly melted the sheet of ice on the sunny side of me until the nearby rock was bare of ice and I could crawl to a safer, unslippery place. The final irony of that experience was that the roll of film I had shot on the poor old ewe later came back from the lab with not a thing on it.

In many ways, "Bighorn!" was my first film, in that I planned it, cared about it, and really believed in it. Even if the original idea of an expansive program about the "World of the Wild Sheep" had proved unfeasible, the more realistic goals I had set for myself—getting close to the bighorn, and filming its head-butting rituals—were richly rewarding accomplishments. It had been my biggest challenge to myself so far, my first personal statement, and I had done something difficult and unique that I could be proud of.

Nevertheless, "Bighorn!" turned out to be a failure financially. I had originally presented the "World of the Wild Sheep" idea to ABC, and they had almost bought it for what would have been an enormous sum at the time. But by the time filming was completed on the bighorn segments, ABC was no longer interested. So I put together a half-hour version of the film instead, and a color advertising brochure, and started the educational distribution aspect of my business that continued up until a few years ago. Although it won several awards, including the Best Western Documentary of 1972 from the Cowboy Hall of Fame in Oklahoma, income from distribution of "Bighorn!" never approached covering the expenses, which were underwritten to a great extent by my generous and understanding parents, and by my own part-time jobs.

The awards that "Bighorn!" received, however, encouraged me to think that perhaps other people appreciated my efforts and even shared my love for this animal. And that encouraged me to turn my attention toward an idea that came to me while I was filming the desert bighorn and asking questions about all those other endangered species—the ones that were on the official list, and perhaps others like the bighorn which should have been, but weren't—or for whom protection without public attention to their plight might still mean too little, too late.

FOUR

AT THE CROSSROADS

The plight of the brown pelican attracted the attention of Theodore Roosevelt, who protected it by establishing our first National Wildlife Refuge, on Florida's Pelican Island, in 1903.

D espite the problems faced by the bighorn sheep, in a way they were lucky. For both the mountain and desert sheep, the sheer inaccessibility of their habitat would shelter them from further human encroachment —at least for the time being. But what about creatures whose last stronghold in the wild was disappearing? Could species threatened with extinction be saved, and if so, what would it take to ensure their future? Certainly more research was needed, and still is, to determine the requirements of animals whose populations are rapidly declining, but all the biological data in the world couldn't save our wildlife without the support of the American people. It's ironic and somewhat alarming to me to think that the same humans whose greed and carelessness have endangered the existence of so many wild things in the first place are also the only ones capable of the foresight and concern that can save these animals. The fate of many species seemed hopeless to me unless enough people cared. I've always found that the more people learn about a particular species, the more they do care, and if knowledge could generate a sense of responsibility, then maybe that, in turn, would generate action. I felt that films could be used as powerful tools in cultivating such a sense of public awareness and concern.

In making "Bighorn!" I had wanted to entertain people as well as educate them. But now I felt an urgency about educating them, and entertainment had to take second place. In the past, my emphasis in filmmaking had been on larger animals with more dramatic lives: the bigger the better. Yet there were many endangered species whose appearance or behavior was not dramatic, like the salt marsh harvest mouse or the Indiana bat, but which nevertheless played important ecological roles, and were in desperate need of protection.

Congress had amended the Endangered Species Act in 1973, and for the first time offered federal protection to threatened, as well as to endangered, species. To promote public awareness of the new law, I decided to document all the mammals and birds on the Endangered Species list. This kind of program would be more hard-hitting than the average wildlife documentary, but I felt that the time was right, the mood of our society was right, and people were ready to listen. In the 1970s, the concept of conservation seemed for the first time to challenge the old-fashioned attitude that confused the wanton development and destruction of America's natural resources with progress.

I wanted the program's title to be as hard-hitting as the film itself. At first I was going to call it "Rare and Endangered," but the more I thought about it, the more this title suggested that the fate of these animals had been sealed—that there was no turning back. Instead, I wanted the film to

These Indiana bats may not appeal to everyone, but they were one of the first endangered species I filmed in the hope of showing that every species is valuable and deserves protection.

show that we had reached a turning point at which we could either choose to protect our wildlife heritage or see it vanish forever. It was important for people to realize that they still *had* a choice. Ultimately, I entitled it "At the Crossroads—The Story of America's Endangered Species."

On the endangered list were many species of reptiles, amphibians, fish, mollusks, crustaceans, insects, and even plants. But for impact, I felt that I had to focus primarily on the larger, warm-blooded animals. Call it prejudice, but my experience as a filmmaker taught me that people prefer their furry or feathered friends to the ones with scales, shells, or chlorophyll. We simply relate more to animals that are closer to us on the evolutionary scale. Sadly enough, there were just too many species of plants and animals on the list to include in one film anyway.

At the time, I had enough money saved up from selling film prints of "Bighorn!" to schools and libraries, and from part-time construction jobs, to at least get me started. I knew it wasn't enough to complete the project, but that had never stopped me before. In fact, looking back on my career as a filmmaker, my penchant for "risking it all"—financially and otherwise—has always been a big factor in accomplishing my goals, although I would not recommend this strategy for everyone.

With this dream in mind and the official U.S. Department of the Interior listing in hand, I set out across the continent to film each of the fourteen mammals and fifteen birds, plus several assorted reptiles, listed as endangered. I was not always without help, as my brother Mark and my childhood buddies, C. C. Lockwood and David Huie, contributed much of their time, talent, and companionship along the way to turn the dream into reality.

Three areas of the United States seemed to have more than their share of rare and endangered species—California, Florida, and the desert Southwest. Part of the reason seemed to be that as the "sunbelt" of the United States attracted more and more people, wildlife habitat was drastically reduced in these areas and sensitive species were the first to suffer or to be displaced. While the first two states had the highest degree of habitat loss due to human encroachment, the deserts of

Arizona presented an additional set of problems. These virtually waterless environments offer unique and specialized niches to suit certain types of plants and animals. The lack of water makes both the land and its inhabitants particularly vulnerable to man-made changes, such as overgrazing, mining, or damming rivers. It's interesting to me that living things in these hostile environments can be so highly adapted to the hardship of desert life, yet be incapable of adapting to the effects of encroaching human civilization. The crucial element, of course, is time. In evolutionary terms, the changes wrought by humans are practically instantaneous.

It seemed logical, not to mention economical, that my brother Mark, who was going to school at the Brooks Institute of Photography in Santa Barbara, could in his spare time concentrate on filming the rare and endangered wildlife in California. Meanwhile, C.C. and I set a course that first took us to Aransas National Wildlife Refuge in Texas, wintering grounds for the whooping crane—the statuesque bird which had originally sparked the elaborate campaign to establish federal protection for vanishing species. There we filmed the whooping crane's elegant and graceful mating dance. To me,

America's tallest bird, the whooping crane, here performs a jubilant mating dance for an interested female (on right) while a year-old juvenile looks on.

the dance symbolized far more than mating—it was a celebration of life and of a bright future for a highly endangered species whose numbers at the time were down to mere dozens. It was the kind of success story we were looking for, one that gave hope that the process of extinction might be reversed.

Next, we headed for the Sonoran desert of southern Arizona in search of a very rare subspecies of pronghorn. Out of once-numerous herds only an estimated seventy-five of these Sonoran pronghorn remained in the several thousand square miles of the Cabeza Prieta National Game Range west of Ajo, Arizona, near the Mexican border. Today, the Sonoran pronghorn are even more critically endangered, due to habitat destruction, particularly in Mexico, which makes up part of their range.

I had never seen the Sonoran desert and was eager to spend some time in this most richly diversified of our American deserts. Here, giant saguaro cacti rule the landscape, with the brilliantly colored Sierra Pinta Mountains as a backdrop. We arrived in April, and our timing couldn't have been better. During the previous month, the Sonoran desert had been blessed with a record rainfall that drenched the parched soil. Cacti have a unique strategy for surviving drought by expanding their thick, fluted skin as their shallow root system rapidly draws in water during a rainstorm, and the trunks of the saguaro cacti bulged from storing as much as a ton of rainfall within their pulpy flesh. But the most spectacular victory over the desert's dryness and heat belongs to the wildflowers. The plants themselves cannot withstand the summer dryness and heat, but their seeds can survive even the worst desert conditions, lying dormant until sufficient rainfall occurs for germination. In a few short weeks following heavy rains, the flowers will bloom, produce seeds, and die. When we reached the Cabeza Prieta, there was only a hint of color dotting the barren landscape. Little did we suspect the wildflower extravaganza that was to follow!

Although impatient to begin our search, after setting up camp we had to pick up our permit to film the endangered Sonoran pronghorn. I had spent months before our arrival, writing letters and contacting all the different agencies that were supposedly in charge of Cabeza Prieta. The list of people and organizations had seemed endless: the Bureau of Sport Fisheries and Wildlife in Washington, D.C., the Regional Refuge Manager of the Cabeza Prieta in Yuma, Arizona, the director of REST, the Regional Endangered Species Team in Albuquerque, New Mexico, everybody but the president himself. And then there was the Air Force, which was using the entire area we were in as an aerial target practice range. I naively assumed the final necessary permit would be ready for us when we walked into the office in Ajo, near Cabeza Prieta. But filming wildlife is never that simple. I wearily explained my intentions all over again and they wearily explained to me that it would still take a couple of more weeks to obtain permission.

I got the distinct feeling that they were trying to discourage visitors in the Cabeza Prieta area. Luckily, I'm not easily discouraged, so C.C. and I decided to do some sightseeing and filming around Arizona while waiting for required permission. We went to Organ Pipe Cactus National Monument and filmed the endangered desert tortoise. At the Grand Canyon, we filmed the Kaibab squirrel, a threatened species that lives only on the north rim—or Kaibab Plateau—of the Canyon. These little animals are to me our prettiest squirrel, with their long tassled ears, glossy black undercoats, and flowing snowy-white tails. Then, near Phoenix, we filmed the reintroduction of masked bobwhite quail, a species that had been decimated in this part of their former native range. Finally, our permit came through, and we headed back to Cabeza Prieta. After all that persistence and waiting, what we received was permission to stay one week.

We set up camp thirty-five miles from the closest major highway. The rugged desert mountains of the Cabeza overlook open stretches of sand broken by sparse patches of grass. Most people would consider this area a desolate wasteland, but to me it was an austere paradise. The land and the climate reminded me very much of the Kalahari Desert of Africa. Like the Kalahari, it gave me a strong feeling of untamable wildness —in fact, the strongest that I have ever felt on this continent. Looking at the jagged profiles of rock formations or the wind-rippled sand made me acutely aware of the timeless forces of wind and water that had shaped this landscape. In fact, with hardly any vegetation to cover the terrain, I sometimes had the strange sensation of looking at time itself.

The Brooks Range of Alaska was actually more remote, but there I had seen oil company helicopters overhead almost every day. In the first week on the Cabeza, the only sign of human beings that we saw was a single set of footprints heading north from Mexico into Arizona. And once we were buzzed by a border patrol plane flying fifty feet above the ground, hunting for illegal aliens desperate enough to cross this desolate country on foot.

With all the bureaucratic roadblocks behind us, Lockwood and I had the time of our lives hiking around, exploring the mountains, and camping under the bright stars. In the first days of combing the desert for signs of pronghorn, we discovered some of their tracks, hardened in the mud-caked ground left by recent rains, and followed them to a grassy plain—the Pinta Sands—where the pronghorn must have come to graze. Judging by the number of tracks we found, it seemed a promising place to set up our heavy camera gear and tripods. To the north, the jagged peaks of the Sierra Pinta loomed above the valley floor. To the south were rolling hills, the blackened remains of ancient lava flows. The bowls and pockets of the rocky hillside provided an ideal natural blind, complete with panoramic view. We aimed our lenses toward the tracks and the Sierra Pinta beyond, and proceeded to wait.

When we had filmed the desert bighorn, we had to set up our cameras at a water hole, then wait for them to come to drink. But we learned from Cabeza biologists that this strategy would be useless for filming pronghorns. Research indicated that instead of drinking water, they obtain sufficient moisture from their normal diet of grasses, browse, and succulents. We hoped this grassy area was the right spot.

Our week was almost up, with no sign of the animals. But meanwhile the annual wildflowers, or "ephemerals" as local people called them, had begun to bloom in incredible numbers. The spectacular array of colors helped keep our minds off the possibility that we might never see, much less film, any pronghorn. Almost overnight, Lockwood and I were inundated by a sea of purple and white, coral and gold, that stretched out to the horizon as far as we could see. For days, acre after acre of yellow, white, and pink evening primrose, and purple sand verbena glowed in the desert sunsets. Then, just as quickly and magically as the wildflowers had appeared, they began to fade, surrendering to the ever blowing wind and the baking sun.

Like the wildflowers, our enthusiasm was also beginning to fade. But we decided to risk getting thrown out, and stay until the pronghorn showed up or until we ran out of food, whichever came first. In the weeks to follow, we found the desert rich with opportunities to film other wildlife. We would each take turns at the blind so that the other could wander off and film or photograph the desert inhabitants: poisonous Gila monsters, ring-tailed coatimundis, bristling peccaries, and a host of other creatures to whom this sun-drenched landscape was home.

Those were my days of wide-eyed enthusiasm, when I turned the camera on whatever animal I came across—endangered or not. Being an opportunist at heart, I would try to get as much footage as I could in any area we were traveling through. Experience had taught me that there was no such thing as having too much good wildlife footage. What I didn't use myself, I thought I could sell to other wildlife film production companies.

Our equipment always had to be kept immaculately clean, which became problematic in the desert, with its ubiquitous sand and dust. The smallest speck of grit could bring our work literally to a grinding halt. We decided, as much as possible, to store all the camera equipment in the truck and to keep the doors closed and windows rolled up. But we paid a price for this meticulousness. The air conditioner only reduced the temperature from 115 degrees outside to 99 degrees inside the truck, which made driving during the daytime something of a sweat bath for both of us, and made us keep a polite distance from each other.

One lazy afternoon, while we were napping in the scant shade of a cholla cactus, the solitude was shattered by the ear-splitting whine of a jet streaking across the cloudless sky. In the distance, we could see its aerial target bursting into flames, the burning scraps of metal momentarily suspended in air before tumbling to earth. It dawned on us that this bomber-to-air target practice might be the reason our permit had been limited to one week. Though it seemed wasteful of money and possibly dangerous to wildlife, this military air show at least entertained us while we waited for the phantom pronghorn to show up. We later learned that the Air Force actually helps preserve the unspoiled quality of the Cabeza Prieta, since much of their gunnery range is off-limits to visitors or development interests. The noise and target remains were a small price to pay in return for protection from human encroachment. Our own encroachment was now several weeks past the permit's expiration date, and we expected that any day an official truck would search us out, but none arrived.

After nearly six weeks, we were convinced that the Sonoran pronghorn was not merely endangered, it was *extinct*. Then one morning I detected a quivering movement in the distant rocky scrub. Were the heat waves playing tricks on my eyes? I've heard of imagining an oasis in the middle of the desert, but who had ever imagined a herd of animals? I grabbed my binoculars. Sure enough, as if from nowhere, a small band of five pronghorn were skirting the edge of the valley, about 300 yards away. In my excitement, I accidentally kicked the tripod as I jumped up, almost toppling the camera in my hurry to roll film.

I had waited a long time to capture what I was sure would be unique footage. Unfortunately, there was nothing unique about the pronghorn's behavior. They walked lazily, grazing on shoots of newly sprouted grass. They looked up, twitched flies off their chestnut-and-white coats, and surveyed the sun-scorched vista, as if wary of some unseen predator. They did nothing out of the ordinary, but by then just *seeing* them was excitement enough for us. Finally, they broke into a lope and moved away from us toward the distant rolling hills, as if the rising midmorning temperature drove them in search of shade. Gathering up our camera equipment, we took off after them, hoping they would pause to graze. But two men carrying ninety pounds of camera gear were no match for the swiftest animals in North America. They disappeared towards the hills leaving us—quite literally—in the dust. It was my first lesson on how rare species do not necessarily equal rare footage.

Having watched wildlife films since I was a boy, I was certain that Sonoran pronghorn had never been filmed before. Now, after a month and a half in the desert, I began to see why. No one, up until now, had been crazy enough to risk snakes, scorpions, relentless sun, isolation, heatstroke, and Air Force targets falling from the sky just to capture on film virtually the same animal that you can see from almost any roadside in Wyoming. Still, Lockwood and I felt a certain satisfaction in being the first ones to do so.

Yet underneath the satisfaction was the uneasy feeling of possibly being the *last* ones to film these rare creatures in the wild. Already, mining and agricultural interests, not to mention off-road vehicles, had begun to scar the landscape in even the most remote sections of the Sonoran desert. C.C. and I packed our equipment into the truck, silently wondering if the Cabeza Prieta wilderness would someday become as endangered as its pronghorn. With C.C. driving, we headed back along the rutted tracks that led to the highway. I turned for one last look, but a curtain of dust rising from behind the truck blotted out my view.

After showers and dinner at a motel that evening, C.C. and I enjoyed a beer at the bar and patted ourselves on the back for a job well done. Little did we know then that congratulations were *not* in order. Several weeks later, we found that the pronghorn footage was virtually worthless. Heat waves rising off the valley floor blurred the animals almost beyond recognition. I had used a 1,000-mm telephoto lens to film them, but they were still too far away, and the long lens only amplified the distorting heat waves.

It was an expensive and disheartening lesson, yet far from a total loss. For one thing, we had witnessed the most spectacular desert wildflower bloom in twenty years, and the thousands of feet of film we'd exposed on other Sonoran creatures turned out beautifully. And even though the pronghorn footage never made it into "At the Crossroads," more than ten years later it was finally used in a *Wild America* program, "Photographing Wildlife," as a prime illustration of the trials of wildlife filmmaking.

When I checked with my brother Mark, I learned that he had already filmed a number of endangered California species

—the California least tern, the San Joaquin kit fox, the tule elk, and the California condor, among others. So Lockwood and I made our way back east to Florida. Here, we planned to film brown pelicans at Pelican Island National Wildlife Refuge, then go on to Everglades National Park to film American alligators, American crocodiles, Everglade kites, and the Florida panther.

Most of these species, though rare, were relatively easy to locate and film—all except the reclusive panther. Try as we might, after many weeks of exploring the Florida Everglades, we had found it impossible to catch even a glimpse of one. Perhaps because so few people had ever seen one, the mysterious lives of these wild cats aroused my curiosity.

While doing my usual research on where, when, and how to find the species I wanted to film, I learned about Les Piper of the Bonita Springs Everglades Wonder Gardens. He had trapped several pairs of Florida panthers in the Big Cypress Swamp region of the Everglades long before it was illegal to do so and had kept them in captivity as they raised several sets of offspring. By then, it was clear to me that filming wild panthers would be harder than trying to film Sonoran pronghorn. It also occurred to me that Les's captive panthers might be a lot better off in the wild than in a cage. So I personally paid him for a young male and female, and planned to film the story of their release into their native habitat, within the protective boundaries of Everglades National Park. Although the two-year-old cats had been raised in captivity, they were by no means tame. And since they had been left with their mother, they were imprinted correctly on a cougar, not a person, so I counted on their natural instinct for avoiding humans to keep them safe.

Once again, I had to get governmental approval in order to release them. But this time, surprisingly, there was no red tape to cut through. The National Park Service and the staff at Everglades Park were more than happy to allow me to film the release of two more Florida panthers into their last stronghold in the wild. They had worked hard to protect the few remaining panthers and though budget constraints prevented them from doing it themselves, adding two more to the dwindling population was fine with them.

So, early one morning, we transported the panthers to a remote section of the Park—an endless sawgrass prairie punctuated by hardwood hammocks, or "tree islands." We stopped the truck near a large hammock, where the tangled growth of gumbo limbo trees, poisonwood, wild coffee, mosses, and ferns would provide shelter and prey for these shy, secretive predators. I rolled film as a ranger sprang the door to their cage. The big cats recoiled, snarling at the humans who offered them freedom. Suddenly the tantalizing scent of the world outside must have awakened their restless instinct. Like bullets, they shot out of the cage and quickly vanished into the tall sawgrass. We leaped on the roof of the truck for a better vantage point, but the swirling sea of grass quickly closed in over the panthers' trail.

C.C., Les, the rangers, and I all shook hands. We had at last filmed one of the wildest symbols of Florida's Everglades.

With my colleague C. C. Lockwood, I purchased two young Florida panthers for the purpose of filming their release into a remote part of the Everglades. Only a few dozen of these beautiful cats remain in the wild.

And, even better, we knew there were two more panthers prowling the impenetrable thickets of the Everglades. Later, I often wondered what became of those two majestic cats. I could only hope that they were able to avoid poachers and secure the future of their kind with a new generation of panthers.

Another creature that once inhabited the hardwood hammocks and cypress swamps of Florida and other southeastern states was the ivory-billed woodpecker. These striking birds, with their glossy black-and-white plumage, prominent crests, and large, ivory-white bills, had always held a special place in my heart, and I wanted to include footage of them in "At the Crossroads." There was only one major problem. No one knew where—or if—any of these woodpeckers still existed in the wild, so I seriously doubted our chances of filming them. However, in one book I had read about them, I learned that these woodpeckers were last filmed in 1935, during an expedition led by Dr. Arthur Allen to explore the swamps of Louisiana. Determined to include this historic footage in "At the Crossroads," I contacted several film archives, but no one seemed to know what had become of it. Finally, dozens of letters and phone calls later, the footage was discovered in a film vault at Cornell University. Happily, Cornell's film library was willing to make it available to me, and I included the flickering black-and-white scenes as a tribute to what had been America's largest woodpecker, and as a reminder that any effort to save them had come too late.

The ivory-bill was particularly vulnerable to humans because it was highly adapted to southern bottomland forests and fed exclusively on the larvae of wood-boring beetles that infected the dying trees. As virgin timber was felled and cleared, and no more trees allowed to mature to old age, such specialized feeding habits ensured the woodpeckers' extinction.

It seemed especially important to me to include the story of the ivory-bill in "At the Crossroads," since their disappearance occurred within this century—recently enough to serve as a reminder that it was *our* responsibility to save this splendid bird. We can't blame this tragedy on nineteenth-century white settlers who recklessly slaughtered the immense buffalo herds, or on eighteenth-century whalers, who killed the last

Steller's sea cow. But how can an intelligent, advanced society such as ours lack the wisdom to preserve the genetic diversity of our planet? There is no reason, no excuse.

Recently, by some twist of fate, we've been given a second chance to retain a sanctuary on this crowded planet for the ivory-bill. In 1985, a small population was discovered in Cuba. Nevertheless, its chances for reintroduction in the United States are slim. Even if there were enough of these birds in Cuba to spare some for reintroduction into this country, there isn't enough old-growth forest left in their former range to support them. Yet if our southern swamps never again echo with the insistent tapping of the stately ivory-bill, for me there's at least some solace in knowing that somewhere in the pine forests of Cuba they still exist.

Sadly, for many endangered animals there will be no second chance. The red wolf is an unfortunate example. At the time we were completing the filming for "At the Crossroads," only a handful of these wolves still survived in Texas and Louisiana. At first we didn't have a clue as to where to find them, but eventually, through reference books, personal contacts, and a good deal of luck, we located a male and pregnant female in a secluded woodland in western Louisiana. C.C. and I carefully constructed a blind near their den, and we filmed the pair going about their canine business of raising a litter of pups, as if unconcerned about their soon-to-be-realized prospects for extinction. Although red wolf blood still flows in a few hybrid canids, the last true red wolf is gone from the wild.

After three years of filming and thousands of miles of traveling, by the summer of 1974 I crossed the red wolf, the last of the endangered species I'd planned to film, off my list. I had finally accomplished my goal of filming every bird and mammal on the Endangered Species list. In retrospect, I think of my travels with C.C., before either of us had homes, offices, and the responsibilities of deadlines, as some of the most rewarding and carefree times of my life. Nowadays I sometimes joke about having to work ten hours a day, six days a week, in order to make enough money to travel the way I used to when I was practically broke. Although I mainly remember the good times, I have to admit there were many trips I took by myself when the loneliness was almost overwhelming. I

A smaller relative of the swift fox, the kit fox (above) *has all but disappeared from our southwestern deserts. This one was photographed stalking mice at night in California's San Joaquin Valley.*

On the other hand, the red wolf (below) *is already extinct in the wild. Before the last ones disappeared, I was fortunate enough to photograph this female with her pups near their den in a backwater Louisiana bayou.*

spent years on the road, without Lockwood or David Huie, filming endangered species such as the red-cockaded woodpecker in Mississippi, the Delmarva fox squirrel in Maryland, and the black-footed ferret in South Dakota, among others. Of the many qualities a wildlife filmmaker must develop, I think the ability to work in total isolation is especially critical.

I had thought that "Bighorn!" had been difficult and time-consuming to complete, but "At the Crossroads" was even more so. Of course, I had realized at the outset that this project would mean traveling to more locations to film more animals than the other program. During this time, I learned that I had no trouble coping with the wild animals: they were *supposed* to be hard to find and to film. But the *human* animal was an element I had not figured on. For one thing, the endangered animals, like all wildlife protected by federal law, were in effect U.S. government property. And to film government property, I had to get government clearance. Which meant dealing with government agencies, biologists, and state game departments.

Sometimes it was hard for me to make sense of these policies. While I had to go through all the various channels, sign stacks of papers, fill out forms in quadruplicate, and swear my unfailing allegiance to my mother country in order to expose a roll of film on an endangered animal, the government allowed biologists to trap, sedate, weigh and measure them, attach ear tags and radio collars, collect eggs, and so on. Though I still feel that both I and most of those government people had the same good intentions, distinct contradictions and earlier abuses sometimes rose to the surface of this bureaucratic quagmire.

I recall an unforgettable experience I had while researching various endangered species we hoped to film in Louisiana. The curator of the University Museum at Louisiana State University in Baton Rouge had offered to let us film an ivory-billed woodpecker skin that the museum had collected and preserved many years ago. When we arrived at the museum, we were taken to a huge room where stuffed specimens were kept. C.C. and I stood there in a state of silent shock while the curator opened drawer after drawer in cabinet after cabinet containing ivory-bill skins stuffed with cotton, hundreds of preserved skins of males and females, juveniles and adults. I could only wonder how many other museums, not to mention private individuals, had collected similar numbers of skins while the ivory-bill drifted toward extinction. I've never researched the topic of "collecting" scientific specimens for museums but I'm pretty sure that I don't want to know any more than that museums are more enlightened today, and most condemn the shameful policies of a previous era.

Today, I'm glad to see a trend toward more cooperation between biologists and filmmakers, as we both work to preserve endangered species, but in the 1970s, it was a different story. In fact, the never-ending hassle of obtaining filming permits was almost enough to make me want to give up the self-imposed mission of filming every endangered bird and

It's predicted that the largest of our squirrels, the handsome Delmarva Peninsula fox squirrel, will not survive until the end of this century on its much-diminished range along the shore of Chesapeake Bay.

A mounted museum specimen of the ivory-billed woodpecker, now presumed extinct in the United States. I was once shocked to be shown hundreds of such specimens stored away in the drawers of a single museum.

mammal in America. I wondered if anybody would even care whether or not I captured these animals on film.

Fortunately for me, my parents never lost enthusiasm for my project, and they came through with moral and financial support when I needed it most. I'd send film back to my home town after it was processed and printed and then call my parents a few days later for the report: "This was good, but that was underexposed," and so on. Often, my mother would make suggestions like "Why didn't you film more of that?" or "Why don't you try to shoot some film on this?" Looking back, I realize that through all those early years it was the patience, encouragement, and generosity of my parents that allowed me eventually to make a living doing what I love most—filming wildlife. And by keeping me going through those tough times, they enabled me to build up an extensive library of footage that, although none of us foresaw it, ten years later would become the foundation of the *Wild America* series.

Hoping to sell "At the Crossroads" to one of the major networks, my brother Mark and I joined forces in Aspen. We rented an apartment together, my first permanent residence since college three years before, edited the film into a one-hour special, and tried to find a celebrity to narrate it so the film would look more attractive to network executives. After much discussion, Robert Redford agreed to consider doing the narration. Mark and I drove to Utah to let him preview the program and discuss the matter with him. But as much as he enjoyed "At the Crossroads" and applauded its message, in the end he refused to narrate the film. He felt strongly, he explained, that a program should stand on its own merits, and not depend on a big name as a selling point. As disappointed as I was, I could respect his feelings.

As it turned out, even his narration probably wouldn't have sold our special. None of the networks were willing to touch such "controversial" subject matter, even if we'd been willing to *give* it to them. So, as we had done with "Bighorn!" we edited "At the Crossroads" down to a half-hour film for distribution to schools, libraries, and conservation clubs.

Knowing that "At the Crossroads" would not be aired on television was hard to swallow. The more limited the audience, the less impact and strength the message would have. I had to convince myself that even though the rewards were not immediate, all the headaches, time, and money we had put into the film would be worth it. Only a relatively small number of people would see it, and the income from educational distribution wouldn't begin to pay back what I had put into it, but there was a certain gratification in doing the kind of work I believed in.

Still, all my lofty ideas and noble aspirations about saving wildlife could not pay the bills. It was time to do films for less idealistic reasons, like earning money. So, in 1975 my brother and I teamed up with John Denver, who also lived in Aspen, and filmed a major portion of one of his television specials. In 1973 and 1974, in between some of our wildlife filming trips, we had done some smaller segments for several of John's other programs, and even though we weren't filming wildlife, it was a pleasure to work with him and his production team once again.

By that time, word had spread of our involvement with endangered species. In addition to writing magazine articles and lecturing on this subject, Mark and I were approached by Lee Mendleson, who usually produced the "Peanuts" specials, to appear in an NBC special called "Wild Places" hosted by Joanne Woodward and Paul Newman. It was our first on-camera interview as spokesmen for the vanishing wildlife and wilderness of America. Best of all, the special included a few scenes from "At the Crossroads," so at least a small portion of our film finally made it to television, and the message I wanted so urgently to convey was given the added credibility of being associated with the names and reputations of Newman and Woodward, who had long been concerned about the same issue.

Meanwhile, C. C. Lockwood asked me to join him in Louisiana to make a film about America's largest river basin swampland, the Atchafalaya. He had come up with enough funding to pay for my expenses and film developing, so I grabbed at the opportunity to leave the hectic, civilized life for the solitude and peace of the natural world.

Most people wouldn't find the dank smell of stagnant water and decaying vegetation of the Atchafalaya swamp to their liking, but C.C. and I felt right at home. The lush woodlands and nutrient-rich waters of this river basin harbored an astounding variety of wildlife—white-tailed deer, black bear, wild turkey, and a profusion of wading birds and waterfowl. By day, C.C. and I listened to the medley of bird songs pouring down from the high branches of the forest canopy. By night, the voices of the swamp belonged to the creatures lingering about the murky, slow-moving waters. The constant drone of spring peepers and leopard frogs was interrupted by a sound which resembled thunder—the bellowing of male alligators, which were uncomfortably close by.

The film we made about the Atchafalaya depicted the importance and fragility of this unique ecosystem by revealing how a rich flow of water-borne nutrients provides critical feeding and nursery grounds for a multitude of creatures. The film was viewed by many people, from schoolchildren to politicians. As a result of aroused public opinion, the Army Corps of Engineers was forced to cancel plans to drain the entire river basin. Subsequently, a wildlife management area was established, and much of the Atchafalaya Basin was saved from development. It pleases me to think that the impact of the film had something to do with that. In a way, it helped compensate for my inability to show all of "At the Crossroads" to a wider audience.

I also benefited in other ways from doing this film, acquiring footage on otters, egrets, black-crowned night herons, and many other species that eventually found their way into a *Wild America* program, "Swamp Critters." Also, spending my days and nights in the damp, brooding swamps of Atchafalaya made me consider how little satisfaction I found in accepting film projects strictly for monetary reasons, as opposed to my earlier goals. The importance of filmmaking in promoting the preservation of wildlife and wild places tugged at my conscience like an unkept promise to myself. There was so much more I had yet to film, so many stories yet to be told. The mournful howl of the red wolves we had filmed for "At

While the black bear is not endangered as a species, much of its habitat, which includes swampland, has been reduced. Louisiana's Atchafalaya Basin is one of the last refuges of this elusive swamp-dwelling bear.

the Crossroads" kept haunting me and certain lines from the narration were etched in my mind: "Unless we change our attitudes, the day will soon arrive when the last living red wolf, howling in isolation, will be answered only by silence."

Sadly, today the red wolf lives only in the memories of those who sought to preserve it and those who sought to kill it. Since the late 1970s it has been extinct in the wild. Was this to be the fate of all wild predators who crossed paths with humankind? While I was traveling throughout the country filming vanishing species, I had seen many sights that made me wonder, and that deeply disturbed me: eagle and coyote carcasses hanging from roadside fences, and park rangers disposing of grizzly bear carcasses in Yellowstone. It made me aware that of all endangered species in America, the most endangered were, and perhaps always had been, the predators.

FIVE

THE
PREDATORS

*The golden eagle is a superb predator, and a superb protector of its young,
as shown by this female which attacked my brother Mark, camera and all.*

I remember the sadness and repulsion I felt as I watched trophy hunters in Africa regularly shoot the big cats—lions, leopards, and cheetahs—without regard for park boundaries or hunting restrictions, and for no better reason than the dubious distinction of hanging a skin on their wall. So many of those hunters seemed devoid of any interest in, appreciation of, or respect for what I can only call their victims. Hunting, for them, seemed as impersonal as picking a can off a supermarket shelf. When I returned to America, and began to actively research and film both bighorn sheep and America's endangered species, I discovered that our own predators were just as persecuted, and even more depleted, than those of Africa. I became increasingly aware of humankind's systematic extermination of the larger, more aggressive carnivores. They were despised and destroyed because they were, in the most basic sense, misunderstood.

So, even while I was filming "Bighorn!" and "At the Crossroads," I was already planning to make a film about predators. I wanted to document the ways in which they are ecologically essential, and to reveal them as the "respectable" creatures they are by dispelling the popular image of them as evil marauders. I planned to point out, in this film, that predators aren't bad or cruel. When one animal kills another for food, there's no wanton behavior involved. A predator generally uses its efficient and effective weapons with skill and speed, and its prey seldom has time for much fear or pain.

Nature doesn't judge. It doesn't condemn and moralize as we humans do. Nature just *is*. And in its complex and wonderful pattern, every living thing interacts with every other living thing. Lichens, for instance, are food for caribou, and caribou, in turn, nourish wolves and bears. And after wolves kill a caribou and eat their fill, foxes and jaegers move in to scavenge the remains. Eventually, microscopic creatures in the soil take over, breaking down the caribou's bones and body, and returning its gift of nutrients to the acidic tundra soil, which in turn nurtures an environment hospitable to lichens. One of my favorite images of this immutable cycle of death and rebirth is my memory of seeing, scattered across the open tundra, slowly decaying caribou antlers encrusted with multicolored, life-sustaining lichen.

Each piece of this immensely intricate system is fascinating and vital in itself. But to me, that moment when predator and prey come together, each fighting to prevail or preserve itself in a struggle that may only last a few dynamic seconds —that moment epitomizes the essence of existence. In a sense, a creature's whole life is spent in preparation for those few seconds. The fox hones its skills from the earliest age— stalking a grasshopper, testing its claws on tree bark, playing with a raccoon tail that its mother brings back to the den. The rabbit is also constantly sharpening its keen senses—wiggling

A predator's whole life is spent preparing for those few moments that mean life or death to its prey, or to itself. This cougar missed the bighorn ram, but later caught a crippled yearling.

its nose to catch a wind-borne scent, flicking its ears to catch the faintest sound, ready at any moment to sprint toward cover. Such everyday activities may go unnoticed or seem inconsequential to us, but they are critical in preparing an animal for that one split second when it must, as either hunter or hunted, flee or fight for its life. In a way, the moment of predation is like the Olympics of the animal kingdom, and each of the contenders is like an athlete who trains for years for the big games, then gets sixty seconds to perform. If the competitor trips and falls, it's all over. Of course, animals don't win any gold medals. What they "win" is far more important—the right to live.

Although some people may think of it as brutal or "blood-thirsty," for me that moment, no matter which animal is the victor, is simply the most exciting event in the natural world. Some people enjoy football or automobile racing or other death-defying sports, but for me, the competition between wild predator and prey for life itself is the most basic "sport" there is. And if you think about it, it seems clear that many of our so-called civilized sports, with their emphasis on the primary hunting skills of speed, strength, agility, and accuracy, owe their roots to this aspect of our own biology and evolution.

In the contest for survival, there is an amazing diversity of ways in which predators have evolved to support themselves and their offspring. When I began filming "At the Crossroads," I became increasingly aware of the great variety of wild hunters on this continent, from the endangered Everglades kite, a specialized bird which feeds on only one kind of freshwater snail, to the weasel, a voracious hunter that will prey on almost any small animal that crosses its path. And I began to film sequences of these and other predators whenever the opportunity presented itself. With each animal I filmed, I came closer to accomplishing my goal of making a program that would depict fairly their necessary role in culling the ranks of prey populations and maintaining a balanced environment. It took me seven years of traveling around the North American continent before I accumulated enough material to show these creatures in their true light, in a film that would eventually be entitled "The Predators."

By definition, a predator is a creature that kills other creatures in order to eat. That's a simple definition for a category of beings ranging in size from the microscopic to the monstrous, from practically invisible fungi to 15,000-pound killer whales. The large carnivores—meat-eating mammals such as wolves, coyotes, bears, and mountain lions—are probably the best known, and are among the most alarming to people. Birds of prey such as owls, hawks, eagles, and falcons certainly live up to the definition. Some people even consider the robin, which kills and eats earthworms, a predator. However the definition or point of view is extended, predators kill animals only to eat—which is where *Homo sapiens* differs from the rest of the predatory pack.

Human motivations for killing go far beyond the basic need for food. One result of this is that our indiscriminate destruction of other animals often results in unbalanced ecosystems. Not only have we mistakenly overhunted many of our prey species, such as the passenger pigeon and the great auk, but it seems clear to me that deep in our primal instincts we also carry a compulsion to get rid of the wild hunters that compete with us for deer, elk, ducks, doves, and other prey, as well as

Dangling its tongue as a lure, the alligator snapping turtle, shown here sunning on a log, will lie in wait for unwary fish and other aquatic creatures underwater. This is just one of a great variety of hunting methods used by predators.

for territory. Cultivating a sense of dominion over the creatures of the earth probably served its purpose in early times, ensuring our survival. Since then, however, we have changed our occupation. We're no longer subsistence hunters. In fact, only some 250,000 hunter-gatherers remain in the world today —less than .003 percent of the global human population. But the instinct to eliminate the "competition" remains.

While I was traveling around the country filming my two earlier specials, learning more and more about predator-prey interactions, I was constantly amazed at how many people despised predators, yet how few were cognizant of their role in a balanced ecosystem. Most people simply failed to realize that the wild predator is not the author of the play, but merely one of the players. By that I mean that nature calls the shots, and even though most predators are at the top of the food chain, their populations are very much dependent upon, and in many ways governed by, prey populations. This may come as a revelation to anyone accustomed to thinking in terms of heroes and villains, of the mighty predator and its exploited prey. Studies at Isle Royale National Park in the middle of Lake Superior, for instance, show that even though there are forty-five moose for every wolf, the number of moose very much limits the number of wolves, rather than the other way around.

Another example, one which had fascinated me for years, was the interdependent relationship that seemed to exist between the lynx and the snowshoe hare. Populations of lynx and hare had been documented for almost ninety years, between 1845 and 1935, in the records of the Hudson Bay Company in Canada. It was found that in certain years the trappers were able to bring in high numbers of lynx furs, and then, every nine or ten years, those numbers mysteriously plummeted. Hare populations also bounced up and down, slightly out of phase with lynx numbers and usually rising or falling one year before the lynx population. In other words, when the cycle reached its zenith, there were enough hares to support a large number of lynx. However, at that point the hares began to die off, due to a variety of environmental factors that are still not totally understood. Consequently, the lynx would starve and die. Of course, fewer lynx mean less predation on the hares, and in time, first the hare and then the lynx populations began to build again, repeating the cycle.

I wanted to film a sequence of a lynx stalking and ambushing a snowshoe hare so that I could talk in the narration about this cyclical relationship, which I felt clearly demonstrated the point that a predator's population is often governed by its prey population. While researching possible locations to find and film lynx, I heard about a trapper who claimed to have regularly sighted one near his cabin in the mountains outside Durango, Colorado. I was more than a little skeptical, since a lynx in Colorado would be extremely rare. Some lynx do still remain in Colorado and Utah, but there are far more of them to the north, in Wyoming and Montana, and to the east in Minnesota and the Great Lakes area. Nonetheless, I couldn't resist a possible opportunity to film the hunting behavior of this wild feline. After contacting the trapper, I learned that while checking his trap lines for pine marten, he sometimes watched a wild cat stalking rodents and hares.

The trapper invited my brother Mark and me to go with him during his rounds to check traps. Shortly after daybreak one morning, we spotted the cat crouched under the lower branches of a towering Englemann spruce at the edge of a clearing less than 100 feet away. We froze for a moment, then slowly and quietly knelt behind a fallen tree trunk and aimed our cameras in the cat's direction. Luckily, we were near a half-frozen creek, so the sound of water gurgling through pockets of ice helped conceal the soft whir of the already muffled camera. Half hidden from us, the cat inched along behind its blind of spruce boughs, and we soon saw what it was hiding from. Only a few pounces away, a snowshoe hare sat chewing the bark from the branch of a young conifer. The hare continued to dine on its prickly meal as its attacker crept closer and closer. Finally the cat emerged from the cover of the boughs, and we could see that it lacked the long black ear tufts of a lynx. Just as I had suspected, it was a bobcat, which closely resembles its lynx cousin. But I was too keyed up in anticipation of the impending encounter to be very disappointed. I held my breath and watched as, ears flattened, belly pressed to the snow, the bobcat moved in as close as it could before suddenly bursting out of the shadows toward the hare.

The hare leaped forward into the air and landed back on the snow, hardly seeming to sink in at all, as its huge hind feet propelled it over the lightly crusted surface with amazing speed.

The age-old footrace between hunter and hunted began. Despite the surprise attack, the hare managed to stay just ahead of the cat's slashing paws, as they zigzagged and circled around the clearing and through the trees. Fortunately for us, the instinct of a pursued rabbit or hare is to outmaneuver its opponent by running in circles, so we were able to film a great deal of the action, as both animals ranged out and around 100 yards or so, and then came back past us several times. Lacking the oversized, heavily furred feet of the snowshoe hare and the lynx, the bobcat was ill equipped to outrun its quarry in snow, and the race was soon over. The exhausted feline slowed to a standstill and, licking an empty paw, watched its meal bound off into the forest.

The nine that got away. Not as adept in the snow as its cousin the lynx, a bobcat misses its chance at a snowshoe hare. For most predators, nine out of ten tries end in failure to catch its prey.

Although the predator in this case turned out to be a bob-cat instead of a lynx, the footage made up one of the most dramatic sequences we had ever filmed. The cyclical preda-tor-prey relationship we had wanted to film, and eventually did film years later, does not truly exist between the bobcat and the hare because of the bobcat's more varied diet. But I knew I could still use this sequence to make another important point, which is that any given individual predator does not have an inherent advantage over its prey—it is not necessarily faster, stronger, or smarter than the animal it may be trying to catch. In fact, studies estimate that most predators miss at least nine out of ten chances to bring down a meal.

So, they're struggling to survive just as much as are the animals they hunt. Perhaps more so, since they are dependent upon an unreliable and often hard-to-catch food supply—un-like their prey, which depends on the more "automatic" an-nual growth of green vegetation. Thus the animals that end up as meals for the meat-eaters are normally not the healthy ones in the prime of their reproductive life, but are the ones that are easiest to catch—the young, old, sick or genetically infe-rior.

The fact that predators kill is often wrongly interpreted by many people to mean that they are destructive. Quite the contrary: predation helps to ensure that disease or physical defects are not passed on to future generations, and thereby promotes the overall health of the prey species through natural selection.

But when people decide to eliminate predators from an area in order to promote game species, the vital checks and balances that control populations within the food chain begin to break down. Since predators in nature are greatly outnum-bered by their prey, the effect of killing even one bobcat, for instance, has a much greater impact on an ecosystem in the long run than killing one hare. For every bobcat that is killed, several hundred hares that were otherwise destined to be the cat's future meals continue to live and reproduce and feed in that same area. Multiply that by the number of bobcats that are killed each year, and it's easy to see how eliminating a few wild predators can wreak havoc on an ecosystem. For this reason, predators need our protection perhaps even more than the prey species we humans tend to favor. Otherwise, what we create is a prey population that grows too large for its normal food supply, and thus becomes vulnerable to starvation as well as to disease and weakened genetic traits.

Even knowing this, people on the whole seem to have a relentless determination to rid the earth of predators. No other animals arouse our emotions like the flesh-eating creatures that have historically competed with us for food. We have both feared and admired them, and for the most part, have made every effort to destroy them. This seems ironic to me, since our own human ancestors evolved from nomadic herbivores to become the most formidable predators on earth, partially by using hunting techniques they learned from watching saber-toothed tigers or roaming packs of wolves.

Even today, many of the various tactics and strategies I use in stalking my subjects with a camera were learned from observing wild pets during my childhood years, and later from

If it cannot catch a large and healthy creature, a predator must settle for something easier. Here the bobcat is about to make a meal of a small deer mouse.

watching wild predators as they hunted their prey. And all during my hunting years, I never felt the aggression toward the wild hunters that I have heard many other human hunters express. I always respected and admired the strength, intelligence, speed, and power of animals that hunt, and I've always thought of them as a link to our long-forgotten past. I believed, and still do, that their instincts are much the same as our instincts and their appetite for meat is no different than our own.

In fact, perhaps one reason civilized people loathe predators so much is because we see qualities in them, such as the instinct to kill, that we ourselves possess, yet don't want to admit to or confront. Or maybe some of our hatred is born out of envy for their free spirit and "nobility." And yet another reason might be that we have, it seems, a basic tendency to hate and fear, to have boogeymen—and boogey-animals. We need bad guys on whom to project blame or disgrace, whether it's the devil, the "dirty commies," or the flesh-eating beasts. Perhaps it satisfies some instinct we inherited from our ancestors to fear, and therefore to avoid, the unknown. For instance, in all of North American history, there is only one documented case of a wolf attacking a human being—and that wolf had rabies. Yet a fear of wolves is almost as common to modern Americans as it was among medieval Europeans. In those days, the wolf was regarded as a sinister animal that symbolized greed, savagery, and witchery, but in this age of enlightened biological studies, what is our reason for such misapprehension?

Certainly there is reason enough for a person camping in the wilderness to fear grizzly bears, but even so, the danger they present doesn't really account for our antipathy toward them. Grizzly bears do attack and kill a very few humans every year, but far fewer than the number that die from bee stings. For the most part, there are ways to avoid dangerous encounters with these animals, which after all, are only doing what comes naturally in such confrontations—protecting themselves and their territory.

Even adding up the attacks over the centuries by wild animals on humans and their livestock, predators still represent little threat to our survival—economic or otherwise.

Nevertheless, we have waged war on them. We have shot, trapped, poisoned, and hunted them with a vengeance that goes far beyond their purported threat to our lives, property, or favorite game animals. With this predator-hatred so ingrained in our society, and with the wide expanses of wilderness carnivores require for their home ranges disappearing at such a rapid rate, large predatory animals face an extremely hazardous future.

Obviously, two conditions must be met to reverse this trend toward the extinction of grizzlies, wolves, mountain lions, and all the rest. The first and most immediate is to preserve naturally balanced wilderness areas, and by that I mean allowing a full spectrum of native predators the freedom to interact with each other and with their potential prey. Even in one of our greatest national parks, Yellowstone, the ecosystem has been largely overgrazed by the too-numerous elk, deer, and bison, animals whose numbers would have been naturally fewer except for the fact that we misguidedly sought to eliminate their predators: wolves, mountain lions, lynx, bobcat, wolverines, and fishers.

Though many people fear and dislike predators, their animal instincts are much the same as ours. This wily coyote eventually outmaneuvered, killed, and ate the rattlesnake.

The second and more long-range condition concerns changing the attitude of most Americans to become more accepting of the large carnivores. Most of the wildlife films that I saw when growing up portrayed predators as villains, which I'm sure is partly responsible for our current attitudes toward them. As Mark and I were learning the ropes of how to produce and market our wildlife films, we saw the need and the opportunity to educate people about these beleaguered animals and hopefully to change the way people react to them. We decided to make, for the first time, a film that showed the predators in their true light—as important, complex, and even beautiful members of the ecosystem.

For "The Predators" we filmed a broad, representative selection of our continent's animal hunters. We found our subjects just about everywhere, from the sky and mountains above, to the water and soil below. What I discovered just beneath my feet was as fascinating and fantastic as what I found on the highest mountain peaks. Among land mammals, predators range in size from one-ounce shrews to 1,500-pound grizzlies. The first time my eyes were opened to this great variety was in 1975, during a trip Mark and I made to Alaska. In those days we worked very closely together (we still do, on specific projects), and in this case we traveled to the McNeil River to film a natural event that was to be included in one of John Denver's specials for ABC. This event was the annual summer gathering of dozens of normally solitary Alaskan brown bears—the largest land predator in North America and in fact in the world. From late June through August, these great bears concentrate along the river's edge to gorge on spawning salmon. Though still territorial, the bears become more tolerant of each other when they gather to harvest this abundant food supply.

We watched and filmed the bears as they growled and fought and groveled for fishing spots along the river. While filming them, we were delighted to discover a miniature predator that had the same aggressive temperament and voracious appetite as the huge bruins. Mark and I were exploring near the McNeil River when we saw a speck of a creature darting about on the ground among a pile of rotting branches. We watched in fascination as what turned out to be a tiny, tireless

*This playful masked weasel, the black-footed ferret, is America's most
endangered mammal.*

*"No Camping" means no garbage scraps to this hungry black bear. Feeding
predators that should be fending for themselves not only weakens their hunting
instinct but also brings them into potentially dangerous proximity to humans.*

shrew ran to and fro, hunting furiously for insects and grubs. We followed along as it stalked and attacked its even more diminutive prey, stopping just long enough to eat what it caught.

Shrews are tiny insectivores—insect-eating mammals—that are found everywhere in North America and are among our most numerous predators. Though they're common, because they're so quick and small they're seldom seen except when the family cat drags one to the doorstep. To my knowledge, they had never before been filmed. When Mark and I returned to Aspen from Alaska, we decided to learn as much as we could about the little-known habits of these scaled-down hunters, and try to film their frenzied behavior.

We discovered that the shrew we had filmed was most likely a pygmy shrew, the smallest predator as well as the smallest mammal, in North America. They stood in marked contrast to the size of the Kodiak brown bears we were filming in the same area. Besides the pygmy shrew, two other shrew species seemed especially interesting to us. One of these was the short-tailed shrew of the eastern states, unique among North American mammals in having venomous saliva, which allows it to kill animals larger than itself. This venom would not have a very potent effect on humans, but is quite deadly to prey as small as mice and voles, which are still bigger than a shrew. The poison is not actually injected into the victim, but rather flows into the wounds made by the shrew's sharp teeth. The short-tail is tiny, less than five inches in length, including its one-inch tail. But its extremely high metabolic rate, driven by a heart that beats 1,000 times per minute, means that it must consume its own weight in food every twenty-four hours. Fortunately for the shrew, its small size and inoffensive habits have allowed it to escape human persecution. In the world of predators, smallness seems to be an advantage—if not in relation to prey, then at least in relation to humans. Imagine our reaction to a bear-sized creature that needed to consume its own weight every twenty-four hours!

We also wanted to film the water shrew, which lives mainly in the northern regions of the continent and is equipped for its aquatic life by having webbed feet and waterproof fur. Its soft, dark-gray coat of dense fur actually traps a thin covering of air, so that underwater it appears silvery in color. To satisfy its mammoth appetite, the tiny water shrew seeks out almost every source of aquatic protein: insects, worms, spiders, even small fish. This restless creature keeps up an incredible schedule that makes me tired just thinking about it—hunting for three or four hours, then resting for only a half-hour or so before hunting some more, day in and day out, summer and winter, for its predictably brief two-year life span.

There was one major obstacle to our goal of filming these fascinating little predators: since they're among the fastest-moving creatures alive, how would a camera capture their quickness without making a blur of it? The answer, we discovered, was to film them at 200 frames per second rather than at the normal 24. By speeding up the film rate in this way, the action you later see on screen is slowed down by a factor of eight. It took us untold hours and dollars to film their hunting behavior in slow motion, and I'll never forget a friend of mine asking me after viewing the sequence, "Why didn't you shoot it in slow motion, so I could see what they were doing?" Even slowed down eight times, the shrew's movements were still incredibly quick.

In addition to containing never-before-filmed sequences on these three species of shrews, "The Predators" was also the first wildlife film to make extensive use of slow-motion photography. In general, a good deal of what might be called my "style" results from this use of slow motion, which allows people to see action and the beauty of movements that would be nothing but a blur if viewed at normal speed. It's allowed me to show, for instance, how a peregrine falcon folds its wings as it plummets like a bullet toward a duck, or how a mountain lion's muscles ripple and bulge as it plunges after a mule deer.

Almost as voracious as the shrews, but larger in size, are the members of the weasel family. On the whole, members of that family, specifically the black-footed ferret, have not fared as well as the shrew. In fact, right now this handsome, playful ferret is the most endangered mammal in North America. It is, as you may have guessed, a predator, although in this case it is in danger only indirectly for that reason. The black-footed ferret, as far as is known, depends entirely on the prairie dog for food and on its burrows for shelter. But because prairie dogs were poisoned to make the land more suitable for cattle and sheep, the prairie dog towns have disappeared, and with them, the black-footed ferret.

In 1972, I had gone along with U.S. Fish and Wildlife Service biologist Conrad Hillman to South Dakota, where we found and filmed what were thought to be, incredibly, the last black-footed ferrets in existence in the United States. Although I eventually included this sequence in "At the Crossroads," instead of in "The Predators," I consider it to be an interesting example of how reducing the numbers of a prey species can have drastic repercussions on a predator that feeds specifically upon it. By 1974, that South Dakota colony had vanished, and it was widely believed that the black-footed ferret too was gone forever. Surprisingly, however, in 1981 a small colony of ferrets was discovered in Wyoming. In the years since that discovery, their numbers have fallen. The official decision was that their only hope for survival would lie

A tiny but ferocious predator, the northern water shrew must meet the demands of a high metabolic rate by consuming its own weight in food every twenty-four hours. Imagine doing it yourself!

in catching them all, breeding them in captivity, and then releasing them into the wild when they were old enough to fend for themselves. I have very mixed feelings about this attempt, and I would have far preferred to see this last remaining colony left undisturbed.

If the black-footed ferret disappears, it will be because we failed to understand the essential interdependence of yet another predator-prey relationship. Just as we cannot kill off all of our predators without greatly diminishing the richness and harmony of the natural world, neither can we kill off prey species on which the predators depend. Otherwise we divest ourselves of a heritage that includes not only magnificent, solitary creatures like the mountain lion, but gregarious, playful ones like the black-footed ferret.

By 1977, we had accumulated an extensive library of footage on North American wildlife, and particularly on predators. I knew we had enough good film to edit into a fine hour-long special on the subject. The trick was to find a market for it. With this in mind, Mark and I approached the programming people at ABC. Ultimately, ABC said they'd be interested in this special only if Robert Redford would narrate it. We knew from experience that they were asking the impossible. We also knew that if we couldn't sell the completed film, we could at least sell footage from it to Survival Anglia, a British wildlife film production company, though that would mean our own program would never come to pass.

When ABC turned us down, the British company viewed our footage and made an offer to buy our best predation sequences, which they would then edit into three half-hour programs. Their offer was far less than the footage was worth, but it would have gone a long way toward paying off a staggering list of debts that were accumulating. It was a discouraging situation for Mark and me. At the last minute, however, a man named Bill Dunne—ironically a former sales agent for Survival Anglia—decided to join forces with us. With his experience in selling programs, and our stock footage library, we felt we might yet sell our original idea of an hour-long wildlife special to the networks.

A hungry grizzly bear, just out of hibernation, is disputing the claim of a wolf pack to the deer they have just killed. The bear, being both bigger and presumably hungrier, won the argument and claimed the deer.

Our persistence paid off when executives at NBC said that they were willing to take a look at some sequences. Though they were impressed with the footage, what they wanted as a final program was, in their words, "an animal cops and robbers show." They wanted to see a lot of animals chasing other animals and killing them, but without any actual bloodshed on-screen. And although killing was okay, showing the predator in the act of eating its prey wasn't. We felt the attitude of the executives betrayed, at best, a lack of knowledge about the natural world, and we found it hard to believe that these were the only themes they had in mind. Such limitations certainly put a crimp in my plan to show predators in their true light, but we knew that we could still work around these restrictions and make some valid points, ones that would possibly dispel some inaccurate myths. I believed we would still be able to emphasize in the narration the positive aspects of predatory behavior and promote an understanding and appreciation for what I considered to be nature's most skilled, efficient, and misunderstood creatures.

Our one-hour special, "The Predators," was finally licensed to NBC for one broadcast. Our exhilaration over this, however, rapidly turned to exhaustion—we were given only five weeks to finish the film! Normally a program of this caliber would take five times that long to complete. Mark and I worked around the clock in our Aspen studio to finish the picture and sound edits. One of us would work from 6:00 A.M. to 6:00 P.M., and then the other would take over for the next twelve hours, seven days a week, for two weeks. With the help of two extra editors, Tom Kennedy and Marc Cerutti, and with John Savage as the narration writer, we managed to finish the program with our health and sanity intact. When the picture edit was completed, we flew back and forth to New York to finalize the sound edit and music score, and to arrange for a narrator.

Since many of the sequences were shot in slow motion, it was necessary to include quite a bit of music in the film, because sound effects just don't work over a scene that has been slowed down. While slowing down the picture can make the action more dramatic and beautiful, slowing down an audio effect, such as the growl of a wolf or the rustle of a leaf, makes it sound distorted and weird. Music could provide an evocative backdrop instead. The trouble is that viewers invariably heard suggestive "bad guy" music over a predatory hunting sequence, and then "good guy" music over a prey animal sequence. We tried to match impartial yet evocative music with *all* species—predator as well as prey—and worked closely with the composer, John Murtaugh, to be certain that this music remained "neutral."

We also wanted to get our point of view across very directly in the narration, in the hope that despite the "cops and robbers" pose required of us by NBC, viewers would come to appreciate the more positive value of predators. When we sold "The Predators" to NBC, we did not discuss the possibility of Robert Redford narrating it, although in the back of my mind I knew he would be the perfect person to do it. The price was negotiated and finalized with only the understanding that the narrator chosen would be subject to the approval of NBC.

As soon as the special was sold, we returned to New York specifically to meet with Redford and once again ask him to narrate one of our programs. He was very busy, but out of concern for the environment and the plight of animals, he was very supportive of what we were trying to do. Since we had already sold "The Predators" based on its own merits rather than on a name, I hoped that this time he might agree to narrate. I'll never forget my conversation with him. "The program is sold," I explained, "and whether you narrate it or not, it's going to be on the air. But if you narrate it, more people will listen and pay attention. More people will get the message, and that's the reason we're doing these films in the first place."

We told him that we knew he could sneeze and make more money than we could offer him, but that it was all our budget allowed, and we'd be very grateful if he'd do it. "Well," he said, "I'll think about it." "There's only one thing," I said. "We need to have a yes or no by five o'clock today, because we're presenting the package to NBC tomorrow, and we have to tell them who's narrating it." It was rather bold and audacious on our part to give Robert Redford deadlines, and also a little foolish, but there was no choice. NBC had purchased the program with the understanding that it be completely edited and delivered in five weeks, and that time was nearly up.

When I called back later that day, Redford conditionally agreed to do the narration, provided he could see the program first. We showed him the film, and he did narrate it, which greatly enhanced the finished product we delivered shortly thereafter to NBC. He received a check for his services, which, incidentally, he never cashed. To this day I've always had a very high regard for Robert Redford, not only for doing so much to help wildlife, but also, inadvertently, for helping both Mark's and my own careers. For that, I've always been grateful.

In April 1977, "The Predators" was completed without so much as a glimpse of blood in the entire film, as NBC had stipulated. The unfortunate result was that the film never showed *why* an animal kills: to eat, and to feed its offspring. The best we could do was to show a cougar scratching some leaves and dirt over a dead bighorn and explain that "after it has eaten its fill, it will leave and come back later." I strongly disagreed with the kind of thinking that prevented us from showing a predator feeding on its kill, but, beyond refusing to sell the program at all, I had little choice in the matter. I reasoned that what we were able to include was at least better than showing nothing at all, or than simply selling footage to other companies, where we would have no say at all about what message it might be used to convey.

"The Predators" was not without controversy, however, both during and long after its production. We included a sequence from Alaska, for instance, in which a man kills a grizzly bear with a rifle. The footage was very graphic: the man stalks and shoots the bear—bang!—and the bear rolls down the hill, dead. We had bought the footage from Duke Ourada, a big-game hunter who had paid a cameraman to accompany him on a hunt and film him killing a grizzly. Over the scene of the hunter looking down at the dead bear, Redford's narration says: "To some, perhaps, the conquest of a noble foe confers nobility on the conquerer . . ." It was a purposely ambiguous statement, intended to leave interpretation up to the viewer. It could mean that the hunter is a noble victor, or it could mean that he depends on killing for a sense of self-importance. When the censors at NBC—their "Standards and Practices" people—looked at it, they said, "Forget it. The phones will be ringing off the hook." They wanted us to take out that scene, and especially that narration line. But Redford stood up for us, saying that he'd pull all of his narration if they did. Had it been only between us and NBC, we surely would have had to give in, but thanks to Redford, our arguments were given more weight, and the scene was left alone.

To some extent, the censors' instincts were correct, because the controversy they foresaw that began after "The Predators" was aired has continued to this day. We still get letters from hunters and trappers who resent certain statements in the program because they think that they're being blamed for our disappearing wildlife. For instance, we showed a sequence of a river otter being trapped and at the same time said that these animals had declined in number. But the implied connection is true: river otter populations were severely reduced over the years in many parts of the country due mainly to the fact that they were overtrapped. But thanks to limited trapping seasons and quotas, and to effective reintroduction programs, the river otter is once again becoming more numerous. We said that, too. Maybe the day will come round again when river otters can be trapped on a virtually unlimited basis, but I doubt it; and it might be to everyone's benefit, especially the otter's, if all of us would consider carefully that nothing in nature is unlimited.

As for that grizzly bear sequence, pro-hunters resented it because we didn't say, "This is great," and anti-hunters resented it because we didn't say, "This is terrible." But our intention was, and is, to report as accurately as we can the situation of American wildlife today, and how it got that way. We try to present the facts as clearly and fairly as possible, letting the viewer draw his or her own conclusion. Naturally, though, some people don't like to hear certain facts that may contradict their own ideas. We received complaints that the narration was biased, but I like to think if we take any side, it's that of wild creatures who otherwise would have no voice.

The money we received for the initial showing of "The Predators" was enough to pay all our bills, buy a new camera, and celebrate success at long last. Though I had my artistic

Playful and gregarious, the river otter is also a clever and fearless hunter. This one is about to pounce on a large but nonpoisonous diamondback water snake.

reservations, the fact was it was a big break for us, and the show received an amazing rating for a one-time wildlife special: a 26 percent share of the viewing audience, which is far above today's average network program.

"The Predators" was not only an important stepping-stone for me, but I believe it also opened people's eyes to the fact that there is no true wilderness without predators. Several years after its premiere, I tried to sell the program as a rerun to NBC and the other networks, without luck. Despite its high ratings the first time, NBC wasn't interested in rebroadcasting it, and the other networks weren't interested in broadcasting a special that had previously aired on NBC. Finally, in 1980, I sold it reluctantly to PBS for far less than I knew it was worth. Ironically, it turned out to be the best move I ever made. "The Predators" introduced me and my work to the public television network in splendid style. It received absolutely terrific ratings. And as a result, several years later, when I approached them with a proposal for the *Wild America* series, PBS executives and program managers were ready to listen.

While "The Predators" eventually paved the way for my future success with PBS, back then, selling wildlife specials to the commercial networks seemed to be the most notable, and the most lucrative, pursuit for me. It also seemed to be a way to reach the greatest number of people with a message of conservation and preservation of our wildlife heritage. But within a year after we sold "The Predators" to NBC, I learned the hard way that dealing with the commercial networks can either make or break you. Little did I suspect at the time that the trials and tribulations of selling my first network wildlife special were downright enjoyable compared to selling my next one.

Of all the North American predators I had filmed in the previous seven years, there was one animal I had taken a particular interest in, and about which it seemed only right for me to make a film—the magnificent, and much maligned, grizzly bear.

THE MAN WHO LOVED BEARS

One reason I like bears so much is that each one I've met has its own distinctive personality. Griz could be affectionate or cantankerous, curious or stubborn, cuddly or mischievous. In short, she was complex and unpredictable, and therefore truly wild.

I t's fairly easy to explain my attraction to bears. Most of our larger native predators are either canines, like the wolf and coyote, or felines, like the bobcat and cougar. They have their counterparts in our domestic dogs and cats, which makes it easier for us to identify with them, if only by categorizing them. Even so, we remain detached from most wild predators. Wild cats are loners, so secretive and elusive that we tend to think of them as anonymous, without distinct personalities. Wolves and coyotes, as creatures of a pack, also seem to lack individual identities. But perhaps because they fit only their own category, bears are easier to imagine as having a distinct personality. Something about them reminds us strongly of ourselves.

Bears are predators, yet like humans, they're omnivorous. Except for the polar bear, they subsist as much on plants as on insects or the flesh of other creatures. They're intelligent and resourceful, yet they're not very adaptable, especially when it comes to adjusting to the proximity of human settlement. They're somewhat more doglike than catlike, yet they too are loners, avoiding each other except for brief encounters during the mating season. To me, there's something about them that epitomizes the old-fashioned term "rugged individualist." Bears can be shy or aggressive, clownish or cantankerous—in short, they're unpredictable and unsociable, which, despite any superficial comparison with humans, makes them truly wild.

Of our three types of native bears—the black, the polar, and the grizzly—the wildest and most unpredictable is the grizzly. And of all the predators that have been extirpated from my adopted home state of Colorado, the grizzly was the one over which I felt the greatest sense of loss. Like the bighorn, the grizzly has been important to me ever since I can remember. I saw my first wild one from a roadside in Mt. McKinley National Park during my first trip to Alaska with David Huie and Charlie Warner in 1968. We were driving around a curve, and there on a boulder outcrop near the highway was an enormous grizzly, poised upright on its hind legs like a statue. Its ruffled, golden-tipped fur shimmered in the late afternoon sun, as I stopped the car less than 100 feet away and just sat there, staring through the open window. The great bear stood looking down toward us for what seemed like minutes, its forelegs lifted, its shaggy body swaying slightly as it sniffed the breeze, trying to smell what its rather poor eyesight probably couldn't quite distinguish. Eventually it dropped onto all fours, lumbered off down the slope, across an open treeless valley, and disappeared behind a low ridge.

I was stunned. No words I had ever read, no picture I had ever seen, prepared me for the height, the massiveness, the sense of brute strength, the sheer *presence* of that bear. Its powerful image lingered vividly in my mind for years, the living personification of the majestic American wilderness as it once had been.

Ten years later, I had another opportunity to see these magnificent bruins up close—too close for comfort, in fact, and not just one, but many bears. In 1975 I returned to the Alaskan peninsula with my brother Mark to film brown bears during the annual spawning run of salmon up the McNeil River. Brown bears—much bigger than black bears, which often occur in a brown or cinnamon color phase—are a larger race of grizzly bear that inhabits the Alaskan peninsula, the

The Alaskan brown bear, a race of grizzly that spends its summers fishing and fighting for spawning salmon, is North America's largest predator.

adjacent islands, and the coastal regions of Alaska. Every summer, as many as 100 of these normally solitary bears stake out fishing territories along the river, arguing and battling for the most advantageous spots. Huge, seasoned old boars, protective sows with their rollicking cubs, impetuous and energetic juveniles, and brash beggar-bears all gather to gorge on the protein-rich salmon and build up their fat reserves for the coming winter. Mark and I had only to point the camera and roll film. It seemed too easy—almost!

One afternoon, as I was lazily stretched out in the cool grass eating a can of sardines for lunch, I spotted a mother and her cubs meandering through the grass on the other side of the river, coming down to fish. I figured the playful cubs would make interesting footage as they watched and learned from their mother's fishing methods. I unthinkingly set the half-empty sardine can down behind me on a rock, and turned my attention to the camera. Not more than a couple of minutes went by before I heard a low grunt just behind me. Wheeling around, I saw a full-grown brown bear—a large male easily weighing half a ton—only yards away. Forgetting the cubs across the river, I instantly sized up the situation, trying to remain calm.

The big bear was almost flat on his belly, crawling through the grass, one paw inching out in front to grab the sardines, using the same method I had seen other bears use to steal a salmon from their neighbor. As is often my habit in remote wilderness areas, I did have a firearm with me: a .44 magnum pistol. Well, it wasn't exactly with me at that moment. It was in my backpack—right beside the sardines. My heart raced as I managed to shrink a few steps away, hoping that the bear wouldn't consider me a challenger for his intended food supply. He gently hooked the can with one of his massive claws and began lapping up the oil-soaked fish. Even with all the salmon in the river, the strong, unfamiliar odor must have been more than his curiosity could stand. He continued to lick the can well after its tasty contents were gone, while I held my breath, hoping that he wouldn't cut his tongue on the sharp edge and blame it on the nearest bystander. The appetizer finished, he turned and ambled off without a backward glance down to the river for a more substantial meal.

With all those juicy salmon running upriver right under their noses, I hadn't thought the bears would be interested in tinned human food. Now I knew better, and I resolved to keep my food supply safely stashed away and my pistol handy and accessible. Not that I wanted to shoot a bear—that was the last thing I wanted to have to do, especially since *I* was the intruder in the bears' domain—but neither did I want to be mauled by a set of four-inch claws that didn't know I meant no harm.

A few days later, while still filming along the McNeil, I had another encounter with a bear in which neither of us was quite as complacent. This old sow was neither as large nor as timid or tolerant as the sardine thief. I'd been following and filming her activities for almost a week, with all my camera gear clanking and creaking wherever I walked. To her, I must have been an exceptionally noisy intruder. One afternoon, while she was out in the middle of the river fishing and I was up on the bank filming her, she apparently decided she'd had enough of my company. Her gestures suddenly became very menacing—she laid her ears back and looked at me out of the top corners of her eyes, with her head cocked at a downward angle and off to the side. Again, I slowly backed away, hoping that I wouldn't have to reach for the pistol, which this time I was wearing, bandolier style, in a holster slung over my shoulder.

As I watched her eyeing me, I hoped that somehow it wouldn't amount to anything more than a staring match. I felt a sickening sense of reluctance to shoot an animal that I felt such a deep sense of awe and respect for—especially one threatened with extinction in the lower forty-eight states, regardless of how abundant they are in Alaska. Worse, the weapon I was carrying suddenly seemed puny and powerless against the sheer size and strength of this creature I was now acutely aware of having encroached upon. After all, she was only minding her own business, whereas I was minding my own *and* hers.

Suddenly, without further warning, she exploded out of the water and charged toward me. Stepping backward, I reached for the pistol, but to my horror, the holster was tangled up with the straps of my backpack. There I was, just like in some kind of a slapstick Western movie, wrestling with my gun and trying to untangle it from the holster and backpack, while keeping one eye on the oncoming animal. Every muscle in me wanted to run, but I knew that would only be an invitation for the bear to chase me. So I stood there, fumbling for my gun while the wet bear streamed toward me—and then suddenly stopped about eight feet away. Luckily for me, this "bluff charge" is the way most bears frighten away intruders. They rush menacingly, then freeze in their tracks. It certainly intimidated me, although I've since speculated that with their poor eyesight, perhaps the reason they charge and then stop is simply to get a better look at what they're charging at.

Thankfully, the old sow never carried out her threat. With a supercilious manner, she turned and sauntered back to her fishing spot in the river. Despite my resolution to keep more distance between myself and the bears, I was charged on two more occasions after that. By that time, however, I had learned the hard way why old-time gunfighters wore their gunbelts on their hips and tied the end of the holster to their lower thigh. And despite my reluctance to shoot a bear, I had even practiced my quick-draw a time or two. Fortunately for everyone concerned, the next two blustery bears repeated the "bluff charge" of the first, leaving my cage rattled but still intact.

However hair-raising, these experiences with bears only served to make the animals more fascinating to me. Between filming trips, I began reading about them extensively, and what I learned was pretty sad. The grizzly, or silvertip (so called because of the grizzled or grayish tips of its long guard hairs), has been relentlessly persecuted over the years to the point where, in the lower forty-eight states, its existence is now seriously threatened. Yet at the time of the Lewis and Clark expedition in the early 1800s, the grizzly ranged from Alaska south to the vicinity of Mexico City, and from western Minnesota to the Pacific Coast. By 1880, none of the Plains states could boast of a single one, and by 1922, there were no grizzlies left in California, the state where they had once been most numerous, and where a southern version of the Alaskan brown bear, known as the "Golden Bear," ironically remains the state symbol. By 1923 the grizzly had been eliminated from

Utah. By 1930 from Arizona. By 1931 from New Mexico. As far as is known, Colorado's last wild-born grizzly was killed in 1979. Today, the grizzly's only security in the lower forty-eight states remains within the protective boundaries of two national parks, Glacier in Montana and Yellowstone in Wyoming.

But even within Yellowstone's more than two million acres, the grizzly bear population has declined significantly since the 1960s, now numbering only about 200. A visitor is much more likely to see a grizzly in Glacier National Park in Montana, which is only one-fifth as large as Yellowstone, but has about the same number of bears. And in neither of these parks is the future of the grizzly secure or free of controversy. Unlike its smaller and less aggressive cousin, the black bear, the grizzly does occasionally attack humans without obvious provocation. Of course, what may not be obvious to a human may be perfectly clear to a bear that feels its territory imposed upon, or which is hungry and comes across a sleeping backpacker that smells edible.

It's a complex situation, but if it came to a choice, I personally would rather have bears in the parks than people, even if it meant I couldn't go there myself. In fact, I think we should set aside areas within certain national parks as preserves for bears that would be entirely off-limits to humans. I would prefer that bears were living there in their own free way rather than have no bears at all.

I was curious to know why not a single national park or wildlife refuge in my home state of Colorado supported a population of grizzlies, especially when historical records clearly indicated that Colorado was once "grizzly country." The sheer number of grizzlies that once roamed the mountains and even the plains of Colorado is attested to by a classic 1919 study conducted by writer and bear expert Enos Mills. In his published research, *The Grizzly*, he tells of discovering signs of forty to forty-five bears during an eight-day hike, and of seeing eleven of them during a single morning—mostly mothers with cubs, reaping a harvest of serviceberries—in an area that is now part of Rocky Mountain National Park.

Equally interesting to me was reading that the first white man killed on, and buried in, Colorado soil was the victim of a grizzly bear attack. The man's name was Lewis Dawson, and he was a member of the Jacob Fowler Expedition that traveled from my home town of Fort Smith, Arkansas, to explore Colorado and New Mexico. On an autumn afternoon in 1821, while his party was camped at the mouth of the Purgatory River, a grizzly bear was seen rustling around in the nearby brush. Dawson and some other men surrounded it and, according to the journal-keeper, the "desperent anemel" attacked Dawson. The gun of his companion misfired not once but three times before one of the party's dogs drove the bear away. Dawson's wounds were so severe that he died several days later and was buried on the spot where the encounter occurred.

Yet for most of the explorers and trappers during the early 1800s, the grizzly was not a significant threat, since records show few fatal attacks. It was when the prospectors arrived later in the century, staking claims and settling the land, that encounters between men and bears intensified. With the advent of newspapers in the West, widespread reports of bear attacks helped to accelerate the spread of their bad reputation. Early settlers and even city folk back East seemed to have an insatiable appetite for "first-hand" accounts of "outlaw bears," which led to bounties on *all* bear hides, outlaw or not. But the single most important factor that sealed the bears' fate was the arrival of ever-spreading herds of domestic livestock. Sheep, cows, hogs, and horses were an inevitably easy catch for this large opportunistic predator long accustomed to much smarter, faster, or stronger wild prey like deer, elk, and bison. A few dead cows later, the grizzly massacre was on.

But overhunting was—and is—only one of the many reasons why grizzlies are now especially vulnerable to extinction. Another consideration is that their reproductive rate is very low. Females don't mate until they are four to six years of age, and then they do so only once every two years, giving birth to no more than one or two cubs each time. The cubs, born during their mother's winter sleep, weigh a mere pound at birth, and don't venture from the den until spring, when they're about four months old. Then the mother bear begins the long and arduous task of teaching them how to survive in the wild. The cubs spend their first winter in a den with their mother, and don't go off on their own until the summer of their second year.

Another reason for their vulnerability is that the wide-ranging bears need large tracts of undisturbed wilderness to search out the broad variety of plants and animals that make up their diet. A grizzly's territorial requirement can extend from 20 to 1,000 square miles. Well-equipped with teeth and claws, and the strength and skills for a carnivorous diet, the grizzly is actually an opportunistic omnivore, which means it will eat just about anything it comes across. In the spring and early summer, bears inhabit lower elevation woodlands and south-facing slopes, where green vegetation is plentiful. As the season progresses, they disperse up the slopes into the aspen and coniferous forests below the timberline, where they gorge themselves on various roots and bulbs, grasses, flowers, insects, and rodents. Toward late summer and fall, the bears are found on the alpine tundra near avalanche and talus rock slides, digging out and eating ground squirrels and marmots. This protein is supplemented with whitebark pine nuts, wild berries, roots, tubers, and fish when available. A grizzly will attack a large animal that is wounded or sick, and has been known to eat other bears as well as moose and bison. But it is more likely to satisfy its appetite for protein by scavenging a large mammal that has already been killed.

After researching the essential habitat requirements of grizzlies, I felt certain at least some areas in the bountiful highlands of Colorado might still support small populations of these bears that would not be likely to interfere with human recreational or economic interests. But all the literature I read indicated that, in this state, grizzlies were a thing of the past. Or were they?

One day, a couple of months after I had returned home from filming the Alaskan brown bears, I was looking at a Colorado state map for directions when something in the fine print caught my eye. Right there in the southwestern corner of the map it read "State Grizzly Bear Refuge." It was the first time I became aware of any area in my adopted home state that might have been set aside for the protection of the great bears and their habitat.

Well, if there were any grizzlies left in Colorado, I wanted to see them. So I drove down to the Bear Refuge in the San Juan Mountains near Pagosa Springs to take a look around. As I hiked around the entire area, I saw that most of it was the kind of remote spruce-fir subalpine habitat that grizzlies thrive in. But though I spent a full week exploring, I found neither tracks nor the typical signs of them, such as clawed trees, rooted-up ground, day beds, droppings, or dens.

What I did see around the periphery of the "refuge," however, were three different herds of sheep, each guarded by sheepherders on horseback, all of whom were outfitted with rifles and dogs. I realized that if any grizzlies *had* been in the area, they would have been shot on sight. The thought that herds of sheep had indirectly replaced the grizzly population gave me the hollow feeling that something essential was missing here—and probably throughout the rest of the Colorado Rockies as well. The white-capped peaks still rose as high as before the white man arrived, the snow still fell as deep, the aspens still shone as golden in the fall, yet these wonders were no longer shared with one of the most magnificent animals that our continent has ever seen.

I later learned that the Colorado Division of Wildlife had established the Grizzly Bear Refuge in accordance with the Endangered Species Act, though the grizzly was only listed as threatened, not endangered. Researchers had conducted a search for bears, putting out horse carcasses, checking for tracks, and using time-lapse 8-mm cameras to see if any grizzlies appeared among the dozens of black bears. When none did, they abandoned the project, partly because of pressure from nearby ranchers. To me, their results, along with the extinction of the grizzly in most other western states, and the drastic number of grizzlies killed during this century alone, made it clear that the grizzly needed to be listed as an endangered species and protected to the full intent of that law. But even today, despite the fact that fewer than 600 still remain in the lower forty-eight states, and despite the fine work of organizations such as Defenders of Wildlife, which specializes in trying to protect predators, these bears are still only listed as threatened. Incredibly, they are also still legally hunted, for sport, in many areas outside the national parks they inhabit.

In the back of my mind I hoped that there might be a grizzly or two left in the deep forests and shadowy canyons of the San Juan Mountains. I felt that any bear that might still survive there had to be pretty smart to have stayed out of harm's way for so long. After talking to hunting guides, trappers, and the biologists who had conducted bear research in the vicinity of the State Grizzly Bear Refuge, I was encouraged to believe that although a grizzly had not been sighted there for decades, a few silvertips might yet roam the forests and scree fields beneath the most remote mountain peaks.

I couldn't help but wonder why certain wilderness areas couldn't be restocked with bears, for the sake of the ecosystem, the same way that game departments do with trout, moose, or wild turkey for the enjoyment of hunters. After all, what was a State Grizzly Bear Refuge without grizzly bears? Perhaps where the bureaucracy had failed, private enterprise might succeed. I assumed that it was mainly a lack of funds that prevented the Division of Wildlife from the restocking. But what if I could raise the necessary funds?

My longtime friend David Speer shared my interest in and concern for grizzlies, and with his financial backing we set up the Endangered Species Restoration Foundation, Inc., with the sole objective of reintroducing a mother grizzly and her cubs into the state of Colorado. Through the foundation, we raised $10,000 and offered it to the Colorado Division of Wildlife if they would use it to reintroduce grizzlies. Their reply was an unequivocal "No"—a surprising response which has not changed to this day. In fact, in 1982, the State Wildlife Commission voted for a resolution against the reintroduction —ever—of the grizzly bear or the wolf into Colorado on the basis that these species represent a threat to life and property. Of course, this decision delighted the livestock ranchers who lobbied for it, and who lease our public lands at rock-bottom prices and then graze them down to the dirt with herds of sheep and cattle, the profit from which goes solely to private pockets.

Although no satisfactory explanation was ever offered as to why the Division of Wildlife wouldn't accept our offer, I suspected that they were reluctant, even for the sake of keeping Colorado nominally wild with a few token bears, to step on the toes of special-interest groups—namely the livestock industry, which provides much of the entrenched political skeleton in our western states. However outmoded the stance of these people, it's going to take a lot of education and a lot of pressure from more enlightened minds in order to get them to see that the predator situation is hardly what it was in the last century. Even then, with a full complement of predators, the "threat to life and property" was hardly what it was blown up to be. And now—well, I couldn't see that adding three grizzly bears to the state's predator population of mountain lions, black bears, and some beleaguered coyotes, could do as much harm as it would do good. If the Division of Wildlife wouldn't do it, I would.

Without their cooperation, however, I had to give up the idea of releasing a female bear with cubs. That plan would take more money, equipment, and labor than I could supply. Instead, I would start with a more realistic goal: to get a grizzly cub, raise it, and then reintroduce it into a certain area in the San Juan Mountains—an area that was, according to my research, the most likely place in the state for it to eventually meet up with another wild, and possibly male, grizzly. There was no guarantee that the cub would be able to survive, or that if it did, it would find another of its kind. But if indeed one or two grizzlies still roamed the remote wilds, there was a chance that the bear I planned to release might pair up with another during the mating season.

While making preparations to obtain a grizzly cub, my brother Mark and I came up with the idea of making a documentary film about what we planned to do. We thought we could dramatize the demise of the great Colorado silvertips by filming the reintroduction of this bear into its native range. By now it was clear to me that a great deal of public sympathy and support would have to be generated to change the minds of lawmakers who felt that the grizzly had no place in the economic development of Colorado. Even though the last grizzly to be trapped in the state was taken in 1952, I figured that some people believed—or wanted to believe—that grizzlies might still inhabit the most inaccessible regions of the Colorado Rockies. But this film would also make the point that once-numerous grizzly bears had been all but completely wiped out. I wanted to show people what they had lost when the largest, and perhaps most intelligent, wild carnivore on earth was no longer a living feature of the Colorado landscape.

Excited by the prospect of making this film, Mark and I spent the next several weeks making calls to find the right candidate to raise. But in the process of locating a grizzly cub, we soon learned more than we wanted to know about the

For many people, the grizzly represents the essence of untamable wilderness. For me, it was the start of fulfilling a dream to welcome this helpless month-old grizzly cub to her new mountain home.

animal markets of the world. There is a great deal of commercial traffic in all species of wild animals, native and exotic, legal and illegal. Grizzly cubs were almost always legally available for sale by American zoos, since at that time the hundred or so bears in the zoos produced about a dozen cubs a year. The legal market was then considered in a glut since all the zoos that wanted grizzlies already had them, and in captivity, the big bears live to be about thirty years old. These extra animals, sadly, cannot be released into the wild, partly for the same bureaucratic reasons that prevented the Division of Wildlife from cooperating with our project. And also, of course, because no mother bear had ever taught them to survive. Thus, many are sold to animal farms of one sort or another, which in the best circumstances means a life of captivity.

We also learned that there are several illegal markets for grizzly cubs, one of which was the circus world. However, more disturbing than these were the so-called "game preserves" that buy cubs, raise them to maturity, then charge wealthy clients for the opportunity to "hunt" them, which sometimes means shooting the animals while they're still in a cage. Such private game "preserves" are for the most part perfectly legal; it's their methods that are sometimes unethical, and almost impossible to monitor, much less control.

The sense of disgust that welled up in me upon learning about this type of trophy hunting was broken by a phone call to the Oklahoma City Zoo. Yes, they had a six-week-old female cub that they were willing to sell, providing I could come up with satisfactory references and licenses, which we proceeded to do. Though I was tempted to try to buy a young cub from a circus, in order to save it from the unhappy and humiliating life it was destined for, such a cub would already have been too old and too confused to begin the kind of survival training I would need to give it. A zoo baby, on the other hand, would be just right.

On the long trip home to Aspen from Oklahoma City, I found out that a carsick baby bear was to be the first and least of many problems to come. A grizzly baby is not much different than a human baby. Formula mixings. Midnight feedings. Burping and crying and cleaning up. But Griz was a *wild* baby, with the true grizzly characteristics of curiosity and intelligence. For a couple of very hectic weeks, I tried to teach the cub to live indoors in the cabin I was staying in at the time. She got into everything. If I left for even a few minutes to work outside, she'd turn the place topsy-turvy—dragging cushions off the couch, overturning oil lamps, opening up all the kitchen cupboards and pulling out the cans and boxes and dishes inside them. I had to watch her constantly, trying to distract her from making a shambles of the cabin by playing and wrestling with her as much as possible. Though her baby teeth and claws were sharp, and occasionally broke the skin, my experience with Griz was that she never bit or scratched out of hostility, but rather out of a playful and experimental innocence. By biting or cuffing her back when she got too

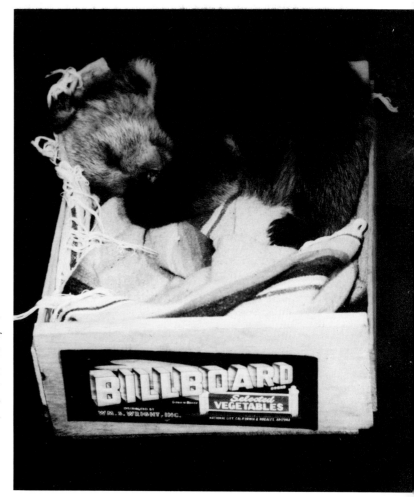

Griz asleep in her box. I cherished such moments of peace. Cute as she looks, and much as I might want to pick her up and hug her, I didn't dare. Awake, she relentlessly exercised a capacity for indoor mischief.

rough, like a mother bear would do, I taught her the limits of what she could get away with.

Fortunately, it was early spring, and I had plenty of reading and writing to keep me busy inside while persistent snow-storms passed over the mountains. When summer came and winter's drifts were sufficiently melted, we journeyed high into the mountains and camped out, to be away from human activity and closer to what I hoped would one day be her real home.

Over the centuries, grizzlies have adapted to a wide variety of habitats, from the semitropical mountains of Mexico to the frozen tundra of Alaska, and in every area, there are variables in food supply, competition, and survival methods. A bear's knowledge of its own specific territory is handed down through generations, from mother to cub. In the short time we would have together, it was up to me to help Griz learn many generations of bear lore so that she could apply it to this particular type of place.

So there Griz and I would be, both of us on all fours scratching around in the dirt and digging up roots and insects and squirrel nut caches. The questions turned over and over in my mind: what's good for a baby grizzly to eat? How would

Griz asleep on the kitchen table. To her, everything in the cabin was an irresistible toy—including the furniture. Like all wild babies, when she tired of play, she fell asleep in the nearest comfortable spot.

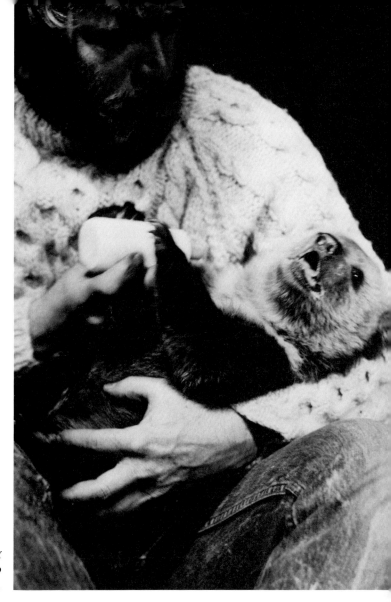

Any baby can be fussy during nursing, and a bear cub is no exception.

a grizzly mother *show* her baby what's good to eat? Through books and conversations with biologists, I learned to identify various grasses, sedges, flowers, and berries that were known to be on the grizzly's menu. But only by my getting down on my knees, gritting my teeth, and nibbling on the plants or berries myself, would Griz imitate me and get the idea. I did draw the line when it came time to show her what insects are good to eat. For that lesson, I would fake popping one into my mouth and chewing it up, then I'd catch another one for her to try.

Griz seemed instinctively to recognize what plants and insects were palatable and nutritious, but trying to teach her how to hunt rodents or to fish was another story. To her, anything that wiggled, jumped, or scurried was to be played with—not eaten. Which was only proper, considering that her mother would have provided for her up to a certain age, just as I was doing, and playing with her food was an appropriate response that preceded learning how to eat it. Nevertheless, when we came to a small stream or mountain lake, I would show her how to look between rocks or underneath rooted embankments where trout would hide. I was surprised how quickly she caught on, but once she had a fish in her mouth, I had a hard time convincing her to actually tear it apart and eat it. She was much more interested in playing "keep away" with it.

While I was teaching Griz to grow up in the wild, my brother Mark often accompanied us and filmed our adventures, as did our friends Steve and Donna Renner. It was hard

Is this affection, or appetite? When Griz was hungry,
anything seemed to be worth a try.

enough just handling a baby grizzly bear, but *filming* her was sheer chaos. While I would be working with Mark to get the camera and sound recording equipment set up and ready for filming, Griz would often run off into the nearby woods. This was preferable to her attempts to help us manipulate the equipment, of course, but without the clever help of Steve and Donna in holding her attention or rounding her up, Mark and I could never have completed the filming.

When she was just six months old, a family of campers in a Volkswagen bus came along the jeep road that ran past the meadow where we were filming. As might be expected, all four of them jumped out to take a closer look at the bear. Knowing how destructive Griz's curiosity could be, we yelled and pleaded with them to get back in and close the door. They respected our warning for awhile and peered out the windows as she sniffed around and explored. Finally, sensing no real danger, they got out and left the door wide open. Of course, Griz couldn't resist investigating this playground on wheels

At three months, with my blessing and encouragement, Griz began exploring outdoors. By that time, the little cabin was a shambles.

and climbed into the bus as the family watched in amusement. A few minutes later, the campers weren't smiling. She completely ransacked their bus, turning it inside out until her curiosity was satisfied. Mark and I knew that to try and dissuade her now would be foolish. By that time, she was a 150-pound bundle of teeth and claws, normally good-natured, but we weren't about to lose a finger because these campers refused to listen to us. Finally, we managed to entice her with some cookies out of their bus and back into our truck, which was bear-proofed. We drove quickly away and I'll never forget the looks on the faces of the campers, staring in disbelief at their ravaged bus.

Another time, she ran away from us and ended up wandering into the yard of a remote mountain ranch house. When we caught up with her, she was tearing off the screen door to get inside, while the frightened ranch wife and her children watched through their front window. Needless to say, it was a little difficult trying to explain what we were doing with a grizzly bear cub. We gave up and just brought them back a new screen door. More than once, Griz got lost, but we would search and track until we found her again, knowing she'd probably starve or get shot if we didn't.

While Griz was very young, she reminded me of a live teddy bear. In fact, one research study shows that cuddly little cubs are one of the most well-loved animals in the world. This must make the grizzly one of our most confusing animal paradoxes. We love the babies and hate the adults. They are incredibly independent and wild, yet can be trained to roller skate and ride bicycles. Physically, they don't look related to primates—and aren't—yet their powers of reason, curiosity, and memory have been compared with those of the chimpanzee. It may be that humans find their intelligence as threatening as their size and strength.

It didn't surprise me that grizzlies rated high on intelligence tests, but the thing that did amaze me in raising Griz was that her personality was very much like that of a human. Griz was every bit as devoted, crafty, playful, manipulative, and loving as my seven-year-old daughter is today. Griz loved to play tricks on me. And she would let me play tricks on her, then go along with it all and pretend to act surprised. She

In Alaska's Denali National Park, a female Toklat grizzly with two cubs confronts a bull caribou with its antlers in velvet, its right hip wounded in an attack by a wolf.

The weakened caribou defends itself valiantly, but its soft antlers are ineffective against the hungry bear which wrestles it down in the river. The bear and her cubs fed on the kill for a week, until high water washed it away.

After an initial confrontation, bighorn rams walk away from each other, then turn, rear, and with their heads tilted slightly to one side, charge each other, their heavy, solid horns colliding with an impact that can be heard a mile away. Sometimes the sound is a smart whack, sometimes a dull clunk, and sometimes it is as sharp and earsplitting as a rifle shot.

Caught by an early snowfall, a pika hurries to gather the last of its "hay crop" and store it away before winter. High-country cousins of the rabbit, pikas do not hibernate and must gather enough food to last for eight months.

A female mountain goat in Montana, with two half-grown kids. Minutes after birth, these agile creatures are on their feet, and within days can follow their mother over the steepest terrain.

The American alligator, its existence in our southern swamps once thought in jeopardy due to poachers and decreasing habitat, is now considered to be holding its own despite these continuing threats.

A serene sunset highlights the primeval quality of Louisiana's Atchafalaya Swamp. Almost drained for development several years ago, North America's largest river basin is now protected and shelters an amazing array of native wildlife.

A badger on Nebraska's snowy prairie chases a prairie dog to its burrow.

While the badger digs for its quarry, a passing coyote senses the opportunity for an easy meal.

The coyote hangs around to watch the work until the split second when the prairie dog is unearthed, whereupon the coyote grabs it out from under the badger's nose.

Largest and most powerful of America's falcons, a gyrfalcon pins down a ptarmigan with its huge taloned feet. Photographed in Alaska, this gyrfalcon is a specimen of an unusual white color phase; more often the species is gray-brown or black.

A female raccoon mates in winter and gives birth in spring to a litter averaging four young. Raccoons are found in each of our lower forty-eight states, are equally at home in rural or suburban areas, and with increasingly frequency are seen even in cities.

A female wandering shrew with newborn young. For this voracious insectivore, motherhood means the added strain of eating enough to maintain her own high metabolic rate—and to feed her babies.

Rocky Mountain bighorn ewe with young kid. Note how well their earth-brown coats blend in with the cliffs, their creamy rump patches echoing the lighter rock tones. Perfect camouflage!

Triplet Alaskan brown bear cubs line up to learn by example from their mother's fishing techniques. Normally solitary, the huge bruins gather by belligerent dozens along riverbanks in summer to feast on spawning salmon.

A pair of young barred owls, a species found throughout the East and Midwest. In daytime, while they rest inconspicuously on a tree limb, owls may be mobbed by scolding flocks of smaller birds, which apparently perceive them as a threat and chase them from tree to tree.

A number of animals are white year-round, but these three creatures are unique in that they change color with the seasons and thus are provided with maximum camouflage protection: brown in summer, mottled in spring and fall, white in winter. From left to right, they are the white-tailed ptarmigan, the short-tailed weasel (or ermine), and the snowshoe hare.

Eyebrows coated with ice, a bull elk, left, nibbles on spruce needles during a harsh Wyoming winter; the elk, below, forage in Yellowstone. With few large predators (such as wolves, bears, and cougars) left to cull their numbers, thousands of elk must be shot or fed by man, or else starve.

loved to slide down snowbanks for the fun of it, then climb up and slide down again. That and "tag" were her favorite games. "Tag" was when she'd rush at me and I'd try to grab her—but miss on purpose. Then I'd chase her and she'd bolt off ten yards, turn, and come running back by me to do it again—and again and again. When she was older and outweighed me, *she* did the tagging and *I* did the running away. What was amazing was that she'd still miss—most of the time—on purpose.

Griz taught me that animals are just as capable of a wide range of moods and emotional responses as people are. They experience fear, anxiety, loyalty, and happiness, just as we do, and I wanted to convey this in the film. Misunderstanding this has been a big reason for the continuing gap in communication between us humans and wild animals like the grizzly. Everyone who's had pets knows that one dog can be shy and retiring, while another is outgoing or aggressive. The same is true for wild animals. They also have distinct personalities.

While Griz was still in captivity in a one-acre pen, she had to be taught about hibernation. This led to a dispute over how and where a bear den should be dug.

Not only different species, but different individuals within a species, can display tremendous variations in emotional response to the same situation.

I think the difficulty humans have in comprehending animals all boils down to the fact that we want everything about them explained by simple answers. We want to believe in the stereotypes we've created—that all deer are lovely and sweet, for instance, and would never bite or kick you, when the truth is that both bucks and does can be ill-tempered and dangerous at times. And we want to think that all grizzly bears are savage and brutal, when I know for a fact that most would rather turn tail and run than attack a human. And I know that at least one, Griz, was not only playful with humans, but sometimes quite affectionate.

All the animals of any species have personalities that are, in most cases, as complex as ours. We don't notice the complexity, I think, because animals' lives seem fairly simple in comparison to ours; they don't regularly have as many different or stressful situations to respond to as we do in our civilized, highly technological world. But anyone can predict that an animal, when cornered or threatened, is not going to act the same as when it is placidly grazing on grass and minding its own business. For instance, people tend to assume that bison are passive and docile because all they ever seem to do is stand around and graze, which is, in fact, what they do most of the time. But if someone goes to Yellowstone Park and fires a flashbulb in a bison's face from a few feet away and gets trampled and killed, the headlines read "Killer Bison on the Loose."

Surprisingly, grizzlies can be as docile as bison as they feed along on plants, insects, or berries. When they do attack people, it's because they're responding as nature designed them to—not as man-eating killers but as self-defensive animals that are programmed to attack anything they perceive as a threat to their cubs, food, or territory. Or that smells like it might be edible, and then resists being eaten. The best way to approach wild creatures is first of all to remember that they *are* wild, and that they don't feel nearly as comfortable with you as you would like to feel with them. Stay still and watch them until they almost forget you're there. Keeping a respectful and observant distance may not be as exciting as seeing how close you can get before an animal runs—either away from you or *at* you—but in the long run, you'll learn more and end up feeling closer to that animal by exercising a little patience and self-control.

At least that's the advice I give when I'm asked, "How did you avoid the dangers inherent in raising a grizzly bear?" Or, "How do you avoid getting hurt while filming potentially dangerous animals in the wild?" I must say that I've been bitten more severely by a domestic dog and scratched more severely by a domestic cat than by any wild animal. Probably the animal that came closest to killing me was a domestic stallion, which almost trampled me to death in a stall when a mare in season was led past. To my mind, wild animals such as the grizzly are no more dangerous than many domestic animals we consider safe.

For that matter, I've always found that factors of weather or terrain, such as unexpected blizzards or rock slides, are far more life-threatening than any wild animal. On several occasions, I've almost paid with my life for being in the wrong place at the wrong time, like the time I got caught on a rocky outcropping off the coast of Alaska during high tide, or got trapped on an icy ledge while filming bighorn in Glacier Park. So when people tell me they wouldn't want to see grizzlies reintroduced into Colorado because of the threat they would present to human life, I'm quick to point out that their chances of getting caught in an avalanche or dying of hypothermia in a sudden snowstorm are far greater than of getting attacked by a grizzly. And *that's* nothing compared with the everyday risk of getting into an automobile accident.

I guess the bottom line is that for many people such as myself, the rewards of venturing outdoors to observe wild animals simply outweigh the risks. It helps to close a gap between us and the rest of the animal kingdom—the gap that developed when civilized people began to lose touch with nature's ways.

Unfortunately, the day when people would want to observe Griz as a full-grown grizzly bear in her native domain was still a long way off. So I anticipated that part of raising her would have to involve instilling in her a fear of humans. Like all bear cubs, Griz was born with a fearless nature and had to be taught how to avoid danger. When we went out hiking, every time we would come across backpackers, I would teach her to run far away as fast as possible. Although she learned to mimic me, because of our close bond I don't think she fully understood that humans were the potential danger she was running from. As she grew older, I hoped that she would become more independent and less interested in human companionship, but that wasn't what happened. She trusted people too much, simply because she had no reason to mistrust them. And for the first year-and-a-half of her life, she had every reason to rely on them, just as she would have on her own mother. Yet I was convinced that her affinity for humans, more than anything else, might cause her death.

Even my efforts to teach her to run away when she heard gunshots had failed. I wasn't at all sure she would run if she didn't have me to run after or to mimic. What I needed to do was far more basic: teach her the *consequences* of trusting humans. I had to train her in a way that nearly broke my heart.

When it came to getting her to go to sleep for the winter, Griz behaved like a reluctant child at bedtime. Actually, she was even worse than that—nipping at my boots, legs, and backside until she finally settled down.

A bear trap was the answer. I could weaken the springs of the trap so that when she was caught in it, it would frighten her more than hurt her. It would teach her the steel smell of the trap, and also that the ones associated with it—humans—were harmful to her and had to be avoided.

One day in late spring, Griz and I set off into the heart of the San Juan Mountains, into a region that we had explored the previous summer. It was long way from any humans or livestock. Knowing that it would be our last trip together into those forested high-mountain valleys, I was tempted to play all of her favorite games with her one last time. But we were here for a different purpose now, and I knew that playing with her would only make it harder on both of us.

We camped for the night in a forest clearing near the bank of a meandering creek. A half-mile upstream, we could hear a waterfall cascading over its rock-carved shelf and thundering into the river's headwaters. The rich, boggy soil flanking the river gave root to a smorgasbord of Griz's favorite delicacies: clover, cow parsnip, and shooting star wildflowers. I felt that if I had to leave her, there could be no better new home than this.

Shortly after moonrise, with Griz curled up outside my sleeping bag, I tried to drift off to sleep. But the crackling of the pine logs in the campfire and the occasional hooting of a great horned owl perched in the silvery branches above us kept arousing my senses. Images of our past year-and-a-half together floated through my mind: Griz sleeping peacefully, sandwiched between blankets in the orange-crate crib; Griz joyfully sliding down a snow-packed slope, gaining momentum, then tumbling head-over-tail at the bottom; me teaching her the finer points of den digging, in preparation for her long winter sleep. I was lucky I had all these memories on film. Griz had the whole summer ahead of her to find her own way in the wild, but this winter she would have to dig her own den.

The next morning, after I stoked the campfire, I took the rusty bear trap out of my backpack. The sight of its curved, saw-edged jaws and heavy anchor chain made me shudder. How many of the great Colorado silvertips had died, their powerful paws clenched between those jagged steel springs, while some hunter or rancher fired the final, fatal shot? Hating every minute, I blunted the teeth with a rock, then heated the trap in the fire to take the temper out of the springs so that they would firmly grip her paw but not cripple her. After it cooled I placed it in the grass and covered it with dirt. Griz was nearby, digging for roots and tubers, a skill she had learned quite well during her first summer. I stood there watching her for a long moment, then called to her. She ran to me eagerly, as if hoping my mood had changed and I was ready to play instead of work at something she didn't understand. Just before she reached me, her foot stepped on the tripping pan of the trap and the jaws snapped shut. I could hardly look. She writhed and bawled in pain. I knew that the knowledge that she was caught, that she was not free, would impress her mind in a way that gunshots had not. I hoped against hope that this harrowing experience would teach her never to trust any human, ever again. Even, and perhaps especially, me.

As much as anything I'd ever done, I hated to be the one to teach her this lesson, and I wondered while I was doing it if raising her had been the right thing to do in the first place. No matter how good my intentions, I had committed one of my own worst sins in betraying her. Calling her to that trap was heartbreaking, and even worse was to sit there, unable to make her understand why I couldn't help her get loose. She finally pulled her sore paw out of the trap, and I could see that she wasn't seriously injured as she ran into a thick stand of spruce and disappeared without looking back.

The plan had worked, but my feelings were wrenched. I wanted her to be free. At the same time, I wondered if it was the best thing for her. It was the last time I saw Griz. I returned to the area from time to time to see if I could find her, or at least find signs of her presence, but each time I came away without a clue as to her whereabouts. I could only hope that, as is the way of grizzlies, she was roaming over the comparatively safe terrain of those remote mountain valleys, and that by autumn she might come across another of her kind. In my last effort to protect her, I kept the location of her release site a secret.

The story of raising and releasing Griz back into the wilderness was eventually depicted in the one-hour special, "The

Griz as a two-year-old was a far cry from the tiny cub I'd carried in my backpack and tussled with as a one-year-old. The hardest thing I ever did was teach her to fear humans, before she went on to her life in the wild.

Man Who Loved Bears." My adventures with Griz were filmed with me primarily in front of the camera and my brother Mark behind it. With Mark's degree in cinematography, at least one of us knew a little about making "people" movies. In some ways, making this special with my brother reminded me of a grown-up version of what we used to do as kids, putting together one of our little home movies starring our wild and domestic pets. Back then, though, the choices weren't so difficult, nor the consequences so uncertain.

Our initial aim had been to produce a documentary film on the status and history of grizzlies in Colorado, including the story of Griz's reintroduction. As we might have expected, CBS—the only network interested in our idea—had other plans for the film. They wanted a sentimental human-interest story about a man and his pet bear, along the lines of the Walt Disney films. They weren't interested in showing maps of the grizzly's original range, or the historical reasons for its extirpation in Colorado. Instead, they wanted a program packed full of drama, comedy, suspenseful cliff-hangers, and happy endings—"warmth and jeopardy," as they put it. And if Mark and I wanted to sell our program, we had to play by their rules, which meant that we would have to include fictional sequences that CBS executives felt would enhance the story line and make the program more interesting to their viewers.

For instance, the film begins with me discovering a male grizzly in the Colorado Rockies, when the truth is, I never saw a grizzly bear there or anywhere else in the state. I simply believed that one or two elusive survivors might still roam the backcountry. But in order to film the sequence of my alleged "sighting" of a wild grizzly boar, Mark and I had to use a tame grizzly owned by a man named Lloyd Beebe, who supplied all the animals for the Disney films. The only reason I felt justified in feigning this aspect of the story line was that nobody really knew for sure whether grizzlies were totally extinct in Colorado. It was conceivable to me that, if a few grizzlies were still alive, it was only a matter of time before somebody came in contact with one of them.

As it turned out, two years after I had released Griz, somebody did, although the circumstances of the encounter were hardly fortuitous for the compatibility of humans and bears. In 1979, a bow-hunter was surprised and mauled by a lone female grizzly in an isolated subalpine region of the San Juan Mountains. Although both his arms and legs were severely injured, the man managed to kill the bear by stabbing her with a hand-held arrow in her neck and chest. The Colorado Division of Wildlife soon afterward confirmed, by tooth and skull identification, that the bear was a sixteen-year-old wild sow grizzly.

I was numb when I first heard of the attack, for fear my

worst nightmare about Griz had come true. But to my relief, the biologist's report eliminated the possibility that it might have been she. Although the bear's death was of course necessary and even a heroic feat from the hunter's point of view, it meant a loss for grizzlies everywhere. Still, it was exciting to think that at least one wild-born grizzly had, for as long as sixteen years, found a sanctuary in Colorado's backcountry. Perhaps there were others.

Since I never saw her again, I could never be sure if Griz mated with a wild grizzly and had cubs. But since the network insisted that we "enhance" the story line of our film with a "happy" ending, Mark and I filmed a wild grizzly sow with cubs in a spruce-fir forest in Montana and used this scene as the film's conclusion, claiming that the sow was Griz with her two cubs. I knew it was the kind of grand finale people wanted to see, and certainly the kind CBS was looking for, but I was never comfortable with this sentimental, faked approach to wildlife filmmaking, especially since the last time we had filmed Griz was that final, painful time we had seen her. We had always been more concerned for Griz as a living creature than as movie material, and it was hard to accept that only as movie material might she have a chance to speak for the real needs of her own kind.

So Mark and I once again bowed to pressure in adapting our documentary style of filmmaking to the network's commerical ways, all with the hope of getting our grizzly bear film on television. We were grateful for the chance to convey our general message about bears, but I couldn't help believing that people would get up from their TV sets more interested in the plight of Griz and her kind if the program hadn't lulled them with an easy, sentimental answer—an answer that didn't require them to think any more about a problem that still hadn't been solved.

Little did I suspect when I was teaching Griz not to trust humans that I should have taken a large dose of my own medicine. Mark and I had made a verbal agreement with CBS that we would complete "The Man Who Loved Bears" and hand it to them in New York by September 7, 1977. The deal was that if we could produce it by that time—on speculation —then we would receive payment after it was broadcast. Even

though I was a country boy from Arkansas, used to a hand-
shake as a promise, the fact that there was no contract or
down payment involved made me feel highly uneasy. But I
remembered the executive at NBC who had bought "The
Predators" telling me once, in so many words, that the television industry was too closely-knit for anyone to risk a bad
reputation by going back on their word. Therefore, he had
said, contracts were a mere formality which were often drawn
up after the fact. So, based on his word, we had completed
and delivered "The Predators," and were promptly paid for
the single broadcast. Just as he had told us, once NBC aired
and returned it, we *then* received a contract to sign.

If that was the way of the business, why was I so nervous?
Because within a few months after selling "The Predators" to
NBC, we had spent every last nickel of profit on filming "The
Man Who Loved Bears." We were flat broke. In order to
complete the post-production process for the bear film and get
it delivered to CBS, we needed a substantial loan, which we
received with the help of our parents, who cosigned the loan
application.

Mark and I worked furiously for the next several months:
editing, hiring a narrator, getting music composed, mixing the
sound tracks, and so on. Finally, on September 7, Bill Dunne
—the agent we were working with on the sale—and I walked
into the CBS office in New York with the completed program,
laid it on the desk of the executive with whom we had made
the deal to buy it, and said, "Here it is!" I'll never forget how
I felt when he looked at us with a blank expression on his face
and said, "Deal, what deal?" and flatly refused to buy the
program.

There we stood, with an hour-long wildlife special, already
tailored to their artificial standards, in our hands, and our
pockets completely empty. Not to mention the financial burden we had placed on our parents for cosigning the loan. More
than at any other point in my life, I felt like I had hit rock
bottom, which indeed I had. Somehow it had been okay to be
a starving filmmaker *before* I got my big break—before I'd had
a wildlife special aired on television. But now, having enjoyed
success, I felt devastated. For the next several months, we

combed the broadcasting world for a market for "The Man Who Loved Bears," but to no avail.

Just at the point when things seemed so bad they could only get better, they did. I met Diane Dale. She was living in Aspen at the time, and by the end of our first date, I knew my life was about to change forever. She was the silver lining behind the dark cloud that had hung over my head for months. With her support and encouragement, and my parents' understanding attitude toward the loan, I made it through the next four months of poverty and apprehension until finally Mark, Bill Dunne, and I persuaded—or I should say *begged*—ABC to buy our special. They offered us what seemed like a king's ransom for two broadcasts in June of 1978, and I was able to pay off the loan. Diane and I were married shortly thereafter, and we took off for a two-month honeymoon in Tahiti.

But before ABC paid us, they did present us with one rather unusual condition. I had had my heart set on Will Geer as the narrator for the program. I'd never forgotten the character he played as the old bear trapper in *Jeremiah Johnson*. His voice and personality were perfect for narrating a film about grizzly bears. So with the help of Robert Redford, who had worked with Will Geer in *Jeremiah Johnson* and had introduced him to us, we were able to convince Will to narrate it. Tragically, he died a few months before "The Man Who Loved Bears" was to be aired, and ABC refused to use the narration of the deceased actor. I suppose they felt it was in bad taste. I disagreed, but didn't feel I was in a good position to argue. After some negotiation, we contacted Henry Fonda to do the narration, and to the delight of ABC, he agreed to record it.

Having the program aired on television did help in the long run to get people thinking and talking about the fact that grizzlies are gone from Colorado and most of the other areas they once belonged. I hoped that people would also see that the bears therefore deserve protection as an endangered, and not merely a threatened, species. Happily, even diluted by its set-up beginning and its "happy ending," not only did that message get broadcast on network television, but for a short time a lengthened version of *The Man Who Loved Bears* was distributed as a feature film to theaters around the country.

Still, despite its popularity with audiences, and despite the fact that many people have told me that *The Man Who Loved Bears* is their favorite of all my films, I had already made up my mind that I never wanted to "go Hollywood" again. I didn't want to do made-up human-interest stories that were shot from a script using tame animals. Instead, I wanted to tell the stories of real animals, free and wild within their wilderness domain, in a truthful and educational manner. It concerned me that audiences, while following a cute and sentimental story line, might easily miss the important message about the problems wild animals must struggle with.

Most Americans of my generation had grown up with the Disney wildlife films, which probably opened their eyes for the first time to the beauty and enchantment of nature. But I felt the time was ripe for a more realistic portrayal of wildlife in America. It was a difficult decision to make, however, because I knew from experience that wildlife documentaries were not what the television networks were looking for, and that I might have to search elsewhere for a viable market for my films. But since it was quite an accomplishment in those days to get *any* wildlife special on network television, much less one of a controversial nature on predators or endangered species, I was encouraged by the fact that I had at least slipped my foot in the door. Despite the many philosophical disagreements we had with network censorship and short-sightedness, I had already come up with another idea to sell to commercial television. This time, however, the subject matter would be enjoyable and agreeable to virtually every-one, even the networks—or so I thought.

The idea had grown out of my rewarding and often comical experiences raising Griz. And in some way I think I needed a change from all the death in "The Predators" and all the negativity of "At the Crossroads." I felt it was time for more positive subject matter. At the instigation and urging of my mother and my wife Diane, I decided to do a wildlife documentary on "wild babies." This time I would show a variety of young animals being taught the skills of survival by their *natural* parents in the wild. After all, I had to agree with the women in my life: what could be more refreshing and uplifting than the eternal renewal of birth and growth?

SEVEN

WILD BABIES

The age of innocence. A young white-tailed deer meets a young timber wolf. Friends for the moment, they will someday be mortal enemies in the struggle for survival.

L ike any new parent raising a first child, I used the trial and error method to teach Griz the survival skills she would need as an adult. And while doing my best to play the role of a wise "mother" grizzly, it became clear that she was teaching me as much as I was teaching her. From Griz I learned the fundamentals of parenthood—patience, protectiveness, physical and emotional nurturing. She also taught me the most important and heartrending lesson of all—how to let go when the need for independence supersedes the need for motherly care and protection. Of course, most human parents learn these things in the eighteen-plus years they normally spend raising a family, but I had to learn a lifetime's worth of parenting skills in the two short years it takes a bear cub to reach adulthood.

My decision to make a film on baby animals was influenced not only by my wife and mother. I was also influenced in a more subtle way by a woman I had hired named Paula Smith, a writer who would replace my brother Mark as my "right-hand man." Mark had branched off from working with me and was involved in producing his own film, "The Incredible Shrew." Meanwhile, maybe I had begun to mellow with age, or maybe it was having a wife and working with a female assistant that opened my eyes to the more sensitive, gentle side of nature.

From that point on, my films seemed to take on a fresh perspective, different from that of the films Mark and I had produced in the days when "the boys" and I traveled around the country in a trailer. Instead of bold, dramatic films laden with pleas to save our wildlife from the pressures of humankind, my emphasis shifted to doing films that simply presented wild creatures living out the most fascinating and appealing aspects of their lives. This approach, I thought, would allow audiences to make their own judgments about how much they value wild creatures and how important it is to protect our wildlife heritage.

"Wild Babies" was the first film to reflect this new direction my career was taking. I filmed the "childhoods" of a wide spectrum of animals, ranging from the American toad, with its copious egg-laying, in which thousands of tadpoles are left by their parents to fend for themselves, to the complex and highly evolved communal parenting behavior of wolves, in which the duties of nurturing a single litter of pups are shared by the entire pack. What was interesting to me was how each of the species I filmed seemed to have a different and unique strategy for ensuring the survival of its offspring. To my surprise, I learned that many of these strategies actually originated in the mating rituals of the parents.

For instance, with many bird species, courtship rituals revolve around an elaborate display of plumage color, movement, and sound. The more impressive the display of a courting male, the more likely he will be able to attract a receptive female. To me, the most interesting avian mating rituals belong to the grouse family. The competition for females among courting male prairie chickens brings the booming grounds, or leks, alive with foot-stomping dances and colorful displays of the inflatable air sacs located on each side of the male birds'

Successful courtship behavior is crucial to the survival of a species. Here a male sage grouse performs a display, "booming" and showing off the colorful air sacs on its neck.

necks. These air sacs make a peculiar booming noise when air is taken into them and then rapidly expelled. Equally impressive is the male ruffed grouse. With his fanned tail and ruffed neck feathers, he broadcasts a loud drumming sound by rapidly beating his wings. Among grouse males, the most eye-catching courtship display will ensure the opportunity to mate with a receptive female. And the offspring of such matings will most likely inherit these successful courtship traits from their parents. This ability to attract a mate is of supreme importance, since the struggle to survive has only one basic goal—to reproduce.

In contrast to male grouse, a bull elk spends more time displaying his strength and potency to other males rather than to females. By directing his heightened sexual energy toward ritualized but nevertheless serious and often dangerous antler clashes with rival males, he strives for the right to mate. The bull elk is typical of the deer family in that he wins acceptance of a harem of cows by virtue of his strength, agility, and stamina, which are often in direct proportion to the size of his

Some mammals, such as bull elk, display their strength and potency not directly to females, but to rival males with whom they fight for the right to mate. These bull elk are sparring in Wyoming's National Elk Refuge.

antlers. His success in passing on these desirable traits comes by the default of other bulls he has driven away rather than by any elaborate courtship rites he performs with the females.

I realized that the mating rituals of the parents had in most cases no direct effect on the offspring. Yet in a long-term, evolutionary sense, the babies were the inheritors of aggressiveness or receptivity that could, in the long run, change the species as much as could actual methods of parenting. The techniques of parental care that exist in the animal kingdom are as diverse and interesting as the various types of mating rituals. In "Wild Babies" I included sequences on how *lack* of parental care is the rule for the offspring of cold-blooded animals, such as toads and catfish. Cold-blooded animals, in spawning thousands and thousands of eggs, better the chances that at least a few of those thousands will survive.

Another evolutionary method by which cold-blooded animals further increase the number of offspring that survive is displayed by frogs and toads, which instinctively gather in large numbers to mate and breed. This behavior, called "explosive breeding," increases the chances of survival by ensuring that all the eggs in the pond will hatch at the same time. In this way, a predator gorging on the tadpoles will quickly become sated and will ultimately eat only a small fraction of the total number of tadpoles. Explosive breeding, like most other reproduction mechanisms in lower animals, succeeds by the sheer numbers of young produced, rather than by any bonding relationship between parents and offspring.

Overproduction of eggs is a very effective form of insurance by which lower animals promote survival of their young. But the types of parent-offspring bonding among birds and especially mammals—where it reaches the highest stages of development—include much more complex strategies for helping offspring reach adulthood. And to me they're much more interesting for the light they shed on human parenting processes. Among higher animals, the structure of the family unit may take the form of one parent assuming the duties of parenthood, or of an extended family where both parents, and even "aunts," "uncles," and older siblings help raise the young. To a great extent, the amount of parental nurturing required by the offspring of birds and mammals depends on how well-developed the young are at hatching or at birth. The two basic degrees of development are called altricial and precocial.

Among birds, the progeny of hawks, owls, eagles, and songbirds, to name a few, are altricial, meaning that they emerge from the egg naked and completely helpless, usually with their eyes closed. This is the case with most birds that build well-constructed nests high off the ground, in trees or on cliffs. The nestlings remain in the nest and are usually cared for by both parents until their feathers are fully grown and they can fly. I filmed a nest of robins and a nest of red-tailed hawks to show how the nestlings of both songbirds and birds of prey need constant care. For many birds with altricial offspring, the time-consuming duties of providing warmth, food, and protection for the helpless young must be shared by both parents.

On the other hand, the offspring, or chicks, of ground-nesting birds, such as waterfowl, shorebirds, and game birds like grouse and pheasants, are precocial. They develop for a longer period of time within the egg, and emerge open-eyed,

The young of birds of prey, and songbirds like the robin shown here, are altricial—naked, vulnerable, and often blind when hatched. Parental attention and care is required until the young are capable of leaving the nest.

The young of many vulnerable ground-nesting birds and waterfowl, such as the Canada goose, are precocial—meaning that they emerge from the egg open-eyed, covered with down, and ready to start fending for themselves.

covered with down, and ready to begin learning to fend for themselves. These chicks are able to leave the nest and peck at food as soon as their feathers are dry, and are only partly dependent on their parents. Since the responsibilities of parenthood are less demanding, in some species these duties are assumed by the female only. Precocial chicks, since they're hatched on the ground, are much more exposed to danger than those hatched in high or well-protected nests. Within hours after they hatch, they must be able to swim or run for cover to escape predators such as raccoons, foxes, or weasels.

However strong a precocial chick may be, if it becomes separated from its mother at an early age, it will soon die. To prevent a chick from straying or lagging behind, a close bond, called "imprinting," develops between parent and young. This learning process begins even before the baby bird hatches out of its egg and ensures that a chick will always be able to identify its parent by sight, smell, and sound. The mother's call, heard even through the eggshell, is the first thing the unhatched chick "imprints" on. Later, immediately after hatching, a chick forms an attachment to the first object it sees. Normally this object is the parent bird, although in the mother's absence some chicks will imprint on other animals or even inanimate objects—which can make life very confusing for them.

Imprinting also occurs in mammals. I learned this lesson the hard way while filming a litter of baby skunks for "Wild Babies." I accidentally approached the litter too closely, and the kits, seeing a large, moving object, started to follow *me*. Not wanting to compete with a protective mother skunk for her litter, I left them behind as fast as possible so they wouldn't have the chance to imprint on me. Once I was out of sight, they returned to their real mother. With mammals—skunks being an excellent example—scent is a very important means of recognition between mother and young, perhaps even more so than sight and sound.

Like birds, mammalian offspring are described as precocial or altricial. Interestingly, the main differences between the two degrees of development of newborn offspring can be seen in two closely related species—rabbits and hares. The offspring of rabbits are altricial, unlike the offspring of hares, which are precocial. Young hares are born, after a slightly longer gestation period than rabbits, in a quiet, concealed spot. They are fully furred, with their eyes open. Rabbits, on the other hand, give birth to blind, furless, and helpless young within a nest lined with soft vegetation and fur. Newborn rabbits are completely dependent on their mother for warmth for the first few days, but hares are born with the ability to produce their own body heat.

The basic family unit for mammals generally consists of a mother and her young. Unlike avian parents, which must leave their young in order to gather food for them, a mammalian mother internally manufactures her offspring's food in the form of milk. This greatly reduces the necessity for a father's role in raising the young. Instead, males of most species expend their energies competing with rivals during the mating season, then mating with as many females as possible. This competitive and promiscuous behavior among males has the evolutionary advantage of assuring that the strongest will pass on his superior survival traits to his offspring.

Lacking the help of a mate in protecting their offspring, many mammal mothers—bighorn sheep, elk, mountain goats, and white-tailed deer, to name a few—band together in "nursery groups." Yet even when grouped together, there remains a very strong bond between each individual mother and her own young. And the longer the period during which the young are dependent on their mother for food and protection, the stronger the bond.

In mammals, this bond can be emotional as well as physical or biological, and some researchers believe it is strengthened and reinforced in the mother by the "baby look" of a young animal. Just as the large, round eyes, shortened face, large forehead, and pudgy body of a puppy make it appealing for a human to pick up and cuddle, these physical features also seem to appeal to the puppy's mother, whose tenderness

The young of mammals also can be altricial, like these helpless, hairless day-old rabbits, or precocial, like the bright-eyed furry offspring of hares.

and affection are as vital to the pup's well-being as is the nutrition it receives from her.

In addition to the attraction of physical appearances, there may be a physiological reason for the powerful bond between parent and offspring. Studies indicate that a rise in a certain hormone level in the mother before she gives birth triggers her maternal interest in her newborn young. This maternal interest—call it instinct if you like—is expressed as a need for continued contact. By licking, touching, and grooming, a mammal mother makes her infants feel secure, which generally means that they will be less likely to venture far from her protective custody.

In "Wild Babies," I included a reverse example of this, showing what happened when a young ground squirrel's curiosity overcame the need to be close to its mother when danger threatened. When a sentry squirrel sounded the alarm that an intruder was nearby, this particular baby stayed above ground instead of following its mother down into a burrow. Luckily for the ground squirrel, *I* was the intruder, and after picking up this baby rodent to take a closer look, I returned it to the safety of the hole where its mother was hiding. Needless to say, a hungry hawk or coyote would not have displayed such good will toward this curious youngster.

Like these mountain goat nannies, many mammal mothers band together in "nursery groups" to protect and care for offspring, without help from males, which, after mating, take no active part in raising the young.

The bond between mother and offspring is thought to be enhanced by the "baby look" of a young animal, exemplified here by this cougar kitten's big eyes and foreshortened face.

In the course of this program, I also tried to relate the behavior of wild parents and youngsters to that of human beings, since—though some people don't like to admit it—our instincts and behavior are not all that different from the rest of the animal kingdom. As with human youngsters, animal "childhood" is the age of discovery and exploration. It is also a time for learning vital skills that will eventually enable the little ones to survive without the protection of their parents. Since I wanted to make "Wild Babies" of special interest to schoolchildren, I used the analogy that wild animal young must attend the toughest "school" of all—the wilderness "school of survival."

From a very early age, all mammals, and even some birds such as ravens and parrots, engage in playful activity. If you watch baby mountain goats leaping and gamboling on seemingly vertical rocks, it does seem that this activity has no other goal or function than simply to have fun. But when I filmed their aerial jumping and twisting, I pointed out in the program that this "frivolous" behavior was critical to survival by strengthening muscles and sharpening coordination and climbing skills. Of course, the goat kids weren't aware that they were preparing themselves for the ups and downs of life: they were simply having fun.

Researchers believe there is a direct correlation between playfulness and intelligence, since the most intelligent animals seem to engage in the greatest amount of playful activity. The reason is simple: intelligence is the capacity for learning, and to play is to learn. Most adolescent mammals rely on learned behavior, in addition to instinct, in order to survive until adulthood and to fit in socially with other members of their species. In this sense, play is merely a practice session —a working out or "rehearsal"—of the social behaviors and motor skills they will need as adults. By contrast, the offspring of most cold-blooded animals rely solely on instinct or on built-in patterns of behavior, and therefore don't expend their energy on playful activities.

There is also a theory that play encourages adaptability and creativity, which lead to innovative modes of behavior. I once watched Griz playing with a can of soup, rolling it around the cabin floor and swatting it with her paw. Finally, she picked up the can and bit into it, puncturing it with her sharp canines. To her delight, the "toy" leaked a delicious-tasting liquid. For the next half-hour, she sat with the can—now a canteen—between her paws, eagerly licking up the dribbles of soup. Of course, a can of soup is not a normal food source for a wild grizzly, but the point is that if Griz had not played with the can in the first place, she might not have discovered its savory contents. It would seem that playful activity allows young animals to distinguish among, and to take advantage of, the greatest number of options, thereby finding better ways to cope with the demands of their environment.

For humans, perhaps a more playful attitude could help us to cope better with the demands of our home and working environments. Griz and the other wild babies I filmed taught me a lot about how a playful approach allows us to see life in a more relaxed manner and helps to soothe day-to-day concerns and tensions. As I remarked in "Wild Babies," perhaps by watching nature's youngsters we can find a way to play less desperately, and to learn more playfully.

For predatory youngsters, such as bears, foxes, and wolves, play tactics consist mainly of stalking, pouncing, cuffing, chasing, and biting—reflecting their instinct to kill for food. They playfully practice these skills on their siblings, and later on insects like grasshoppers, until they are ready to accompany their parents on a hunt. By contrast, youngsters of prey species, such as deer or pronghorn, play games involving agility and speed—skills which will later enable them to escape their enemies. Yet one form of play common to the young of both predator and prey is the rough-and-tumble game of push and shove that establishes a hierarchy of dominance, first among the siblings in a family, then in later life among adults competing for territory and mates.

For the progeny of highly social animals, learning rules of rank and dominance at an early age serves to minimize unnecessary conflict within the social structure of the group once the animal reaches adulthood. To me, the most interesting example of highly structured social behavior is to be found in wolf packs, so for "Wild Babies" I filmed adult timber wolves raising a litter of pups. Within a wolf pack, only the dominant or "alpha" male and female reproduce, the female normally giving birth to a litter of from four to six pups. In this way, with so many "aunts" and "uncles" to interact with, more food and attention is devoted to each pup, and the young wolves quickly learn social skills that will help them fit into the pack as adults.

As the offspring of any species mature into adulthood, the once-powerful bonds that held the family together begin to weaken. For higher mammals, the separation between mother and young comes about gradually, beginning with the weaning process. Eventually the youngsters venture farther away on their own for longer periods of time, finding their own food and defending themselves from danger. For birds, the acquisition of flight feathers by fledglings marks the beginning of the end of their parent's duties. The sensory information of touch, sight, scent, and sound, which served to establish and reinforce the ties that bound a family unit together, is communicated to a lesser degree as the babies grow up. Finally, the bond between parent and offspring is severed, sometimes forcibly, after the secrets of survival have been passed on to a new generation.

Unlike most of my earlier films, my primary intention in making "Wild Babies" was not so much to show how much of our valuable wildlife heritage we have lost, but rather to show the importance of the familial bonds that exist in nature and how they relate to our own human family life. Just like human children, nature's youngsters also hold the secrets of the past and the promise of the future. Learning this, I hoped, might enable viewers to empathize more with wild creatures and their increasingly difficult struggle to survive and raise offspring in our crowded world.

Another way that I hoped to help people relate to and understand wild animals, besides comparing similarities in our behavior and instincts, was by showing human interaction with animals. I thought people might be more likely to pay attention, remember, and learn from scenes in which a person is watching, touching, or even being chased by a wild creature than if I showed only the animals by themselves. That's why I sometimes like to appear on-camera to dramatize the points I'm trying to make. For instance, if I put my finger next to a tiny hummingbird's nest in a cedar tree, people can see its size in relation to my fingertips and will realize how exquisitely small and fragile this creature's home and nursery really is, which I hope will give them a greater appreciation for the bird itself. On the other end of the size scale, I've also approached a wild boar on camera during mating season and been chased up a tree, and once filmed a female moose as she chased my camera crew farther away from her calf. These instances were included to dramatize the fact that any wild animal should be approached only with great caution.

I hope that when people see myself or another person being chased on camera, they will interpret it as a signal to keep their distance from creatures they might not have considered dangerous. Filming such scenes does occasionally put myself or my camera crew at a bit of a risk, but I like to think that in a way we are the rodeo clowns of the wildlife filmmaking business. Because we know pretty much what to expect from a wild animal's behavior, we are able to dramatize what might happen to a less experienced person in the same situation, and still avoid the consequences.

I'll never forget an instance in Yellowstone Park that made me realize just how naive people can be about wild animals. I was with C. C. Lockwood filming the elk bugling and mating sequence that is seen in "Wild Babies." We had our sound recording gear set up at the edge of a forest clearing, and were recording the bugling of a large bull elk in the middle of the meadow. This amazing, eerie call serves as both a battle cry to rivals and a love ballad to receptive females during the rutting season. We were curious to see whether this particular bull would recognize his own voice, or consider it a challenge from a rival, when we played it back to him.

The instant he heard his own mating call, he became enraged—slashing the air with his antlers as if doing battle with an invisible enemy. Then, bewildered and out of breath, he paused for a moment and snorted. Catching our scent, he charged straight for us. We ran behind a nearby clump of aspen trees, which effectively shielded us from his piercing antlers. Since the animals in Yellowstone are relatively used to people, we were only about 100 yards from the road and in sight of other tourists. Just as the bull was calming down, we looked around to see a woman, dressed in hot pink shorts and matching blouse, a camera dangling from her neck, walking across the meadow directly toward the bull elk. In her outstretched hand was a piece of enriched white bread. Needless to say, the elk soon spotted her and began pawing and thrashing the earth with his antlers. Heedless of this obvious warning, she continued to walk toward this highly irritated 1,000-pound bull elk with his massive rack of twelve sharp tines, thinking he was going to nibble a piece of bread out of her hand, just like a squirrel in the park back home. In all fairness to her, our own proximity to the elk had probably bolstered her sense of security. When we yelled at her to get back in her car, she threw us a "mind your own business" glance, just as the elk decided to charge. She shrieked, spun around, and ran, dropping the bread and reaching her car barely seconds before the elk reached her.

Of course, we may have been partly responsible for unwittingly antagonizing this bull, but no matter whose voice he thought he was hearing, he was in no mood to be approached by anything other than a cow elk. Part of the reason I act as "rodeo clown" in some of my programs is not only to show people that some animals *will* chase you, but also to show when and why they are *most likely* to chase you. As I noted in some of my subsequent programs, like "Watching Wildlife" and "Photographing Wildlife," animals at certain times of the year can be especially dangerous. Males are more dangerous in the fall when they are fighting for mating privileges, and females are more dangerous in the spring and summer when they have young to protect.

Even while I try in my films to teach how to avoid dangerous animals, I also go out of my way to get close to and touch wild animals, as long as I don't think it will put them or myself in danger. In "Wild Babies," I appear on camera picking up a baby ground squirrel, and my wife, Diane, is shown walking up to and gently touching a baby pronghorn hiding in the sagebrush. I wanted to show how the fawn's first instinct is to stay motionless and out of sight until the moment when Diane touches it and causes the fawn to bolt for its mother.

Of course, I'm well aware that wild parents with offspring in a nest or den are much more sensitive to human presence than at other times of the year, and that the young then are more vulnerable than at any other time in their life. Still, I think it's sometimes defensible for a filmmaker to put an animal at some small, temporary risk, in order to show, for example, how a baby pronghorn avoids detection, or how a parent bird feeds its young, so long as a word of caution is introduced. As a result, many millions of people might better understand, respect, and care about wildlife of all kinds. More and more, the survival of a species depends on its relationship to the human species—on how well we understand its needs and how much we value its existence.

But in filming wild animals with young, there are many precautions that can be taken to minimize the stress of one's presence. The most important is to keep plenty of distance between yourself and the animal's den or nest. For more sensitive species, such as foxes or bears, I use a telephoto lens and set up my camera out of sight of the animals, either inside a tent or behind a natural blind. Since most mammals have a keen sense of smell, it's important to remain downwind of them. For animals which are not highly sensitive to human presence, such as tree-nesting birds, it's a simple but time-consuming matter of setting up a blind at some distance from the nest, then moving it a little closer each day, until one is within filming range. This gives the birds time to accept the strange-looking object in their territory. Also, it's best to get into the blind before daybreak, so as not to disturb them at their day's activities. Then there are less sensitive species such as the porcupine, which is slow-moving and relatively unwary of humans. To film a mother porcupine with her baby, I simply followed them around with my camera, moving as slowly as possible, and before long they accepted my presence.

By 1979, I had accumulated enough footage on wild babies to edit into a one-hour special to sell to the networks. However, by this time, two very important changes were taking place in the wildlife filmmaking business. First of all, the commercial networks had almost completely lost interest in broadcasting wildlife programs. Even *Wild Kingdom*, the National Geographic specials, and Survival Anglia's wildlife specials, all of which had found a niche in the commercial television industry long ago, were no longer being bought. Consequently, these wildlife production companies had to find new markets through syndication and Public Television.

That was the bad news. The good news was that, although the commercial network ratings for wildlife programs were at an all-time low, which is why the networks weren't buying them anymore, the educational distribution of my films was at an all-time high. Schools, libraries, and wildlife organizations were purchasing release prints of my earlier films as fast as I could supply them. Although educational distribution was the bread-and-butter income of my business, I was still hoping to sell "Wild Babies" to a major commercial network, thinking it just might be the kind of noncontroversial, entertaining program they would be interested in.

However, there was a catch-22 involved. The networks would only broadcast one-hour specials, while schools and libraries were only interested in buying a fifteen- to thirty-minute format. So I had two choices. I could either edit "Wild Babies" into a one-hour program with the hope of selling it to the networks, as I had with "The Predators" and "The Man Who Loved Bears," or I could make two separate half-hour films to sell educationally. Of course, I wanted to do both. That way, if the networks didn't buy it—and there was a good chance they wouldn't—I could still depend on income from educational sales of the two half-hour programs. After carefully studying the footage, I came up with a plan.

While filming for "Wild Babies," I had happened to shoot a great deal of footage on two animals in particular—timber wolves and white-tailed deer. I had filmed each species during the course of raising their offspring—the social behavior of a wolf pack raising a litter of pups, and a doe giving birth to, nursing, and raising her twin fawns. Besides this footage, several years earlier I had filmed an interesting predation sequence of a wolf pack hunting a deer, which had yet to be edited into any program.

I felt that the life stories and predator-prey interactions of these two species could make an interesting film that would stand on its own, so I decided to edit a half-hour program called "The Wolf and the Whitetail," along with a half-hour program on "Wild Babies." In this way, I would have two films that could be distributed educationally. And, since a good portion of "The Wolf and the Whitetail" was made up of sequences of those two species in the process of raising their young, I edited together another one-hour film, called "Wild Babies," composed of these two half-hour formats, to sell to the networks.

The sixty-minute program began with the first fifteen minutes of the half-hour version of "Wild Babies," introducing the courtship rituals of various species. Following was the entire story of "The Wolf and the Whitetail," beginning with the courtship of the alpha male and female, and leading into the play and perils of the wolf pups and the whitetail fawns. Then I concluded the sixty-minute film with the last fifteen minutes of "Wild Babies," depicting the familial bonds of other species of wildlife, such as a mother porcupine, raccoon, and moose with their respective offspring.

It was a lot of trouble to go to, but when ABC-TV considered buying the one-hour format for an "After-School Special," it suddenly all seemed worthwhile. However, when I showed them the completed special, their reaction was once again fairly predictable. In their words, the program needed more of what they called "warmth and jeopardy." They weren't interested in the day-to-day lives of wild animals going through their courtship rituals or bringing food to the nest to feed their growing offspring. They wanted to see more babies barely escape the jaws of villainous predators, while the mother risked her life to rescue her young. And, of course, all the animals had to live happily ever after.

They weren't looking for what I had to offer, and they declined to buy the program. So "Wild Babies" and "The Wolf and the Whitetail" were separately released for educational distribution, and I finally abandoned the idea of selling wildlife specials to the networks. I knew that there were somewhat manipulated reasons for the reduced ratings that network wildlife specials had been receiving, mainly having to do with the networks' refusal to advertise these specials. But after finally accepting that network specials were a thing of the past, I came up with Plan B. My own personal market analysis had revealed that PBS was quickly filling the niche for wildlife programming left vacant by the commercial networks with highly popular wildlife specials and series such as *National Geographic* and *Nova*. When I contacted the PBS

Play is an integral part of growing up. A baby bighorn's antics while navigating steep cliffs are also its first leaps and bounds toward learning crucial survival skills.

program directors, they informed me that what they were looking for was a continuing *series* of programs on wildlife rather than for one-time specials. Although the immediate rewards of money and recognition would not be as great as with commercial television, my Plan B was to sell a wildlife series to PBS.

By this time, I already had several completed films which could form the foundation for such a series, and I also had an extensive library of unedited wildlife footage that could be used as the basis for other programs. Instead of selling my best material to other companies as stock footage for them to make programs out of, I thought, why not use it myself? My initial idea was to do a series of seven one-hour programs entitled *Life in the Wild*. The subject matter would be wildlife around the world: the pandas in China, the dolphins of Hawaii, and the Marco Polo sheep in the Himalayas, for instance, in addition to the North American wildlife I had already filmed.

Because of the worldwide travel involved, the series would be very expensive to produce. I knew PBS did not have the budget to buy this type of series, so I would have to find a corporate underwriter to fund the production. Big corporations generally have a sizable advertising budget, and will often sponsor, or underwrite, the production costs of high-quality, educational programs on Public Television. This means of advertising effectively enhances their corporate image in the eyes of the extensive and well-educated PBS audience, in addition to displaying their name and logo on air for several seconds during each broadcast. So I made a deal with a PBS affiliate in Chicago, WTTW, which had contacts with the major underwriters of Public Television. If they could come up with corporate funding for the series, they would get a percentage of the underwriting funds and I would produce and own the films.

After several major corporations had been approached to underwrite the series, Shell Oil was the only one that seemed interested. But just when it looked like we were close to coming to an agreement with them, a program aired on PBS called "Death of a Princess" that effectively blew our chances right out of the water. The program was a rather negative portrayal of the royal families of the oil-producing Arab nations, and was ironically sponsored by one of the larger oil companies in this country. As a result, this oil company received a great deal of angry feedback from business associates in Saudi Arabia for being associated with such an offensive program. To our dismay, Shell Oil also decided to stay away from the underwriting business for an indefinite period of time.

After two years of inquiries, we still weren't able to fund the *Life in the Wild* series either through corporate sponsorship or through the SPC, a funding organization within PBS made up of program managers who vote once a year to buy certain programs for the Public Broadcasting Service. So, for me, it was back to the drawing board to try and come up with an idea for a wildlife series that would sell. In my mind there were only two probable reasons why we couldn't find a sponsor for the series. One, because it was too expensive, or two, because the subject matter wasn't unique and interesting enough. After many brainstorming sessions, I came up with an idea that I hoped would take care of both problems at the same time.

I would do a series strictly on the wildlife of North America. Since less traveling would be involved, the series would be cheaper to produce. Even more important, I remembered my experiences with the success of my home movie on Alaska versus the dismal failure of my more sophisticated professional movie on Africa. Once again, I speculated that Americans had seen enough of exotic species from faraway places. They might want to see and learn about the creatures that are found in their own backyards, or that can be found in the various national parks that millions of Americans visit each year.

This approach, I calculated, would set the series apart from all other wildlife programming, most of which featured exotic—especially African—wildlife that a great majority of Americans would never have a chance to see in real life. Not that I don't think lions, hyenas, zebras, giraffes, and elephants are fascinating. I do. But all of them have been filmed time and time again. They've been filmed poorly and they've been filmed beautifully, but above all, they've been filmed to the point of predictability. We've all seen films on African lions, yet many people have never seen a program about American mountain lions, or, for that matter, chipmunks, shrews, or white-tailed deer—animals that are more easily seen and that live in nearly every area of our country. The popularity of my earlier films such as "Bighorn!", "At the Crossroads," and "The Predators" reinforced my belief that American people want to see programs about American wildlife. And, after discovering and filming the great diversity of wild creatures and wild places found on this continent, I knew that *I* did!

I think we've become somewhat bored with the exotic, and now prefer to rediscover the familiar. Besides, I felt strongly —and still do—that the American landscape holds all the allure, variety, and dramatic intrigue of Africa, or any other place in the world, and I was excited by the prospect of showing people, through my films, what was right under their noses all along.

So I called the series *Wild America* and promoted it as "the first television series ever to focus exclusively on North American wildlife." The series, as I envisioned it, would be made up of ten half-hour programs, four of them being films I had already produced: "Bighorn!," "At the Crossroads," "Wild Babies," and "The Wolf and the Whitetail." Since this would be a no-frills, low-budget series, I had to give up my pie-in-the-sky ideas of hiring Judy Collins to sing the theme song or having Leslie Neilsen do the voice-over narration. I also had to sever my ties with WTTW, since I would be marketing the series myself, and the rock-bottom budget would not support the expense of an "agent" selling the series for me.

In 1981, I returned to the annual PBS program fair, for the second time, in order to seek funding for *Wild America* from the SPC program managers. With four of the programs already completed and enough stock footage for the other six, I offered to sell the series at a price that was far below what anyone else could have ever shot and produced the programs for. It was an offer they couldn't refuse—and they didn't. Perseverance had finally paid off, and a new wildlife series was born. Just a few months previous to the birth of *Wild America*, Diane and I had our first child, a daughter whom we named Hannah. That these two joyful highlights of my life happened within six months of each other is still a delightful mystery to me. I like to believe that my newborn daughter was the lucky charm that helped to clinch the deal with PBS, but in truth, luck had little to do with it. "The Predators" had already aired on PBS, so they were familiar with and respected my work. I think they were delighted to have the opportunity to purchase inexpensive wildlife programming from a recognized producer, although I don't know whether or not they realized then what a bargain they had bought.

When the elation of selling *Wild America* to PBS began to subside, the next step was to hire a staff of talented, dedicated people. Paula Smith had by then been working with me for the past two years as a writer and assistant. I immediately hired John King, who had gone to school with my brother Mark at the Brooks Institute of Photography, as a picture and sound editor and part-time cameraman. John had previously worked with Mark and me on the John Denver specials, and had helped us film and edit some of our own earlier network specials.

Shortly afterwards, two other important people came on board, receiving on-the-job training in both the office and in the field. Michelle Brandt-Morton came all the way from Florida to work with me, initially as a researcher with a degree in wildlife management, and then quickly stepping up to learn picture and sound editing. Since then, she's also taken on duties as a scriptwriter and cameraperson. Greg Hensley started out with the unglamorous job of cleaning our educational release prints, and soon graduated to being a cameraman specializing in time-lapse photography. He also spends part of his time as a sound recordist and picture and sound editor.

Normally, a producer tries to hire the most experienced staff he can find to get a newly created series off the ground. But at the time, I simply didn't have the budget to hire a full staff of the best-known people in the business. As a result, each member of my staff had to learn new skills and wear the hats of two or three different job positions. But all of them were eager and quick to learn, as well as talented and flexible. Fortunately, my previous experience in making wildlife specials on a shoestring budget had forced me to do much of the writing, and picture and sound editing myself, so I had a thorough knowledge of each of these aspects of post-production. I spent as much time as I could teaching and overseeing my staff, while still managing the business and financial aspects of running a television series. It was a frantic, chaotic year for all of us, but with a great deal of teamwork and dedication, we managed to get the programs completed and delivered on time.

Because of the low budget, I also had to wear many hats. Not only was I the producer, director, and main cameraman, but also the narrator and host of the series. It was a lot of responsibility for one person, but perhaps in the long run, I think it was one of the secrets to the success of *Wild America*. With my extensive involvement in each of the programs, I was the common thread woven through them, ensuring they were all of the same style and quality. One *TV Guide* reviewer described the series as "home-grown television," which I personally found very flattering, whether or not it was meant that way. Although the series is not produced in a posh studio in New York City using the latest and greatest production equipment, people were, and continue to be, amazed at the standard of professionalism and accomplishment achieved by our small but dedicated staff.

Even so, I do have to laugh at all the mistakes we made in that first year. In our overzealous attempt to make the series a smash hit we edited as much action-packed footage as we could into each half hour, then threw in as many interesting facts as would fit into an almost continuous stream of narration. To top it off, more than fifteen minutes of each half-hour program was accompanied by background music in addition to all the sound effects. Needless to say, those early programs now seem a bit "crowded."

Now, of course, we do things a little differently. The programs are much slower paced, and it seems that each year we cut back even further on narration and music in order to let the action and the natural sound effects speak for themselves. But despite the earlier overkill on action, music, and narration, the immediate response from the PBS viewers during the premiere episodes of *Wild America* in Year One was very positive. The PBS program managers were pleasantly surprised that such an inexpensive wildlife series, produced by an independent production company, could prove so popular. It seems another expression of the American dream: that a low-budget "sleeper" series should succeed, one based on the belief that Americans are interested in and concerned about their own heritage of wildlife, a heritage that has contributed immeasurably to the greatness of this nation.

The high ratings *Wild America* drew made us feel somewhat hopeful that PBS might buy the series for a second year, which they did. Yet there was little time to bask in the glory of our initial success. Having used up most of the good material in my stock footage library for the first year of *Wild America*, the footage for the second year of the series had to be specifically shot for each program. Nevertheless, my staff and I were ready to produce ten new wildlife programs the likes of which no one had ever seen before—and this time without having to bow to any network censors and their unrealistic notions about wild creatures and how they live.

Unlike commercial networks, Public Television has always been in the admirable and perhaps enviable position of

"Wild Babies" was in many ways the beginning of the Wild America *series. Here at our lab in Denver we mix a dozen or more rolls of sound effects, music, and narration rolls onto a single sound track.*

being able to take risks and to break new ground, since it does not have to be concerned with editorial control by advertisers. With PBS's financial backing, we were ready to film all those things that we thought were important and interesting, but which had always been censored out of network programs: birth, death, mating, and predation. All the main events of an animal's life. And we set out to do just that in the second year of *Wild America*, with two of my all-time favorite programs, "Born To Run" and "Hog Wild!"

EIGHT

BEAUTY AND THE BEAST

While filming "Hog Wild!," I came across a nest of newborn wild piglets. The spotted one on the left shows that this litter carries a predominance of genes from domestic hogs.

I t was not until the second year of *Wild America* that I realized how much producing a series of wildlife programs, instead of individual specials, had changed my career. I was still intimately involved in every phase of post-production. I approved each picture edit, I read and corrected each script before I recorded the narration, and I listened to every sound-effects edit and music edit before a program went to the sound mix, where all the sound tracks were combined onto one track. But the thing that had changed most from my pre-series days was that I no longer had the time to shoot all of the footage for each of the ten half-hour programs. Instead, I needed to hire additional cinematographers to film either specific sequences for a certain program or, rarely, to shoot the entire program.

For me, this was an ironic situation, and somewhat frustrating, since my cinematography skills were the primary basis of my reputation as a wildlife filmmaker. The situation reminded me of a cop who is so good catching criminals out on the street that he's promoted to captain and ends up pushing pencils and shuffling paper—which was just how I was spending an increasing amount of my time. The business and financial aspects of producing a series were interesting and challenging, but I still wanted to research and shoot every scene of every program in the *Wild America* series. Of course that was impossible, but there were two programs in the second year that I took a special interest in and decided to film myself. One was "Born to Run," about the pronghorn, and the other was "Hog Wild!" about wild swine.

These animals were especially appealing to me because, of all the wild creatures that still roam this continent, none are more lovely than the sleek, graceful pronghorn, and none more homely than the bristling, ungainly wild hog, usually called the wild boar. I called them "the beauty and the beast," and filming a year in the life of each of these species was a fascinating study in contrasts, beginning with physical appearance. The pronghorn is the size of a small deer and sports a handsome two-toned coat of reddish-tan and white, punctuated by a snowy white rump patch. The bucks have a black throat band, which accentuates their protruding dark eyes, black nose, and the coal-black pronged horns on their head. The females usually grow only small, prongless spikes, but both sexes are equally graceful and lightfooted as they race across open prairie.

Whereas the pronghorn's movements seem effortless, the wild boar moves through swampy thickets at a gait that is stiff and awkward by comparison. And its physique is anything but lissome. Basically, the wild hog has a long nose, short neck,

An all-American native, the pronghorn is the sole surviving member of a large and ancient family of hoofed mammals. This pronghorn is scent-marking a mullein weed.

and a stocky muscular body covered by coarse, bristling guard hairs. Because most wild swine today are the hybrid offspring of European wild boars and feral, or free-roaming, domestic hogs, they come in all shapes and colors—from fat and spotted to lean and uniformly dark in color. Their incredibly tough and wily temperament is backed up by razor-sharp tusks, which are longer and more prominent in male boars than in female sows.

The evolutionary histories of these two creatures are as unlike as their appearances. The pronghorn of today is the sole survivor of a large family of prehistoric hoofed mammals that once populated the North American continent. Its ancestors ranged in size from the diminutive stature of a jackrabbit to an animal that was much larger than the present-day pronghorn. A wide variety of horn configurations also occurred throughout their evolution. Some species had long, vertical horns, some spirally twisted horns, and some even had four to six horns sprouting at different angles from their heads. These prehistoric pronghorns did not cross the Bering Strait land bridge from Asia during the Pleistocene epoch as our other native hoofed mammals did. This unique creature, found nowhere else in the world, was already here. For over twenty million years, through frigid ice ages and dry interglacial periods, the pronghorn evolved along with other animals and plants, and with the changing landscape of North America. Although it was given the scientific name *Antilocapra americana*, which translates as "American goat-antelope," it is not closely related either to present-day goats or antelope, nor for that matter to any other living hoofed mammal. Thus, although they once had numerous relatives, they are now the sole surviving members of their own taxonomic family, Antilocapridae. Though they are often called pronghorn antelope, or simply antelope, their correct common name is pronghorn.

Less than two centuries ago, pronghorn herds drifted across our rolling grasslands by the millions, along with seemingly endless herds of bison, bighorn, deer, and elk. Those were the days when the wildlife on the plains of America rivaled that of Africa for sheer numbers. Biologists estimate that pronghorn populations peaked at an incredible 100 *million*—surpassing even the number of bison—by the time the white man began to settle the prairies and desert plains. They swelled the ranks of what was most likely the largest concentration of herd mammals that the world has ever known.

While the pronghorn is truly an American native, the wild hog is anything but. Domestic swine were first brought to this continent in the late 1400s by Spanish explorers who relied on them for food. But many of these animals escaped to multiply and flourish in the American wilderness. Later, in the 1800s, European wild boars were brought over from Germany and Russia to be released on private hunting preserves. These wild boars bred with feral, once-domestic swine which had escaped the barnyard to run wild.

Although today's wild hogs are for the most part a mixed strain of feral pigs and European wild boar, they do have a close relative that is native to this continent. The peccary, smaller but similar in appearance to the European wild boar,

European wild boars, long-nosed and stiff-bristled, were brought to the New World by settlers for sport. Many escaped, mated with domestic hogs, and multiplied to become at best a mixed blessing.

ranges from the southwestern deserts of the United States and Mexico down into the tropical jungles of Central and South America. This New World counterpart of the Old World swine is distinguished by a scent gland on its back, which is used to mark its territory and communicate socially with other peccaries. We included a brief segment on it in "Hog Wild!," and later celebrated its native status in a program called "All-American Animals."

While the peccary, and especially the pronghorn, have always run wild and free, no farm animal has reverted back to that state quite as readily as the domestic hog. Its domesticity is merely a thin veneer over its inherent wildness, and the intelligence and adaptability of these creatures are apparent in the way domestic pigs can easily survive and fend for themselves outside the barnyard. These wild swine inhabit most of our southern states, and have been steadily increasing in numbers and in range. They have spread up the east coast as far as New Hampshire, and west across southern Texas. They can survive the cold, but find more food in warmer areas like Puerto Rico, Hawaii, Florida, and California. In California, wild hogs double their population every six years, and in other areas, like the Great Smoky Mountains National Park in Tennessee, they pose a threat to many native species of plants and animals because of their destructive rooting and eating habits.

These aggressive omnivores compete with native deer, squirrels, bears, and other animals for acorns and nuts. And they compete with other creatures for plants, grubs, lizards, snakes, frogs, and rodents. They also feed on rare lilies and endangered salamanders, a fact that does not endear them to the National Park Service, which manages the Great Smoky Mountains National Park for the protection of *native* plants and wildlife. It's been shown that wild hogs also cause soil erosion by plowing up the earth with their snouts in search of roots and tubers. At the same time, other than humans, dogs, and an occasional bear or alligator, no predators remain to feed on the hogs. For all these reasons, the wild hog's increasing numbers do not qualify it as a success story—if success is defined as whatever is good for the environment as a whole.

Yet, while hogs in the Smokies are viewed as exotic pests,

Similar in appearance to the European wild boar is the collared peccary of our American Southwest. Eating cactus, spines and all, presents no problem for this resilient native.

in western Europe, where their numbers are fewer, wild boars are looked upon as friends of the forester. By rooting up the ground, foresters claim, the pigs help to aerate the soil, and the pigs also bury nuts and seeds, thereby regenerating the woodlands. Farmers on both continents, however, see the animals as a nuisance because of their costly habit of digging up planted fields of crops.

One thing that wild hogs and pronghorn do have in common is that they are both increasing in numbers at present, although the pronghorn nearly became extinct at the beginning of this century. This was due in large part to the fact that for some unknown reason, pronghorn refuse to jump fences. The only way they will cross a barbed wire fence is if the bottom wire is high enough off the ground for them to crawl underneath. This inexplicable reluctance to jump fences made the elegant creatures easy to round up and slaughter in the late 1800s, when pronghorn tenderloins were popular dinner fare. Tragically, hunters often left the rest of the carcass to rot, and this wastefulness became another factor in their decline.

Even today, the pronghorn's refusal to leap fences continues to place it in danger, since on today's extensively fenced ranches, herds cannot move on to new feeding grounds. They therefore often starve, especially in the winter when food is scarce and storms bring them up against snow-choked fence lines. Fortunately, today more and more ranchers are cooperating with game departments to put up fences only where they are necessary and functional, and to string the bottom wire high enough off the ground to allow pronghorn a way to crawl under.

Another thing that wild hogs and pronghorn have in common is that both are popular game animals. They are hunted not only for their tasty meat, but just as often for their trophy heads—the pronghorn for its distinctive inward-sweeping

What's a young pronghorn to do when it can't get over or under a fence? Civilizing the West with barbed wire nearly wiped out the otherwise agile pronghorn, which for some unknown reason refuses to jump fences.

hooked horns and the wild hog for its curved, sword-sharp tusks. Ironically, both animal populations are on the rise for one simple reason: hunters want more of them to hunt. Many game departments encourage the expansion of the ranges of these two species by transplanting them into management areas where they can be legally hunted. In fact, wild boars in the Great Smoky Mountains National Park are regularly live-trapped and then released into open hunting areas outside the park. This way sportsmen can have the pleasure and satisfaction of hunting the animals, and park personnel are relieved of the job of eradicating them from within park boundaries. Because of their popularity with hunters, it looks as though these two animals are here to stay, for better or for worse. Certainly it's better to manage the hunting of a native animal such as the pronghorn so that its population remains stable, or even increases.

However, the wild hog serves as a prime example of the destructive effect a non-native species can have on our continent's wildlife and wildlands. It also exemplifies that the benefit of introducing an exotic game species into a wilderness area for sport usually fails to outweigh the threat presented to the ecosystem by such non-native competitors for food and space. It's an important distinction to make: because a given animal is wild doesn't mean it automatically should be protected. The effect it has on its environment and the degree to which it maintains the balance nature has set within an area determines its suitability.

Despite their popularity with big-game hunters, neither the pronghorn nor the wild hog would rate very high on a list of America's best-loved animals. At least not compared with deer, eagles, or even bears—animals which have always held a prominent place in our hearts. I think the attention we pay to certain animals is sometimes just a matter of public relations, and that's another reason why I wanted to make these programs about the pronghorn and the wild hog. Because I had never seen a film about either of them before, I had a hunch most people knew little, if anything, about them, even though neither is rare or difficult to observe in its respective habitat.

Since wildlife cinematography came into being forty or fifty years ago, many "ordinary" species have been passed over in the pursuit of filming only the most dramatic or exotic creatures. I have to admit that I've been guilty of this myself. When I drove through Wyoming on my way to film bison, elk, and grizzly bears in Yellowstone, I would pass herd after herd of pronghorns grazing next to the highway. Sometimes I would see them racing through the sagebrush, long legs outstretched and white rump patches flaring. It never occurred to me then that their life story might be as interesting as the more dramatic wildlife I was going to Yellowstone to film. Of course, I had earlier spent six weeks on the Cabeza Prieta filming the endangered Sonoran pronghorn for "At the Crossroads," but then my interest was due to the fact that it *was* rare, and very little was known about it.

Back then, I guess I was as guilty as the next wildlife cinematographer of wanting to film either rarely-seen animals like the Sonoran pronghorn, or to film rarely-seen behavior, such as the dramatic head-butting ritual of the bighorn sheep. During the early years of my career, I was under the vague impression that people wanted to see in a program only what they couldn't see for themselves in real life, or at least what they couldn't normally see along a highway. To a certain extent, I'm sure that's true, and that is the reason for the popularity of "The Undersea World of Jacques Cousteau," the National Geographic specials, or the BBC Natural History Unit's fascinating film work on microscopic plants and animals.

It was while filming sequences for "Wild Babies" that I realized the uncommon behavior of familiar species could be just as interesting as the common behavior of unfamiliar or exotic ones, and that I might not be alone in valuing each creature for the unique complexity of its means of survival. In this instance, raccoon babies were trying to reach the far bank of a stream by following their mother across a fallen log. One baby lost its balance, plopped into the water, and fretfully paddled toward shore. Seeing this, the mother raccoon seemed to decide that swimming lessons were a prerequisite to log-climbing lessons, and slipped into the water herself, enticing her youngsters to follow.

In another instance, I experienced for the first time what

an interesting animal the pronghorn really is. While driving through Wyoming, Diane and I stopped and got out of the truck to walk around and stretch our legs. About fifty yards away, we saw a pronghorn doe near the side of the highway. She acted nervous about our presence, and we couldn't understand why she didn't run away. At about that moment Diane nearly stepped on her well-hidden fawn lying motionless, curled up under a clump of sagebrush.

I later read that a newborn pronghorn is practically odorless, to the extent that even a coyote can pass within a few feet of a fawn and not smell it. As an extra protective measure, for several days after birth the fawn lies as still as possible, while the mother grazes. After only three or four days, a baby pronghorn can run beside its mother, at which point it uses speed, rather than concealment, to escape predation. For this reason, we eventually called our program on the pronghorn "Born To Run," and my brother Marshall and I later actually did film a sequence of a coyote chasing a baby pronghorn.

A couple of years after I filmed Diane finding the baby pronghorn, Marshall and I took a trip to Yellowstone Park— something we have done every summer for the past fifteen years—and along the way happened to discover another peculiarity about pronghorns. On our way there, we stopped occasionally to explore the prairie arroyos of northern Colorado, and the Red Desert around Rock Springs, Wyoming. On one of these exploratory hikes along a prairie gully, we found several pronged horns lying about, some half-covered with dirt. Surprisingly, the horns were very lightweight and completely hollow inside. Although we kept our eyes open for any skeletons or evidence that pronghorns had died in the area, we could not find a single clue as to where the horns had come from. We were curious to know how these appendages happened to be separated from their skulls, since animals with horns, like bighorn sheep and mountain goats, wear the same pair for life, whereas animals with antlers, like deer, elk and moose, shed them each year. Or so we thought.

When we got to Yellowstone, we asked a biologist about our odd finding and he informed us that the pronghorn is the *only* animal in the world that sheds its horns. It is also the only animal with horns that are branched or pronged. The basic difference between antlers and horns is that, for one, antlers are made of solid bone and grow from a protuberance of the skull called a pedicel. They are nourished in their yearly growth by a blood-rich tissue, called velvet, which covers the outside of the antlers until they reach their full season's growth. The velvet then dries up and is rubbed off as the animal prepares for the fall rutting, or breeding, season. When the breeding period is over, the antlers are shed, which reduces the amount of energy needed to carry their weight through the winter. In the spring, the growth cycle begins again.

Horns, on the other hand, are made up of a combination of substances. They consist of an inner core of bone, growing as a direct extension of the skull, and an outer sheath of keratin —a hard substance similar to our fingernails. Horns are usually permanent structures that continue to grow throughout the animal's life. Each winter, however, the pronghorn's unique horny sheath drops off, leaving only the bony core covered by a soft layer of hair. In spring, the sheath begins to grow again. The female also has horns, but they are much smaller than the male's and aren't shed as regularly.

Personal experience combined with research made me realize that the pronghorn's life story was even more fascinating than I had first suspected. Of all its qualities, speed was the most impressive. Not only can baby pronghorns run thirty miles per hour at a mere three days old, but as adults they are supposedly the second fastest animal in the world, right behind the cheetah. I say "supposedly" because I'd find this ranking easier to believe *after* I saw a cheetah catch a pronghorn.

Unlike my encounters with pronghorns, my experience with wild hogs before shooting "Hog Wild!" was minimal. The only ones I had ever heard about in my home state were called Arkansas Razorbacks—the University of Arkansas football team, named after a type of wild boar that has a prominent, aggressive-looking ridge of stiff hair along its backbone. But the animals themselves are not common in Arkansas.

I had seen a wild pig only once in my life, during one of my teenage jaunts into the Arkansas woods. One frosty morning I was hunting deer in dense undergrowth along the Arkan-

sas River. It was below zero that morning—exceptionally cold
for Arkansas—but the weather appealed to my sense of adventure. I was stalking through the woods, carrying a high-
powered rifle and treading as carefully as possible through the
dry, ice-encrusted leaves. Despite my care, I stepped on a
twig and snapped it. Instantly, a large animal leapt up about
twenty or thirty feet ahead of me and ran crashing off through
the brush.

I followed it, thinking it might be a bear, since deer don't
make that much noise. While possibilities flashed through my
mind as to what kind of creature it could be, the animal slid
to a stop and poked its head out of the undergrowth, seeming
to glare back at me. In the instant I realized I was chasing a
wild boar—a large, mean-looking one at that—it burst out of
the brush and charged straight at me. With no time to ponder
my options, and with rifle at waist level rather than at my
shoulder, I pointed rather than aimed, and literally shot from
the hip. The boar stumbled and fell five feet in front of me. As
I bent down to inspect it, I realized I was shivering, either
from cold or from excitement—I'm still not sure which. I ran
back to my house and enlisted two friends to help me haul
that 250-pound critter out of the deep thicket to where we
could dress the carcass and divvy up the meat.

My interest in making a program about these feisty wild
hogs for *Wild America* originated from an old idea I once had
for a network special that never quite made it past the drawing
board stage. A few years before the series was acquired by
PBS, I had researched and written a script entitled "The Joy
of Pigs," based on a magazine article about the different pigs
of the world. This was after I had already sold two wildlife
specials to the networks, and I was always trying to come up
with new and interesting subjects that I thought the networks
or cable companies might buy as one-hour programs.

"The Joy of Pigs" was to be a humorous and informative
look at the swine of fact and fiction, depicting their history in
America as descendants of the European wild boar, and including sequences on wild hogs from all over the world, such
as the warthog of Africa and the bizarre babirusa of the Ce-
lebes and Molucca Islands, whose upper tusks, rather than

growing downward on the outside of its mouth, grow upward, puncturing the skin and curving backward toward the fore- head.

This program would also have explored the pig's cultural role in our society, with cartoon clips and references to Porky Pig, the Three Little Pigs, and the popular Muppet character, Miss Piggy—all of which I hoped would make it appealing to a commercial network. I was even more interested in the se- rious role of swine in our culture. I wanted, for instance, to include a sequence on "mini pigs," which have been bred smaller specifically for research purposes. These pigs are so physiologically similar to humans that they are used to study the effects of alcohol and other chemicals on people. Even barnyard swine would have their moment in the spotlight, with a sequence on domestic pigs, often referred to as "Corn on the Hoof," since nearly one-half of America's corn crop is consumed by pigs.

When I delved into the subject, I felt that a program on pigs could mean another network success. At the time, a kind of porcine madness seemed to be sweeping the nation. *New West* magazine had nicknamed 1979 the "Year of the Pig," and swine-related stores, books, and products were popping up everywhere. I thought Miss Piggy would be the ideal host for "The Joy of Pigs." So, between writing letters to wildlife departments in Surinam, Africa, and Germany, and tracking down hog-calling contests in the southern United States, I would call London—where "The Muppet Show" was then being taped—to discuss with Miss Piggy's manager the pos- sibility of having the popular Muppet host the special.

Alas, Miss Piggy's manager wasn't interested, and neither were any of the networks or cable companies. Still, the theme stuck with me because pigs, though not particularly attractive animals, are highly intelligent and their history is very much intertwined with our own. Wild boar hunting has historically been the sport of kings, and such hunts were recorded by Homer centuries before Christ. Although "The Joy of Pigs" was not appropriate as a *Wild America* program concept be- cause of its cultural analysis of pigs as portrayed in cartoons and art, and because it included wild hogs outside North America, it did inspire me to do a half-hour program on the wild swine of North America. Since, after all, the descendants of the European wild boar were breeding with feral hogs and running wild throughout the southern states, "Hog Wild!" struck me as an appropriate title for the program.

Once my staff and I decided upon the programs we would produce for Year Two of the series, our next step was to thoroughly research the subjects involved and come up with shooting scripts for our cinematographers to use as guidelines.

Razor-sharp tusks backed by an aggressive disposition are typical wild boar traits. More than once I've been chased up a tree by a mean-looking face like this one.

This opened up another niche in the office for a person who could take care of researching and writing cinematography outlines, someone who knew wildlife and who could write. A woman named Karen Chamberlain, a published writer with a degree in zoology, turned out to be just the person I was looking for. She helped me to coordinate with various cinematographers what needed to be filmed and where and when to film it. While she was working on other Year Two programs, I had time to do most of the research on "Born To Run" and "Hog Wild!" myself.

Among the things that fascinated me about pronghorn are the specific ways in which they are so perfectly adapted to the harsh, open deserts and prairies of North America. I wanted to show why this animal has survived on the prairie while other grassland inhabitants either became extinct, like the plains wolf and the plains grizzly, or have been greatly reduced in numbers and pushed into the mountains, like the bighorn, bison, and elk.

Mixed grass plains, sagebrush basins, shortgrass prairies, and southwestern deserts are the ancestral home of the pronghorn. Eons ago, as the Sierras and the Rockies rose, becoming a barrier for rains blown east from the Pacific, the vast inland area to the east became too dry to support much beyond grasses. The result is an immense band of prairie, some 600 miles wide and 2,000 miles long, that still stretches from the Rockies eastward to Ohio, and from Texas to northern Canada. It is the world's largest and richest grassland.

The climate of this grassland is as extreme as its soil is rich. Temperatures may soar to a sweltering 110 degrees in summer, and in winter plunge to −40 below. But the pronghorn is exquisitely adapted to cope with this environment. Like some other ungulates, including deer, the pronghorn has a coat of dense, hollow hair. But the pronghorn is unique in that as large cells of air become trapped within and between the hairs, specialized sets of muscles just under the skin allow the animal to raise or lower the hairs, adjusting the angle, and therefore the amount of insulating air, according to the temperature. Its ability to adjust the angle of its hair is also important in another way. When a predator such as a coyote, bobcat, or eagle threatens, a sentry pronghorn erects the hairs of its white rump patch, flashing a highly visible warning signal that can be seen for great distances.

Not only is the pronghorn able to spot an approaching predator from afar and warn other herd members, it is also able to escape from almost any potential danger. The pronghorn has evolved extra-keen senses of sight, hearing, and smell, along with its amazing speed. It relies on tall, rotating ears, which can pick up sound from a mile away, and on extraordinary eyesight, equal to that of a human with eight-power binoculars. Large and luminous, the pronghorn's dark eyes are situated well to the side of its face in protruding eye

Ultra-keen eyesight and hearing have helped the pronghorn survive for millions of years. This young star of "Born to Run" displays the large, wide-set eyes and long, rotating ears typical of its kind.

sockets, which gives it a wide-angle field of vision and limits the effectiveness of any predator that tries to creep up from behind.

On the open plains, the most successful means of escape for a large animal is to outrun its enemy, since there is little in the way of protective vegetation or hiding places. In the pronghorn's speed—up to sixty miles an hour in short sprints —and endurance can probably be found the most significant key to its survival on the open plains. This speed is due in part to the structure of its leg bones, which are slender and delicate, yet proportionately ten times stronger than those of a cow. Even its habit of eating only small quantities of forage at a time leaves it always ready to run. The pronghorn swallows small bites of its food whole, without chewing, and after the food has fermented in its four-part stomach, the softened cud is brought up during resting periods to be chewed, swallowed, and finally digested. In this way, the animal is never slowed down by the weight of a full stomach.

The pronghorn's varied diet demonstrates another aspect of its adaptability. In the spring it eats mostly grass. In summer, it browses on rabbit brush, bitter brush, and juniper, along with forbs (broad-leafed flowering plants) such as dandelion, clover, larkspur, and Russian thistle. In winter, it depends primarily on sagebrush. The fact that pronghorn don't generally compete for the same food with domestic cattle, and only to a small extent with sheep, is another factor contributing to their survival on the open range. As usual, the less a wild animal competes with human economic interests, the better its long-term chances.

The pronghorn is a true survivor, not only in terms of millions of years of geological change, but also in terms of the more recent changes resulting from human settlement. Overhunting in the 1800s, and the ubiquitous fence lines of the plains in our own century, nearly wiped out the huge herds of pronghorn. Today, thanks to transplantation programs, protective legislation, and cooperative landowners, pronghorn populations have recovered and these animals now number in the hundreds of thousands.

After reading all the books and literature I could find on this swift creature, I decided that the format of the film should be chronological, going from one spring through the seasons to the next. This scope would encompass all the major events that I hoped to film, such as does giving birth in springtime, males fighting with rivals in the fall, shedding their horns in winter, and so on. Since I no longer had the time to spend an entire year out on the prairie waiting for all these seasonal events to occur, I figured out the peak times for fighting, mating, birthing, and so on, and showed up then, for about three of the most critical weeks during each season. Usually, I traveled alone, but on several important trips my brother Marshall came along to help with camera and sound.

When working under the deadline pressure inherent in producing a wildlife series, you have to make the job as quick and easy as possible. Careful research increases the chances that you will be at the right place at the right time. But unfortunately, you either get males fighting during those several weeks in the fall, for instance, or you don't. A second try means waiting until the next year. This method of filming wildlife is obviously more of a gamble than the sit-and-wait-for-months method of my earlier years, but if you do your homework, it's generally possible to get the footage you're after. In making wildlife films, what most people call luck is really a result of research and planning.

Doing your homework also helps you to find out what I call the "fun facts," or biological quirks of an animal, which I then try to capture on film. Pronghorn, for example, have feet similar to those of the deer family, except that they lack the two little dewclaws—an extra first and fourth toe—that deer have on the back of each leg. They possess only the main middle pair—the toes of their cloven hooves. No one knows quite why the dewclaws were lost, but some speculate that it may have to do with the evolution of a streamlined leg, with no protrusions to catch on sagebrush or even create friction with the wind.

I also wanted to show how the pronghorn is able to run so fast and so far. Its windpipe, lungs, and heart are much larger and better-developed than those of other animals its size, enabling the bloodstream to supply more energy-boosting oxygen to the muscles. And when these prairie speedsters run, they keep their mouths open, dampening the dust with their saliva, and taking in a much greater volume of air than animals that run with their mouths closed. To show this, I used telephoto close-ups of them running, open mouths drinking in the wind.

As with the pronghorn program, I wanted to show the major events in the life of the wild hog, too—fighting, mating, and giving birth. But in planning "Hog Wild!" I had a little more leeway than I'd had with "Born To Run," since hogs are found in relatively warm climates, where they breed and give birth year round.

My film crew and I traveled to coastal Georgia, about ten miles south of Savannah, where we filmed most of "Hog Wild!" on a private hunting preserve. It was an enormous, 20,000-acre tract of land, where hunting was managed by the landowner, and where people came to pay 300 dollars to bag a boar with large tusks. It was a great place for hunters looking for a guaranteed trophy. However, it was not so terrific for a family vacation. I had brought my wife Diane and our two-year-old daughter Hannah with me on this trip, and soon learned that doing so wasn't such a good idea. Diane called the hunting preserve and lodge "The Pig Farm." In addition to the wild hogs running loose—sometimes literally at the front door—there were fire ants and rattlesnakes all over the place. We couldn't take our eyes off Hannah for a moment when she was outside, and inside, well, let's just say that the old hunting lodge was definitely not the Hilton Hotel.

The rest of the crew consisted of my friend David Huie and my cousin Steve Stouffer, who came along to help with recording sound. It was hard, messy work filming hogs in the

Wild hogs usually avoid humans, but on the other hand, they won't hesitate to run off cameramen who intrude on their privacy during the mating season—as we found out while filming them in Georgia.

wet Georgia swamps. But that didn't stop us from having the time of our lives. It almost seemed like we were kids again, a reminder of the days when David, Steve, and I used to run around in the Arkansas woods, exploring and hunting, only this time we were hunting with a camera and getting paid for it. I suppose our sense of danger and excitement had not changed much from our childhood years, since the high points of the trip were when we got chased through muddy marshes, and up trees, by the wild boars.

One day, for instance, we came upon some boars that were following a sow in heat. We decided to trail along, hoping we might film them in the act of mating. But the boars didn't particularly like our intrusion. They'd sniff the air to catch our scent, then turn and charge, with their heads lowered and tusks slashing. I would run to the closest tree and shimmy up ten feet or so, tucking my legs under me. Below, the boars would swing their heads and snort in frustration. After a few minutes, they would remember the sow and wander off, looking for her again. Then I'd climb down and continue to follow them. I scrambled up a tree more than once, diverting the attention of the boars, while David and Steve stayed back to film the action. Twice a boar charged right for David, sending the camera and tripod flying and David

running for cover. When we lost their trail, we would stand quietly and listen for them squealing in the distance. Hogs have terrible eyesight, but they have terrific hearing, and they communicate with each other in a pig language of grunts and squeals.

Pronghorns were also a real challenge to film, but in a different way. Unlike hogs, their eyesight is very keen, and their habitat is wide open, with few places where a cameraman can conceal himself. Fortunately, pronghorn are surprisingly curious animals, and weren't very shy or afraid of us. They rely primarily on vision to warn them of danger, and would ignore us as long as we kept out of their "flight distance"—an area with a radius of several hundred yards within which, if they are approached too closely, the whole herd takes flight. The pronghorn we filmed were also on private land, but were not hunted, and therefore were much less wary than those which are hunted on a regular basis.

We had permission to film pronghorns on a 10,000-acre livestock ranch near Medicine Bow, Wyoming. The rancher was very forward-thinking—he actually happened to *like* coyotes, for instance. Since coyotes were not hunted on his ranch, we could approach them, too, up to about a hundred yards— a comfortable filming distance with a long telephoto lens. By contrast, in most areas these wary, clever wild dogs are rarely even seen by day, and usually only from far away.

For two weeks in the spring, after most of the pronghorn fawns had been born, we followed coyotes around and actually filmed—for what I believe is the first time ever—a coyote chasing and attempting to kill a young pronghorn fawn. The day it happened, we had set our cameras up on top of a ridge overlooking a prairie basin, where we could see several does with their young fawns. We saw one fawn lie down by a clump of long grass, while its mother grazed. After a while, a coyote showed up, trotting in the direction of the well-hidden fawn and sniffing the air and sagebrush as if it sensed that where there are does, there are fawns nearby. Although the coyote could not catch sight or scent of the odorless fawn, it trotted past within a few feet of it—close enough to make the baby panic and bolt for its mother. In a flash, the coyote spun around and streaked toward the spindly-legged animal. The youngster instinctively ran in wide circles, keeping barely inches in front of the coyote. Finally the coyote lurched for the fawn's hind legs and tripped it. Instantly the wild dog had the bleating fawn pinned down by the back of its neck. To our astonishment, at this moment the doe came running in at full speed toward them, kicking the coyote away and sending it tumbling head-over-tail. As the coyote regained its footing, she chased it half a mile across the prairie and completely out of sight. A few minutes later, the mother rejoined her fawn and gave it a nudge as if to say, "Don't ever panic again!"

It was an unbelievable sequence to have been able to film, and it came as a terrific surprise to me because of what I'd seen in Africa. When a jackel or hyena got hold of a baby gazelle, the mother usually behaved as if she were helpless to save her young. Very rarely did a mother gazelle or antelope respond with the kind of vigor and determination displayed by the pronghorn doe, and never did we see one able to force the attacker to drop its hold on her offspring. I later asked the rancher if he had ever witnessed this before, and he told us that he regularly saw pronghorn does chasing coyotes out of the area where their fawns were hiding. He added that despite this unusual protective instinct on the part of the does, many fawns do fall victim to swift and cunning coyotes.

Interestingly, many others die before they're even born. Pronghorn have a curious reproductive trait in which the females produce three to eight embryos, of which only two typically survive to full-term birth. The others are miscarried very early in the pregnancy. Perhaps this is a survival tactic to better the chances that the strongest possible babies are born. Twins are the rule for pronghorn. A female pronghorn becomes ready to breed at fifteen months of age, and usually produces a set of offspring every year thereafter, during the seven to ten years of her life.

The offspring of wild hogs have survival problems related to birth, too. In Georgia, we discovered a typical "nest" constructed of branches and vegetation, which a female hog breaks off and carries in her mouth to heap into a large brush pile. Within the protection and warmth of this mound, she gives birth to from three to twelve piglets. While one particular sow was away feeding, I crept up to the nest and, pushing away the brush, looked inside. I found six wiggling, squealing newborn piglets, and a seventh one dead, still wet from birth. With so many piglets to a litter, one or more of the hungry little ones are often smothered or crushed in a crowded nest as they search for their mother's warmth and a nipple to nurse on. Because of these factors, plus pressures resulting from predators and disease, only about half of the babies live to maturity.

Wild hogs more than make up for their losses, though, by breeding year-round, the females often having two or three litters a year. Hypothetically, a sow breeding continuously for ten years could, if all her daughters did likewise, have 7 million descendants in that time! Of course, in the wild, their actual reproductive rate is not nearly that great, but it is still high enough to force them to expand constantly into new territory. Wild hogs are the most prolific large mammal in North America.

The pronghorn, on the other hand, must now rely on human help to repopulate their original range. Near Craig, Colorado, we filmed a pronghorn transplant program that was being conducted by the Colorado Division of Wildlife. They rounded up herds of pronghorns by chasing them with a helicopter into a large overhanging net. Once the herd was directly beneath the net, a whole string of blasting caps was simultaneously fired, releasing the net from its supporting poles and bringing it down on top of the pronghorn. The net pinned the animals to the ground while the biologists rushed in and hog-tied their legs. Then the animals' blood was tested and they were aged, tagged, put into trucks, and hauled off to Utah to be released.

This trap-and-transplant method is the means by which surplus herds in one area are used to repopulate other regions of their original range. However, in the process of rounding them up, six out of about 100 animals died. Most were killed by stress-induced shock. One died when the center net pole fell on it and broke its neck. Several females, in the course of being rounded up, trapped, and handled, miscarried their fetuses. This wasn't the natural elimination of extra embryos during the early stages of pregnancy. These fetuses were older, more developed, and were miscarried due to stress.

While we were filming, I picked up one of those tiny forms from the trampled earth, and examined it in my hand. I knew that some viewers might find it distasteful that I would show a dead pronghorn fetus close up on film. But it was such a well-developed and fascinating miniature replica of the adult that I found it beautiful, and it was dramatic held in a human hand. To me, the scene portrayed the irony that some pronghorn die so others can live. I could have made the same point by showing the adult pronghorn carcasses, but that might have been just as offensive. And by filming the tiny figure of this unborn creature, I was able to make two points: one, that pronghorns naturally miscarry a definite proportion of their potential offspring; and two, that this was not such a case.

But the animals that died were not wasted. The men of the Colorado Division of Wildlife gutted the carcasses quickly and expertly, and the meat was carefully preserved for human consumption. Most people involved in game management are very much in tune with nature, and most of them are hunters, so they know how to take advantage of a fresh source of protein. Also, some of the gutted females contained younger,

A pronghorn fetus, this one aborted as the result of stress on its mother during a trapping and transplanting roundup. Pronghorns also naturally abort all but two fetuses in earlier stages of pregnancy.

less-developed fetuses, and these were autopsied to learn more about the species and the environmental factors that affect them. One can condemn the Colorado Division of Wildlife and say that they've killed six pronghorn. Or one can praise them, and say that they've made it possible for countless others to survive and reclaim their historic range. Paradoxical situations and trade-offs are as commonplace in the managing of wildlife as they are in nature itself. That was several years ago, and hopefully by now methods have been invented that reduce the stress and handling problems, so that even more animals can be successfully transplanted.

Both my mother and Diane tell me I try to jam too much information into each program, but I like to show as many aspects as I can of an animal's life: how it survives in its environment, what factors typically cause its death, and especially what its relationship to humankind is. There are always some facts that people would rather not hear, but the journalist in me feels it's important to tell the whole story, and not purposely to exclude the more distasteful facts if they make an important point.

All of which is to explain why, in "Hog Wild!" I included what I thought was an incredible sequence of two hogs mating, although I was sure that some viewers would think it went beyond the bounds of good taste. Indeed, some did. But the whole process was so unusual that I took the risk. We showed not only the unique corkscrew-shaped penis of the boar, which is eighteen inches long, but also how it twirls around like a drill bit as the animals copulate, the better to deposit sperm deep within the female's uterus.

To me, there's nothing offensive about nature's ingenious inventions to ensure the survival of a species, whether it's the reproductive organ of a hog, which evolved as a means for successful transfer of sperm, or the odd-shaped nose of an elephant, which evolved to better secure food and water. I wasn't too worried that this footage would ruin our good rating on PBS, because I knew the great majority of viewers were sensible enough to simply think it an intriguing fact about hogs. But for the first time since the series began, I was a

The well-camouflaged poorwill, a relative of the nighthawk and whippoorwill, has a distinctively wide mouth for catching bugs, and is the only bird that hibernates instead of flying south.

I find few things in nature as delicately beautiful as the tiny, meticulously made nest of a hummingbird. Covered with lichens for camouflage, this nest contains a pair of tiny white eggs.

A pronghorn fawn can run thirty miles an hour within a few days of birth. This one outran the coyote for several minutes before being caught. Luckily, its mother was nearby and came swiftly to the rescue

America's only marsupial, the opossum bears up to fourteen young the size of honeybees, which immediately migrate through her fur to her pouch. There they nurse for several months. When they emerge, they cling to their mother's back for a few more weeks, learning to feed and care for themselves.

Thick-bodied and swamp-colored, the cottonmouth moccasin is aptly named for its white mouth and throat. Found in our southern swamplands, it is one of America's four poisonous snakes.

The Blair's, or gray-banded, kingsnake, seen here next to a blooming prickly pear cactus in Texas, is one of our most beautiful snakes. Like other kingsnakes, it is a constrictor which often feeds on other snakes.

In the cold, shallow waters of Colorado's Maroon Creek, my brother Mark and I filmed the story of the brook trout, a fish noteworthy for spawning in autumn rather than spring or summer.

The elaborately spotted brook trout, a native of eastern streams, has been widely introduced throughout our western states.

Some of the story was filmed in an indoor aquarium, to show how eggs develop into sac fry and then into fingerlings.

A gravid (or ripely pregnant) female deposits her eggs.

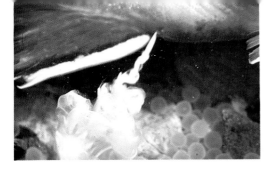

The male fertilizes them with his milt.

Shielded by pebbles, the eggs develop into sac fry, absorbing the nutritious yolk as they grow first into striped fingerlings and finally into mature, brightly spotted fish.

Nature is rich with hues as diverse as the species she creates. Color often has a distinct evolutionary function, and roseate spoonbills like these are most brightly colored at the height of the mating season.

A cutthroat trout in Yellowstone Lake dramatically gulps down a redside shiner.

Our native cutthroat trout, marked by a vivid red-orange slash at the throat, becomes even more colorful as the spawning season approaches.

*The snowshoe hare is the mainstay
of the lynx's diet—but the hare
is hardly an easy catch.*

The exquisitely marked ocelot is an increasing rarity among North America's wild cats. In the United States, its range barely extends above the Mexican border into Texas.

Wolves howl to call the pack together for hunting, to confuse their prey, or sometimes just to hear themselves sing. Their long, drawn-out song is one of the wildest, most spine-chilling sounds in nature.

little concerned about the reaction of PBS's program managers. Public Television stations do not have any censors as such, but they are licensed by the Federal Communications Commission and therefore subscribe to general policies of fairness and acceptability. And the people in charge of national programming for PBS review every program before it's cleared for airing.

To their credit, PBS didn't cut the sequence; in fact, they didn't even complain about it. I did find out later, though, that some individual station program managers had cut the mating sequence on their own. That's fine with me; they know their audiences and it is their prerogative to pull anything that their viewers might consider objectionable. But on commercial television, the mating sequence would *never* have aired. To my way of thinking, PBS deserves a lot of praise for airing a natural history "first."

That a few people found this sequence objectionable doesn't diminish my sense of pride in "Hog Wild!" Though I've tried to mention only the fun or interesting aspects involved, filming it was very hard work from start to finish. The hogs were potentially dangerous and the conditions were uncomfortable at best. Walking around in those Georgia swamps meant that my feet were always wet. We wore boots, of course, but they were almost always full of muddy marsh water. When I finally got home, the skin on my feet began to peel—layer after layer after layer—for a period of almost six months. I was diagnosed as having something akin to "jungle rot." Finally, just as I was getting concerned that I wouldn't have any skin left on my feet, the condition cleared up.

But filming difficulties aside, the hog is such an unlikely star of a show, that it's one of the reasons I like the program so much. When "Hog Wild!" aired, people in California, Florida, Georgia, and North and South Carolina wrote in, amazed to have seen things about the hogs that even they, who lived in the states where hogs were common, hadn't known—their fighting behavior, their destructive feeding habits, even the fact that they're not native to our continent. Probably what surprises people most about hogs is their high level of intelligence. Some experts believe they are smarter than dogs because not only can they learn the same tricks as a dog in a shorter amount of time, but swine have been known to solve problems by "thinking" them through rather than by mimicking a trainer. This capacity for independent thought is one way of defining intelligence in animals, and pigs, along with primates, seem to be especially capable of it.

I'm also proud of "Born To Run." Making this program was extremely satisfying for me, in that I set out to document every vital aspect of the pronghorn's life, and I did. The same is true for "Hog Wild!" In fact, I have to say that these programs are two of my all-time favorites. Why? Mainly because each of them show the complete cycle of one animal's life. Unlike "Hog Wild!" and "Born To Run," most of the *Wild America* programs in Year Two compared and contrasted several animals within a related group, such as the "Wild Cats" of North America, or the members of the deer family in "Antlered Kingdom." In this sort of program, the trick is to film a few of the most interesting aspects of each animal and briefly discuss how they are typical of or unusual for the family or category in general before moving on to a sequence of another related animal. This approach merely touches on the major events in the life history of each species, instead giving a broad, overall insight into what features make major categories of animals closely related.

Another approach that we use in our programs is to start with a even broader concept, such as the Year Two program, "Animal Oddities," which was composed of a medley of two-to three-minute sequences on unrelated species. The common thread in this episode is to show some unusual or odd aspect of behavior or appearance of each subject, one that in most cases contributes to its survival. This type of film devotes even less time to an individual animal's life history, but viewers nevertheless have found the format entertaining and educational.

These diverse formats of the programs in the *Wild America* series are intended to create something for everyone, with some of the half-hour programs containing a great deal of information on one species and others containing a little information on a number of species. From the letters and comments we receive from viewers, this seems to be the best overall structure for the series. Yet I think I will always be more inclined to film programs devoted to the life story of one particular animal. This is the classic format for wildlife films, and though I've never been reluctant to break rules, it really is the most satisfying approach for a cinematographer. It allows me to get thoroughly acquainted with, and to better understand, a particular animal in relation to its environment.

From my experience with the wild hog and pronghorn programs, the most difficult thing about doing these half-hour programs is editing all that great footage to just a half-hour's worth of material. I constantly have to ask myself, "What is it that viewers want to see, and how might that differ from what I want to show?" When I was filming in Georgia, for example, I was somewhat surprised by the violence associated with managing and hunting wild boars. I saw at least a dozen hogs killed by hunters who used hounds first to track them down, then hold them at bay until the hunters arrived. Once a wild boar was cornered by the barking dogs, the manager would release a specially trained bulldog that ran in and grabbed the boar by the ear. Such a grip was often more than a mouthful for the dog, especially when it got hold of a big, fierce old boar. In fact, the life expectancy of a bulldog was measured by how many boars it could be sent after. On the average, a dog was good for about twelve boars, by which time it had usually either died of wounds or become permanently disabled.

I once went with a manager from the hunting preserve, who had been paid by a farmer to capture a wild boar and remove it from his property. The hog inhabited a patch of woods adjacent to the farmer's crop fields. The manager wanted to live-capture the hog and transport it back to the hunting preserve to turn loose. So we took the dogs to the farm and followed them as they sniffed the ground and took off, yelping feverishly after the fresh scent. When the dogs had located the hog, the manager released his pit bull, which seized the boar's ear in a death grip while the hunter moved in to grab the boar's hind legs, throw it to the ground, and rope its legs together. Then the live, trussed-up, hoarsely squealing animal was carried out of the woods, slung upside down with a long pole between its legs, just like the wolf in "Peter and the Wolf." Hunters don't normally carry game that way, but in this case, it wouldn't be a good idea to swing a live wild boar over your shoulders, or it would slice you with its tusks.

I didn't want to offend anyone's sensibilities with the violence and bloodshed of a real wild boar kill, but I thought it *was* important, as well as honest, to show how these animals are tracked down using hunting dogs. So this became the only hunting sequence in "Hog Wild!" Despite my reticence, some viewers were still upset by the violence inflicted not only on the hog, but on the dogs. I had filmed some hounds surrounding the enraged boar, which used its quick reflexes to outmaneuver one of them, and with the slash of a tusk, gave it a gaping wound. After the boar was hog-tied, I filmed a hunter stitching up the bleeding hound with a needle and thread. The narration over this scene explained that this dog was lucky.

Ironically, one audience that was highly offended by this film was an auditorium full of wildlife filmmakers. In 1985, our entire staff attended an International Wildlife Filmmaker's Symposium in Bath, England. The audience was composed mostly of British filmmakers from the BBC and Survival Anglia, along with other Europeans. When I showed "Hog Wild!" as a representation of American wildlife filmmaking, their reaction to the film was, in a word, *shocked*. Not because of the mating scenes—although one woman from Canada did run out of the room during the scenes showing the boar's penis —but because of the bloodshed and violence depicted in the sequence of the captured boar.

I had picked this film to exhibit not only because it is one of my personal favorites, but because I had thought that many Europeans were hunters and would therefore be interested in a film on a game animal popular in both Europe and in the United States. Well, those that do hunt are a relatively privileged few among the upper classes. And, by and large, they hunt on private pheasant reserves or in Africa. So, much to my dismay, I found out that ordinary people in England *don't* hunt, and furthermore that they don't even like hunting. On the other hand, they *do* love their dogs. After the film was shown, we found ourselves verbally attacked by the normally calm and mild-mannered English. How could we possibly show such a thing? My response was, "This is what *happens* during a wild boar hunt. Sometimes dogs get killed and sometimes even people get killed. I don't necessarily agree with these hunting methods, I'm just showing the way it is."

Well, the point is that I thought I was already soft-pedaling the killing and hunting. I thought that I was showing the least possible bloodshed that could be shown, by filming a live capture instead of trophy killing. In the course of living with and filming the hunters in Georgia, not only did I *not* show what were—in my opinion—very bloody and disturbing scenes of animals being killed, gutted, and skinned, but I certainly didn't show what *I* thought was the most shocking thing of all.

On the preserve were some feral pigs that weren't thought to look like "real wild hogs," because they had a lot of domestic genes and therefore were chubby and spotted rather than dark and lean. Hunters didn't care for the spotted ones because they looked "tame." They preferred those that looked like the European wild boar—this solid, dark coloration supposedly indicated a somehow "wilder" animal, which of course it doesn't.

On this particular hunting preserve the management was trying actively to breed for wilder-looking traits and away from the more domestic-looking pig traits. So, while I was there, they would sometimes catch and barbeque young domestic-looking "shoats"—thirty- to fifty-pound hogs. Early one morning I had the dubious privilege of witnessing a rather bizarre tradition, as the hunters took a bulldog out, caught half a dozen of the younger male shoats, and with the flick of a very sharp knife, removed their testicles. Then they turned each of the squealing pigs loose, minus its pear-sized reproductive organs, and returned with a plastic bag of these trophies to cook up in the bunkhouse for—what else?—breakfast.

These "mountain oysters" were, I must say, very tasty, though they came as a bit of a shock at six A.M., especially after having seen them attached to their owners less than a half hour before. The reason for these castrations was twofold: the neutered males would grow up to be more tender when later harvested for camp food, and more important, these males would be unable to pass on their "domestic" traits.

Had I shown all *that* on film, I'm absolutely certain that

my British audience would have passed out cold midway through the program. I can only say that I do go out of my way to respect the sensibilities of whatever potential audience I might have. But of course, it's impossible to please all of the people all of the time.

The personal satisfaction I derived from filming "Hog Wild!" and "Pronghorn" was great, and I was eager after those experiences to find another similar project. There *was* another animal whose life history I had wanted to film for ten years, ever since Mark and I had filmed the bobcat-hare predation chase for "The Predators." Like the wild boar, the relatives of this creature roam throughout Europe and Asia. And like the pronghorn, its anatomy is uniquely specialized for an unyielding environment. The animal I'm referring to is the lynx, and it prowls a part of the North American landscape that I had yet to fully explore—an immense stretch of coniferous forest that encircles the subarctic globe.

NINE

IN THE GREAT NORTH WOODS

An almost-full-grown Spud climbs a tree near timberline to look around. The most arboreal member of the weasel family, the fisher loves to climb—not just trees, but anything, as my family and I learned.

The expression "the great outdoors" means many things to many people. To rural midwestern youngsters, it probably means the wooded hills beyond their parents' farmland. To retired folks traveling around the country in an RV, it might mean a campground nestled in a quiet grove of trees a mile from a major highway. To a hunter, it may be the remote backcountry his hired guide takes him to each autumn. For me, the great outdoors is anywhere mother nature still reigns over the land—where the natural cycles of life and death remain unbroken by human intervention. Although such places are rapidly disappearing, there are many relatively unspoiled landscapes still to be found on this continent. So many, in fact, that it's hard to decide which is my favorite.

I certainly love the wide open prairies of our country's heartland and the sun-soaked deserts of Utah and Arizona, where far-reaching horizons meet cloudless skies. But I'm also partial to the open, lawnlike areas under the scattered pines in the Black Hills of South Dakota, and to the oak woodlands of northern Arkansas. Without a doubt, the magnificent panoramic vistas of the Rocky Mountains are unequaled anywhere on this continent, although I must admit that people, condominiums, and ski resorts are taking their toll on the high country. These areas are all wild or rugged, but if "pristine and unspoiled" is used as one of the criteria to decide, then my choice would have to be the great north woods.

In ecological terms, this region is an immensely broad band of forest, giving way on the south to prairies and plains, and on the north to barren arctic tundra. These woods extend across not only North America but girdle Siberia and Scandinavia as well. Their distinguishing feature is the predominance of conifers and evergreens such as pine, fir, and spruce. This coniferous belt, some 1,200 miles wide from north to south, is also called the boreal forest, after the Greek god of the north wind, Boreas. The Russian word for the subarctic forest area is "taiga." I simply call it the "north woods."

On the U.S. side of the Canadian border, the great north

woods reach as far southeast as the Adirondack and Appalachian mountains. The major portion, however, lies above the lower forty-eight states, in the central provinces of Canada. Beginning in the northeastern corner of Minnesota, and interrupted only by lakes and ponds, these forests run across the northern shore of Lake Superior, then extend further north to embrace most of the top of the continent from Alaska in the west to Labrador in the east.

For a person walking up to the edge of this evergreen forest, the close-standing density of tree trunks and the musty odor of decaying needles might give the woods a somewhat foreboding and uninviting aura. But as you enter this somber realm, your eyes grow accustomed to the darkness, and you begin to feel the quiet coolness and smell the spicy resin of evergreens. It is a land that fairy tales are made of—where Hansel and Gretel might have walked through the woods sprinkling bread crumbs to find their way back home.

I love the sensation of entering the depths of this forest, leaving behind the sky and the sun's warming rays and then, moments later, being enveloped by a cool, dark shelter. It's like walking through a wall which separates day from night. Maybe I feel that way because some primordial instinct tells me that the deep woods mean security, cover, and camouflage. Maybe I instinctively know that this is a place where a hunter can hide, both from his prey—so he'll be able to stalk it more easily—and from potential enemies that might stalk him. For whatever reason the northern woods might appeal to my cave-man instincts, on a more conscious level I love them because they are home to fascinating animals perfectly adapted to the challenges of this harsh, subarctic wilderness.

Many species of plants and animals to which this coniferous forest is home can be found on both the North American and Eurasian continents. The largest member of the deer family, the moose, or European elk, browses on willows and aquatic plants, while the slightly smaller caribou—called the reindeer in Europe—feeds on moss and lichens and tree bark. High up among the evergreen branches, also on both continents, is found the great gray owl, with its feathery feet and fabulous face. The owl might share its perch with two arboreal (or tree climbing) members of the weasel family: the pine marten and the wolverine. But my favorite denizen of the deep north woods is the beautifully furred lynx, which silently prowls the forests of North America just as it does those of Siberia and Scandinavia.

The agile lynx is the only wild cat specifically adapted to these northern forests. Its legs are long and almost gangly-looking in proportion to its three-foot-long body, and its feet—broad, fur-covered "snowshoes"—are twice the size of a bob-cat's. These adaptations enable the lynx to walk or run easily

The Great Gray Owl, with its mysterious face and feathered feet, can be found in northern boreal forests around the world.

through deep snow, hardly sinking into drifts that would swallow another animal of similar size and weight. Although the lynx weighs about the same as the bobcat and has a similarly soft-spotted gray coat, it looks heavier because of its thicker fur. In our southern states, bobcats are more rust-colored with distinct dark spots, but in the northern part of their range, they are almost the same color as the lynx, and they even have ear tufts similar to the lynx. The only sure way to tell the two animals apart is by their tails. The lynx has a completely black tail, while the bobcat's has a white underside.

Distinguishing between these two feline cousins is made easier by the fact that the lynx's range begins where that of the bobcat leaves off, with relatively little overlap. The combined range of these wild cats covers the whole of our continent, with the bobcat living in all of the lower forty-eight states south into Mexico, and the lynx inhabiting the Rocky Mountains, the forests of the northernmost states bordering Canada, and the whole expanse of northern woodland in Canada and Alaska.

While the bobcat may be found in more open country and even in rocky desert terrain, the lynx is strictly a creature of the deep boreal forest. Here it preys on voles, lemmings, grouse, and even deer, but one species in particular is critical to its survival: the snowshoe hare, an animal which also has broad, furred feet adapted for traveling over the thinnest crusts of snow. I had always been fascinated by the mystery of the lynx's intimate relationship with the snowshoe hare, in which the populations of both animals rise and fall almost in unison, and through the years I had stayed in touch with a number of trappers in the north, asking them to please keep their eyes open for a den-site where a family of lynx might be found.

To complicate the matter of filming them, lynx have extraordinary night vision and often hunt in darkness, which would reduce my chances of filming their predatory behavior. But to my advantage, lynx in general are the least shy of North America's wild cats and can sometimes be observed at close range. This was something I had learned years before when I saw a lynx for the first time, in 1975 at Katmai National Monument on the Alaskan peninsula. Mark and I were staying at

The bobcat on the left and the lynx on the right are similar-looking feline cousins, but the longer-legged lynx, with its long ear-tufts and black tail, is better adapted to life in the great north woods.

a campground there, near the Brooks River Lodge, and each evening we fished for salmon. Every few days, at dusk (which lasts during the Alaskan summer from 10:00 P.M. to midnight) we caught a glimpse of a lynx slinking through the forest clearings and stalking the snowshoe hares that fed in a meadow near the campground. Unfortunately, it was hard enough to see the action, much less film it, so we didn't even try. We could see the lighter colored lynx since it stood out against the dark forest understory, but the hares were in their summer brown pelage and were very hard to observe in the low light. Sometimes we would follow the lynx through the trees for a mile or so and were always amazed at how it would allow us to approach to within ten yards of it. It would look back from time to time and show a little concern if we got too close, but it was basically unbothered by our presence.

Besides observing that lynx are not very shy, another observation that I've made of them relates to the old adage "you are what you eat." I find that lynx are very "hare-like," particularly in the way they sit on their haunches and tuck their long hind legs up under their bellies. Another reason that both predator and prey sit this way is to de-ice their fur-covered feet by pulling off the little snowballs that form between their toes. The luxurious silkiness of the lynx's coat is much more like the hare's soft fur than like, say, a cougar's short, stiff hair. And finally, something about the lynx's personality sets it apart from other wildcats. Its nature is relatively docile, calm and restrained—more like that of the snowshoe hare. In fact, some naturalists have called the lynx nothing but a long-legged, short-eared, oversized hare—one that happens to eat other hares.

As a result, the lynx has something of a dual personality. Most predatory animals, such as grizzlies, wolverines, or hawks, never seem calm and docile to us. Instead, they exude a sense of contained power and potential violence waiting to be unleashed. But the lynx is different. Even though it kills for food, to me the lynx kills "nicely." Quickly and efficiently this skillful hunter pounces on its prey, its long canine teeth piercing the victim's skull and killing it instantly. I've never seen a lynx "play" with its prey, wearing it down into a state of exhaustion and shock before dealing the final blow. I even think of its face as having a curious, almost kindly expression, with its ruff of sideburns and its long ear tufts. This unusual combination of calmness and aggressiveness is probably one reason that the animal is so appealing to me. I often feel that I share this nature with the lynx. Our society expects males to be strong and protective, yet at the same time sensitive and gentle. Although these characteristics are at opposite ends of the spectrum, I like to think that I've successfully combined them in my personal life. In other words, I've consciously tried to be more like a lynx.

Another way I emulate the lynx is in my use of snowshoes whenever walking through deep snow. Although I must add that after a snowshoe race that Diane and I entered for fun near our home in Colorado, my respect for the lynx increased. Have you ever tried to "run" in snowshoes? It's about as impossible as riding a bicycle underwater. Despite the fact that our movements were nowhere near as fluid and graceful as those of a lynx running through deep powder, we did manage to win the race.

For most purposes, narrow, lightweight cross-country skis would be much more swift and efficient than snowshoes. But the problem with using them to track and film wildlife is that they don't give enough support to an adult carrying a sixty- or seventy-pound pack of equipment, to keep him or her from sinking into the snow. Snowshoes, on the other hand, with their webbing and their wide, teardrop-shaped frame, provide a broad base of support which distributes weight more evenly. Nowadays the modern trend is toward aluminum-framed snowshoes with neoprene webbing and bindings, but I stick with the traditional version: wooden-framed snowshoes with woven rawhide mesh and leather bindings. I still have one old pair that I've used for most of the twenty years I've been filming wildlife. They work beautifully, and they just seem better for the outdoors.

My respect and admiration for the lynx stems from my feeling that it is simply the most beautiful predator in North America. I wanted to devote an entire program to its life story —a program to be called "North Woods Lynx." I thought the program should be centered around the predator-prey interaction of the lynx and snowshoe hare, since their lives are so closely intertwined. Various trappers and biologists with whom I had been in contact over the years had suggested places where I might easily find and film a few of these animals. As it turned out, I ended up filming sequences for the program in three different areas: northern Minnesota, Montana, and Ontario, Canada.

To film the predation sequence, for instance, my three-man filming crew, consisting of myself, my brother Marshall, and Greg Hensley, concentrated our efforts in Minnesota during the winter months. There were several reasons for this. First, locating lynx would be less of a problem in winter, since it's easier to track animals in snow. Second, the lynx's diet would be relatively restricted to hares, since they are one of the few prey species that do not hibernate, but remain active all winter long. And finally, for aesthetic purposes, I wanted to film snowshoe hares in their winter pelage because I thought that their pure white coats would be more dramatic than their chestnut-brown summer fur.

In the effort to get a good predation sequence for the program, we first traveled to Superior National Forest in northern Minnesota, where a biologist studying lynx/snowshoe hare interactions helped us locate our subjects, pointing out areas on a map where high densities of hares had been sighted and consequently where lynx were likely to be found. After talking to him, we checked into a motel and started to organize our camera gear while discussing our shooting plans. It may surprise some people to know that we often check into motels while on the road filming, rather than "roughing it" by camping out. Not that I wouldn't prefer to camp out, but it's a matter of practicality. Camera equipment such as lenses, camera magazines (the housing that holds the rolls of film), and so on must be kept immaculately clean, which requires dirt-free living quarters where we can take everything apart and spread it out to clean it each evening. We also need a handy electrical outlet for overnight recharging of the batteries that power the cameras, especially when filming in low temperatures that quickly drain them of electrical energy.

That week in Minnesota was cold, gray, and cloudy—not exactly ideal filming weather, but unless it is raining heavily, we almost always proceed with filming. We do so not only because we can't afford the time or expense of waiting for clear skies and warmer temperatures, but also because I feel it's important to show nature in all her moods. So Marshall, Greg, and I set out at dawn each day to look for lynx tracks in the spruce-fir wilderness of Superior National Forest. While snowshoeing through the deep powder, we would occasionally spread out, up to a mile apart, to look for signs of lynx. If one of us saw fresh tracks or caught sight of one, but were too far apart to use hand signals, we'd speak via walkie-talkies that we carried with us.

Early one morning, I spotted some fresh lynx tracks crossing a forest clearing and immediately called on the walkie-talkie for Marshall and Greg to come join me. As all three of us followed the tracks, I glanced upward, as I often do while tracking, and caught sight of a half-hidden lynx staring at us from the limb of a spruce tree. We all froze in our tracks and stared back at it. We knew what came next: very slowly we moved behind the nearest clump of trees with our camera gear, and silently, patiently waited for the lynx to come down out of the spruce to hunt its next meal. We hoped to then be able to stay within filming distance of the stealthy cat.

At times like this, while crouched in the cold waiting for an animal to make its move, a million things go through my mind. I worry that there's fog on the front of the camera lens, or worse yet, inside the eyepiece of the camera itself. I wonder if the freezing temperatures are making the film too brittle to run through the camera, or if it's making the fluid head on the tripod so stiff that there's the possibility of breaking something when I try to pan. When my feet reach the point where they're so cold they're almost numb, I get concerned about frostbite, so I wiggle my toes as much as I can. And I've found that I actually feel warmer if I imagine sitting by a fire at the end of the day with a cup of hot chocolate in my hands.

I could almost taste the hot chocolate when a slight movement by the cat jarred me back to reality. It stretched, yawned, then jumped out of the tree and slipped away across the snow. Very slowly we shouldered our gear and began to follow it. After about a mile, it finally caught sight of a hare. This potential meal happened to be preoccupied, pushing its way through the new snow to carve out a route to its feeding area, which hares generally have to do after a snowstorm obliterates their trails. The lynx immediately stopped in its tracks and sank to its belly, then—head down and intent on its prey —began to inch its way toward the hare. While its attention was focused in this way, we had time to position our cameras and film some stalking behavior before the cat had crept as close as it was going to get without alarming the hare. Then, suddenly gathering its muscles, it hurled itself like a lightning bolt.

The flushed hare sprang away, but rather than running straight into the dense forest where the snow was thin, it stayed out in the deep fluffy powder of the meadow and circled and zigzagged, trying to outmaneuver the cat and gain a few inches of headway. Just as one of the lynx's outstretched front paws was about to hook the hare's hind foot, the hare leaped up into the air, then dove headfirst into the snow. I couldn't believe my eyes! The hare had simply disappeared under a flurry of deep powder, completely confounding its pursuer. The cat slid to a stop, peered at the spot where the hare had disappeared, and pushed its nose down into the snow to sniff —while the hare popped its head up out of the snow about three feet behind the cat, then bounded away while the puzzled lynx was still staring at the place where it dove in. And this happened not just once, but several times. Sometimes the hare did its dive in and out without losing its momentum. But sometimes it carried its trick to the extreme, and amazed us by traveling for several yards beneath the light snow, doubling back past its attacker without being detected.

I had never read or heard of this escape behavior before, so I was as surprised as the lynx when I first witnessed it. On our way back to the motel that particular evening, we were pretty excited about our discovery. We also tried to figure out what each of us had filmed. Marshall said, "Well, I got the stalking and the beginning of the chase. I was focused on the hare after it flushed until a couple of trees blocked my view. What did you get?" And I replied, "I had the 300-mm lens full-frame on the lynx, although it was hard to keep it in focus because of the hare's quick turns. But I kept on it, and hopefully it stayed sharp most of the times the hare dived into the snow." And then Greg added, "Well, I shot the action wide and got both the lynx and the hare in the frame, from when the cat began stalking to when the hare got away." From our three combined vantage points, camera angles, and lens lengths, we could tell that we had managed to film a complete sequence of the stalking, the chase, and the escape.

We filmed a lynx chasing a hare several more times, although on all those occasions the hares remained above the snow. Since the "snow dive" was such a successful ruse, it seems that it would have entered the hare's repertoire of great escapes many generations ago. But since we observed it performed by only one lone hare, we decided it had to be a learned, rather than an inherited, trait. Though we didn't film a statistically significant number of chases, it seemed that about two out of three hares were caught within 100 yards or not at all—assuming that the lynx had been able to stalk close enough in the beginning for an advantageous rush. The hares that did not try the snow dive had to be very fast, or very lucky, to escape.

But luckily for us, if a hare was not caught immediately, both animals would usually circle back past the hiding place (or "form," as it's called) where the prey was flushed in the

Like its primary prey, the snowshoe hare,
the lynx has extremely large, fur-covered feet that
enable it to travel easily over deep snow.

Just as certain animals have adapted to snowy habitat
with large, furry "snowshoe" feet, so the ptarmigan in winter
grows a feathery covering for its oversized toes.

first place. The reason for this is that the hare prefers to stay within a familiar area, and tries to use quick turns and natural obstacles, rather than long-distance endurance, to escape. Like any hunted animal, the snowshoe hare knows every log and bush, every possible hiding place and escape route in its home territory, and uses them to advantage in trying to out-maneuver a cat. Because the hare's home ground is relatively limited, we were able to film most of the action during each of these chases, instead of just filming the tail end of a lynx bounding straight off after its prey and disappearing into the woods.

Over a three-month filming period—several weeks at a time in different locations—we observed lynx chasing snowshoe hares on a dozen different occasions. Of those twelve chases, we were out of filming range for about half of them, and for most of the rest could shoot only varying degrees of the action. From those five or six chases that we did film, though, we were able to edit together the two complete chase sequences that appear in the final program. That's a pretty good indication of the amount of time and footage involved in obtaining most sequences for a wildlife film. In general, we work with an average filming ratio—the amount of footage exposed compared to the amount of footage used in the pro-

gram—of about 20:1. This means that for every minute you see of a finished program, about twenty minutes' worth of film was exposed.

Not only do we have to film twenty times the amount of footage we will eventually need, but the resulting sequence, or "story" as it were, is often constructed in the editing room. This may be a bit of a shock to people who like to believe that they are seeing the action as it happened moment by moment in the wild, but that is the case only about half the time in any wildlife film. In the editing process, it's necessary to take, for instance, a scene of a lynx sneaking up on a snowshoe hare from one roll of film and splice it together with a scene of a lynx chasing a snowshoe hare from another roll, and so on, until a complete story, with a beginning, middle, and end, is constructed. Those scenes might have occurred a minute, an hour, or even a month apart. Of course, the scenes selected for the final edit will all have to have occurred on a sunny day, or all on a cloudy day, so that the lighting will be consistent.

Sometimes, in the course of filming wildlife for the series, we are lucky enough to film a single event, such as a predation chase, from start to finish, so that the resulting sequence or story is edited the way it actually happened. An example is the sequence we filmed for a program on the "Controversial Coyote," where a pack of four adult coyotes relayed each other to chase down a jackrabbit. The actual chase took about seven minutes and we edited it into the program just the way it happened. But normally the process of making a film requires condensing time, while still putting together the story as accurately as possible.

Although the editing process distorts the reality of time and space to a certain extent, the lynx-hare chase, and indeed all the sequences that make up the *Wild America* programs, do capture the authentic and vital forces of nature set in motion—the instinct to kill for food, the drive to eat and reproduce, or the determination to protect offspring. The bottom line is that it doesn't matter how many minutes a lynx sits in wait for a hare to make the wrong move, or whether the chase occurred on a sunny or overcast morning. What is important to understand is that every movement, every feature of the animal's anatomy, every decision made by an animal to attack or to escape represents millions of years of perfecting, or at least maximizing, the ability of the species to survive. This is what intrigues me most about the natural world and this is what I try to relate in my films, as dramatically and as accurately as possible.

In contrast to the lynx-hare chase, which was the action high point of the program, we also filmed a more "philosophical" sequence in which I inspect a juvenile lynx we found lying curled up dead, as if asleep in the snow, at the base of a spruce tree. It could have been the victim of some feline disease, but judging by its poor condition, I suspected that this young lynx had died of starvation. During the bitter winters of the northern forest, not much in the way of vegetation is available except conifers, whose tough resinous needles provide little sustenance for vegetarian creatures. The snowshoe hare is one of the very few species that can eat and digest this limited diet, which in turn means the lynx does not have a broad spectrum of prey species to feed upon. And if the snowshoe hare's cyclical population happens to be at a low ebb, the lynx too will have a difficult time surviving a long, cold winter. We filmed this dead cat to make the point, in the narration, that sometimes the predator, not the prey, ends up the loser in the contest for survival. Especially in winter, a young lynx's lack of hunting experience is compounded by a limited food supply. Yet for the wildlife that has evolved in those northern lands, winter is simply another season of the year, another challenge to stay alive. It never ceases to amaze me how, in one way or another, most wild animals do very well in meeting that challenge.

Another north woods animal that is as tough as the environment it lives in is the elusive wolverine. Like the lynx and the snowshoe hare, it is uniquely adapted to cold latitudes. Its coat is composed of a layer of dense underfur plus a layer of longer, coarser guard hairs that prevent moisture from condensing and freezing on the coat. The wolverine, too, has "snowshoe" feet, which in winter grow short, stiff hairs that add to the size of the feet and assist the animal's movement across snow and ice.

I learned a good deal about the wolverine during my filming trips to Montana and while talking to trappers in the region where we filmed lynx. During all the time we spent looking for lynx in the evergreen forests, I saw a wolverine only once. It was climbing the trunk of a spruce tree, and when it saw us, it leaped about twenty feet down and landed in the deep snow, then scrambled over some fallen logs and disappeared under a sweep of low-hanging branches. The wolverine's reclusive nature, plus its habit of wandering immense distances in its remote habitat, have made this creature one of the world's least observed animals, which is what piqued my curiosity.

The wolverine is known for its fierce temperament, its scavenging and trap-raiding ways, its musky smell, and its bearlike, bowlegged lope. What I learned about this animal, through reading and talking to a man who had trapped them for twenty-five years, was much more complex than that. For one thing, its keen sense of smell, with which it can locate food several feet under the snow, is exceeded only by its unbelievable strength. It can be said that for its size, the wolverine is the strongest of all North American mammals. Trappers claim that its jaws are so powerful that it can literally chew through heavy steel mesh or break the metal chain anchoring a leg-hold trap. Its teeth, however, suffer badly in the process, with many or most being broken off or shattered.

To fuel its muscular thirty-pound body, the wolverine spends most of its time searching for carrion. However, it is also capable of catching prey ranging in size from a mouse to a moose. With its short, stocky legs, chasing down a larger animal such as a deer or a caribou would require more speed than it can muster, so it has other methods of tackling prey larger and swifter than itself. One way is by using its long-distance endurance to follow a large animal through deep snow at a slow but steady gait until the intended victim becomes too exhausted to flee or fight, or until it flounders helplessly. Then the wolverine hurries toward its struggling prey and jumps on its back, delivering a fatal bite with its powerful jaws to the spine or the throat.

The wolverine is an arboreal creature, and another strategy of attack it uses is to crouch in the branches of a tree until an unsuspecting deer passes beneath. The wolverine then leaps onto the animal's back, its long claws gripping until it can deliver the final bite. Lynx and bobcat have also been known to bring down prey in this manner. As dramatic as this hunting of large prey might seem, it should be made clear that this is unusual and is successful only if the prey is already weakened.

The wolverine is first and foremost a scavenger. Paradoxically, it both competes with, and depends upon, bigger predators of the north such as wolves, lynx, mountain lions, and bears. The ability of these creatures to bring down large game increases the supply of carrion for the wolverine. Though it competes with other meat-eaters for the carcasses of animals that have died of old age or starvation, and has even been known to drive much larger animals such as bears or mountain lions away from their kills, its dependency upon them is such that the wolverine has difficulty thriving in areas devoid of more successful predators. The wolverine often follows wolf packs in winter, not only because traveling is made easier by letting the wolves break trail, but mainly because it eventually may be able to snatch away some of the wolves' kill.

Its habit of stealing food has outraged many a trapper who

The wolverine is a wandering, misunderstood loner, a bad-tempered scavenger of rare stamina capable of performing almost unbelievable feats of strength.

discovered his trapline robbed. Like most scavengers, the wolverine is an efficient opportunist, and when it comes across a trapline offering meat baits or trapped animals, it will move from trap to trap removing and eating the contents of each, usually without getting caught itself. As if that weren't enough for a trapper to contend with, the wolverine will sometimes drag away the uneaten portion, with the trap in tow, and bury it for a later meal.

Much ado has been made of the wolverine's bad temperament. The animal was described in an 1892 account as "a ravenous monster of insatiable voracity, matchless strength and supernatural cunning; a terror of all other beasts, the bloodthirsty monster of the forests." It's been nicknamed "skunk bear" because it looks like a small bear and smells like a large skunk; "evil one" and "devil bear" because of its fierce disposition; and other names too colorful to print. It's a creature of legend. Some have said that it can kill a full-grown moose, others that it can drive off an entire pack of wolves from their kill. I was curious to learn if the wolverine really deserved all those names, and if the legends about it were true. I saw the need to shed some positive, or at least realistic, light on this misunderstood loner, so I decided to do a program on it that would be entitled "Wolverine Country." The same trapper with whom I had been in contact while searching for lynx also helped us to locate and film some of these fiercely elusive creatures in the breathtakingly beautiful Bob Marshall Wilderness Area—or "The Bob," as locals call it—in Montana.

Unlike the lynx, which can be tracked in snow or filmed near its den, the wolverine is much harder to follow because of its tendency to roam faster and farther than a person on snowshoes can travel. On the other hand, the wolverine does have some characteristics, such as an incredible sense of smell and a voracious appetite, that worked to our advantage when attempting to film it. Because it's the ultimate scavenger, and because especially during the lean winter months it will travel miles to find meat, I figured that if I introduced a road-killed deer carcass into an area known to be inhabited by wolverines, sooner or later an animal would show up to feed on it.

In mid-February, I drove to Montana, picking up a road-killed deer along the way with permission from the Montana Division of Wildlife. When I arrived at the wilderness area, I transferred the carcass onto a dogsled which I had rented in advance and headed out into the backcountry of The Bob. The next morning, I found a good spot to place the carcass, near a small open brook. Then, using a clump of trees as a natural blind, I waited that entire day and most of a second day for a wolverine to show up.

However, the first animal that was attracted to the bait late that second afternoon was not a wolverine but a *wolf*—an animal now even rarer in Montana than the wolverine. A few minutes later, another wolf showed up. Judging by their friendliness toward one another, the second was probably the first one's mate. Hardly had they begun to feed on the carcass when a wolverine appeared, shuffling belligerently over a nearby ridge of snow and sidling cautiously toward the wolves,

To film wolverines, I took a dogsled team deep into Montana's Bob Marshall Wilderness, where motorized vehicles, including snowmobiles, are prohibited.

its coal-black eyes glinting and its tiny ears flattened against
its head. As the wolverine got within a few feet of the carcass,
it hunched its back like a cat, bared its teeth, and let out a
weird deep-throated gurgling, then lunged toward the wolves.
The wolves leaped away, then returned to circle the carcass
nervously. Their empty stomachs seemed to be urging them
to risk a fight, while their instinct told them that this was not
an animal to be dealt with easily. Finally, tails tucked, the
wolves retreated from the frozen deer and abandoned their
windfall to the skunk bear.

It must have been a lean winter in those parts for my bait
to have worked so effectively. Two more days passed, and
another wolverine showed up. The newcomer rushed at the
first wolverine with a great show of fury, but stopped just short
of a fight. I was prepared to see the two wolverines meshed in
a mass of slashing claws and flying fur. But what I saw instead
was a classic "cussing contest." Using a variety of deep-
throated chuckling noises that combined snorting, growling,
heavy breathing and just plain weird wolverine words, the two
sized each other up. The first wolverine had already fought off
two wolves and wasn't about to give in to another of its own
kind. And the newcomer, not wanting to risk receiving a permanent injury from its more belligerent opponent, circled
around "chuckling" for an hour or so before it finally loped off
into the trees to continue its solitary search for food.

Due to their long fur, it was impossible for me to determine
the sex of either animal, and I have no idea whether any factor
besides food was at stake. I was able to watch and film not
only the confrontation over the carcass, but also the victorious
wolverine eating its fill, then leaving the area to rest and digest
the huge quantity of meat it had consumed. I later trailed it
by dogsled and then on snowshoes for hours until the animal
got so far ahead that I couldn't keep up.

Although we were never able to film a female with young
or find an active den, we were pleased with the footage of the
two wolverines together, and with the evidence that their behavior toward others of their own species might be less aggressive than has been reported by other sources. And I was
especially pleased since I had never seen much at all about
wolverines on film before. Unlike the "North Woods Lynx"

program, which focuses on the whole life history of the wild cat, "Wolverine Country" centers mainly around the necessity for the wolverine to feed and scavenge during the long winter months.

As is often the case, the legendary feats of this animal are probably exaggerated, but I must admit that when trappers claim that wolverines can eat steel, it's not as far from the truth as one might think. Of course, they don't actually "eat" metal of any kind, but I have it from a reliable source that they can chew through 11-gauge steel-reinforced wire fencing, and from my own experience I know that they can quite easily bite through the frozen bones of a deer carcass.

A white camouflage outfit and snowshoes—strategies borrowed from northern forest species like the snowshoe hare—helped me track and film wolverines in winter without disturbing their activities.

Personally, I have a great deal of admiration and respect for this often maligned creature because it's such a fierce survivor in an extremely harsh and inhospitable land. It doesn't hibernate, it hunts by day and by night, and it has been observed in boggy arctic tundra as well as on 13,000-foot mountain passes. So it may be said that neither time of year, nor time of day, can deter the wolverine from its far-roaming, scavenging way of life. With claws like a bear, teeth like a wolf, and a disposition like—well—like that of a "devil bear," it's a formidable adversary when competing with wolves, or even bears, over a carcass. So its reputation of being able to drive off larger predators from their kill is well-founded, although I'm sure as often as not it works the other way around.

As the largest land-dwelling member of the weasel, or Mustelidae, family (the sea otter is the largest of all), the wolverine exhibits to an extreme many typically mustelid traits. It is unusually elusive, and has a ravenous appetite and a pugnacious disposition. North America's weasel family falls into four main groups, based primarily on body shape: the typically long, slender mink, marten, weasel, and fisher; the large, flat-bodied, low-slung badger and wolverine; the bushy-tailed skunks; and the sleek, streamlined otters, of both fresh and salt water. All are meat-eaters, and all share other trademarks of the family: five toes on each foot, anal scent glands, and fine fur—sometimes too fine for their own good. Many mustelids have been greatly reduced in range and in number by overtrapping to meet the demands of the fashion world.

During the same year "Wolverine Country" was being made, I began filming a program about another mustelid called the fisher. "Fisher" is actually an unfitting appellation, since fish are an almost negligible part of the diet of these creatures compared to some of the other members of the weasel family. It has been speculated that the fisher received its name from old-time trappers' reports about it stealing fish baits from their traplines.

Unlike "Wolverine Country" or "North Woods Lynx," which were planned, "Fishers in the Family" came about quite by accident. I was driving along a mountain road on the way home from a filming trip one early spring day and passed a dead animal along the road. I didn't recognize it at first, so I stopped the truck and backed up. To my amazement, it turned out to be a female fisher—an animal that looks like a darker, larger pine marten. Fishers are thought to be rare throughout most of the Rockies, but with her long sinuous body, short legs, weasel-like beady eyes, and pointed snout, this one was unmistakable. It was sad enough that she had been killed by a car, but even worse, I could tell by her swollen teats that she had left kits in a nest, perhaps somewhere nearby—babies which would soon die without her warmth and milk.

As wet, heavy flakes of spring snow drifted down, melting on the dark asphalt, I recalled a promise made to myself after raising Griz that I would never have another wild pet. But under the circumstances, I felt that I had to at least try to find the now-orphaned fisher kits. I started to backtrack, following the female's trail in the light snow. But as the woods whitened, this became increasingly difficult. Finally, as I stopped to listen and look around once more before turning back, I heard faint crying sounds coming from underneath a fallen log. Sure

Contrary to its name, a fisher does not catch fish—but it does eat porcupines.

enough, the log was hollow, and inside it were two furry little fisher babies, mewing almost like kittens. Breaking my promise, I nestled them inside my coat and took them home with me.

Diane had mixed feelings about the new additions to our family, but she soon warmed up to their adorable, fuzzy little faces and clumsy playfulness. We named the male Spud because he looked like a fat little round potato, and the female Porky because she was equally pudgy, and because fishers are one of the very few animals known to eat porcupines. I was amazed to learn that fishers are the only animal whose skin, muscle tissue, and digestive systems can actually dissolve the thorny quills that normally cause fatal infections in other animals. I also read that the method by which fishers prey upon porcupines is often debated. Some books said that the fisher uses its lightning-fast reflexes to flip its prey over and attack the porcupine's soft, unprotected underbelly. Others made a more macabre claim that the fisher deftly avoids the porcupine's tail swipes by biting its victim's face, until, from shock and loss of blood, the porcupine succumbs to the fisher's attack.

In any case, their habit of preying on porcupines (which strip and girdle the bark from trees, thus killing valuable timber) has made them friends of the forester and has helped bring them back from the brink of extinction in a number of places. Presently, they are being reintroduced into their original range to help control the destructive porcupine populations. It's a happy ending to a rather sad story, since the fisher was sought for its exquisite fur and was nearly trapped out of existence in the lower forty-eight states during the first half of this century.

I quickly read as many facts about them as I could, and I also consulted with my friend Dr. Greg Hayes, a veterinarian specializing in wildlife, who gave the fisher kits the proper vaccinations against rabies and other diseases. It was hard to know what we had really gotten ourselves into as foster parents, since I had never heard of anyone else raising fishers as pets. All we knew about them is that they look like a cross between a mink and an otter in size. They have the sharp teeth and the agility of a weasel, but also the claws and climbing ability of a squirrel. The most arboreal of all the weasels, fishers not only climb trees, they climb *anything*. Curtains, shelves, even people. As they grew, the fishers would climb right up my pants leg, continue up my back, use the top of my head for a launching pad, and take a sailing leap across the room. They're extremely acrobatic, which in the wild comes in handy for chasing squirrels, but in our home, their climbing and leaping antics occasionally proved disastrous. They would swing from hanging lamps or jump from the kitchen cabinets across the room and land in the trash can, spilling its contents all over the floor.

All in all, though, the fishers came at a wonderful time for us. Our daughter Hannah was almost three years old when I

My daughter, Hannah, greets the orphaned fishers. Raising them taught me and my family—especially Hannah—invaluable lessons about wild animals, and about ourselves.

brought them home, and she fell absolutely in love with them. They were wonderful playmates for her, and she was with them almost constantly. What began as an unexpected sighting of a rare, road-killed animal slowly developed into a wonderful story: Hannah and the fishers growing and playing together. I started to film it as a home movie, just as I had filmed similar stories with my brothers and sisters when we were young, but I soon realized that it would make a perfect *Wild America* program. Later, as I was teaching the fishers to hunt on their own, I realized that the second half of their story was similar to that of Griz: learning to be self-sufficient so that they might someday be released to live freely in the same terrain where their mother would have raised them. In this way, "Fishers in the Family" grew into a two-part program.

Knowing that porcupines are a mainstay of the fisher's diet in the wild, I kept my eye open for one to introduce to Porky and Spud. One day when the fishers were about four months old, while I was driving down the road with them in their carrying cage in the back seat, I saw a porcupine amble across the road and disappear into an aspen grove on the other side. I took them out of the car and carried them into the grove to see what they would do. Surprisingly, they simply sniffed at the slow-moving animal and bolted off into the woods to look for smaller, less prickly rodents. Maybe not *all* fishers eat porcupines, I thought, or maybe Porky and Spud were too well-fed to bother. Or maybe they were just too young.

One of the biggest surprises of all in the course of raising the fishers was that, just like Hannah, Diane fell head over heels in love with our adopted pets. The reason it surprised me is that she generally enjoys the company of people more than that of animals, while I'm often more the opposite. When I first brought them home, I figured that the duties and responsibilities of 3:00 A.M. feedings, cage cleanings, and such, would naturally fall on me. It wasn't long, however, before Diane had taken them under her care, feeding and playing with them, to the point where some friendly rivalry developed among the three of us over whose turn it was to feed them.

In the end, I'm convinced that Diane was even sadder to see them go than I was. We released them in the fall of the same year that I rescued them, into a dense spruce-fir forest near where I had found them. We put out a feeding station for them, but by that time they had already learned to hunt and never did take any of the food. Nevertheless, I did see them once later that autumn and again during the winter, and learned that somewhere along the way they had also learned to hunt porcupines: the last time I saw them they greeted me from the branches of a spruce tree, at the base of which lay the snow-covered carcass of a half-eaten porcupine.

To the best of our knowledge, the fishers still continue to live contentedly in the wild, where they should be. We've heard from a man who drives snow-cats through the area that he's seen one or the other of them every now and then, or noticed their tracks.

The personal satisfaction I got from making "Fishers in the Family" was derived not from filming any once-in-a-lifetime predation sequence such as I had for the lynx program. Nor did it come from any memorable winter wilderness experience. It came mostly from introducing American television audiences to a rare and little-known animal, one which was once found in many areas of the country. On a personal level, I loved having the chance to share with my own family some of the fun I'd had with wild animals when I was a child. The fishers' curiosity and energetic personalities reminded me of Foxy the fox. Like him, they had to investigate everything in sight, turn over every rock and log, and chase anything that moved. And like Griz, they were playful, affectionate, and quick to learn, although I have to admit that teaching Griz to dig for tubers and roots was a lot easier than trying to teach the fishers to hunt and eat a porcupine.

Diane and I loved to watch them wrestle and run in the meadow where we took them to play and hunt ground squirrels, but I think it was Hannah who got the most benefit from watching them. Kids can learn many valuable lessons from raising animals, both wild and domestic. She learned how to be gentle and sensitive toward other living things, and she accepted the responsibility that goes with caring for an animal. But most of all, even at her early age, she began to learn the first steps toward being a good parent herself by helping and watching us raise the fishers—how to be loving, yet firm at times, and how to let go when you know deep inside that it is time to set a young one on its own. Though Hannah has many years to go before she will be a parent, I think these lessons will stick with her and perhaps give her that extra edge of understanding and patience.

Each animal—lynx, wolverine, and fisher—in the name of progress and often for the price of its pelt, has been pushed farther and farther north toward the tundra and now thrives, in most cases, only in remote places. Because of this, most people won't ever have the chance to see them in their natural habitat. But making programs such as "North Woods Lynx," "Wolverine Country," and "Fishers in the Family" might, I hope, generate some understanding and appreciation for these seldom-seen creatures. After completing these programs, however, I was ready to take *Wild America* in a new direction, not only figuratively, but literally as well.

TEN

GO EAST, YOUNG MAN

*In our increasingly crowded, congested, managed world, I
sometimes wonder if wildlife is still really wild. With his perfect
poise and uplifted tail—a "flag" to warn other deer of danger—
this buck shows me the answer.*

F or much of my early filming career, I had unintention-
ally followed Mr. Greeley's famous bit of advice, and
gone west. West was where the bighorn and grizzlies
were, and somehow that direction had always implied
a sense of frontier, of true wilderness, in a way that east did
not. But now that I'd grown a little older, and especially after
a winter spent traveling between Colorado and the great north
woods, I was ready to turn my sights toward the Atlantic. I
realized it was a part of the country about which I knew relatively little.

Most of the programs we had made so far were set partly
if not totally in the western half of the country, and more and
more often this fact was being brought to my attention. People
from Maine or Virginia were writing to me and saying things
like, "Hey, your programs are great, but how come you don't
have much to say about wildlife in the east?" And they'd tell
me about star-nosed moles tunneling under their backyard in
Maine, or Brant geese they'd seen on a visit to the Virginia
shore. And people in New York and Delaware were writing
their local PBS stations, saying things like, "We enjoy this
series because it shows us bighorn and elk and grizzlies and
other animals that we never get a chance to see in the wild,
but we've put out a nesting box for wood ducks on our property
and would love to see a program about them."

So, the PBS people began passing on the word, kind of
nudging me a little, reminding me that after all, *I* was the one
who had named the series *Wild America*, and "America"
wasn't limited to what you could see from a 14,000-foot peak
in the middle of the Rockies, any more than it's restricted to
what you can see from the top of the Empire State Building.
At the same time, they sent me sheaves of demographic studies to turn my attention to the fact that a great percentage of our
audience does happen to live in the eastern half of the country.

Of course, I was well aware of these statistics already, at
least generally, and I *had* already spent a good deal of time all
along the eastern seaboard, in Georgia and the Carolinas, Virginia, New York, and Connecticut, filming species on the en-

dangered list for "At the Crossroads." I don't think there are necessarily more endangered species in the east than in the west, but at just *one* national wildlife refuge in Maryland—Blackwater—I had filmed three endangered species: the Delmarva fox squirrel, the red-cockaded woodpecker, and the southern bald eagle.

What I learned in those early filming trips was that it's definitely more difficult, and therefore more expensive, to film most creatures in most places in the East. Wherever animals have learned to fear people—whether because they're hunted or simply because there are a lot of people around to fear—it's going to take far more time and patience to film them than if those same animals had never developed any shyness or fear in the first place. In the filmmaking business, time and patience are synonyms for money. And that's the primary thing that there's just never enough of.

But that's more of an excuse than a reason, and when I think back, there *were* a number of good reasons for the heavier emphasis we had been putting on the western half of the country. I certainly hadn't intended to slight our eastern audiences, but assumed that other people would be interested in the same kinds of wildlife that I enjoyed researching and filming. And in my early years at least, I tended to think in terms of greener grass. By this I mean that I grew up in Arkansas with cottontails and doves, raccoons and red foxes, wild turkeys and white-tailed deer, and on rare occasions a black bear or wild hog for added excitement. I'm in no way saying that familiarity breeds contempt—I enjoyed and admired those animals while I was growing up, and I still do—but I think familiarity does breed, well, familiarity. If I looked east, or northeast, what I saw was basically the same kind of animals that I had already hunted or filmed in the woods behind our family's house.

But if I looked west, well, just like Horace Greeley said, I saw new horizons, new opportunities to grow up with the country. The scale was very different—not only the scale of space, with broad prairies and plains and great mountain ranges and deserts, but also the scale of wildness, or at least of size. For one thing, the East had virtually no predators left, or rather, no large ones, and as I've mentioned, predators to me have always represented a balanced ecosystem, a natural harmony at work in the environment.

I think that the concentration of urban life in the East has crowded out the larger life forms. It's now necessary to go down into Mexico to film jaguars; they're no longer found in Alabama. It's necessary to go to Wyoming to film elk; they're no longer found in Pennsylvania. It's necessary to go as far as Minnesota or Montana or Alaska to film wolves; they're no longer found in Vermont or New Hampshire. My first impulse when I started making films in college, in fact, was to go as far west and north as possible—to Alaska—where the grass, at least figuratively speaking, is as green as it gets, and where million-acre refuges still protect, at least partially protect, a way of life that's as ancient as the continent itself. Where huge herds of caribou still migrate 600 miles to their calving grounds, and where packs of wolves still tend to their business of culling the weak and sick from the herds. And where the clashing horns of Dall sheep rams still set the rocks ringing.

But after having spent enough time in those new areas to satisfy my initial curiosity, I was glad to have a little extra incentive to renew some old acquaintances. I headed east— both northeast and southeast, but southeast was first. Although the American South is geographically east, the deep South, especially swamps and river basins like the Atchafalaya in Louisiana, is distinctly different from the rest of the eastern part of the country, and obviously from the West, too, for that matter. Our southern marshes, estuaries, and swamps are breeding grounds for the richest, most complexly interdependent association of plants and animals that we have. Because of this complexity, they are also highly stable environments; remove one element and another will fill its place almost immediately. These shadowy bottomlands and impenetrable swamps are as wild as any place in the world. The bellow of an alligator is as primal and spine-chilling a sound as you'll ever hear. It's easy to get lost, or drown, or to sink up to your ears in quicksand, which is what happened to me while I was making the "Swamp Critters" program. I've had some of my most difficult filming experiences in these wet and secret places, and some of my most rewarding ones. And as usual when a place has proved challenging, I can't wait to go back to it.

East is east, unless it's south—and filming the wildlife of our southern swamps and bottomlands has always held great appeal for me. Filming from a blind like this one above the water helps me blend into the scenery.

In fact, I planned and researched a whole program called "Swamp Bear" just to give myself the opportunity to do some real exploring in the backwoods bayous of Louisiana, one of the last strongholds of the bear in the South. The result of this filming trip may well become the all-time most difficult *Wild America* "adventure search" program, since the bear itself nearly turned out to be a phantom. But in trying to find and film one of the bears, we shot footage on so many other interesting aspects of swamp life that what had been planned as one half-hour program grew, in the editing room, into two.

The "swamp bear" is not a distinct species, but simply a black bear that lives in the swamps. Or rather, not so simply: it's estimated that there are no more than 600 bears left in the six-state area from east Texas to South Carolina, with most of them in Louisiana, Mississippi, Alabama, and Georgia. A needle in a haystack would be easier to find—all you'd have to do is roll around in the hay. The needle, unlike the bear, is not going to do its best to keep out of your way. After long weeks spent poling through shallow swamps by flat-bottomed pirogue, wading through mucky marshes, and encountering creatures as diverse in size but similar in temperament as mosquitos, water moccasins, and alligator snapping turtles, we did eventually track down and locate a bear. However difficult or unpleasant the experience sounds, it was exciting and worthwhile. Part of the thrill for me was filming what hadn't been adequately documented before.

But I'm getting away from my story. Just as there were a lot of good reasons for filming wildlife in the West, so there were just as many for turning our attention to the East. From the beginning, I really did want the *Wild America* series to give a balanced overview of all of American wildlife—not only the big, magnificent mammals, but also the smaller and easily overlooked ones, as well as amphibians, reptiles, fishes, and birds. I've always been drawn to the surprising, the amazing, the incredible, and it's certainly true that the eastern United States has its fair share of unusual creatures. And from the letters and feedback we were getting, I could see that other people were interested in them, too. So, three years into the series, with so much good audience response, we were in a position to sit down around the office lunch table and say

"Well, where do we want the series to go from here?" The unanimous vote was that each year's ten programs should provide a balance of east and west, north and south, large and medium and small. Each year we would do at least one film on birds, one on a cold-blooded species, one "how-to" program, and so on. And each of these programs would be set in a different part of the country—the more specific the location, the better.

Once we started thinking "east," the possibilities seemed endless: "Pennsylvania Whitetail," "Otters of the Adirondacks," and a program about the woodcock in Maine, which we called "Timberdoodles of Moosehorn," just to mention a very few. Here was a way of celebrating not only a specific wild animal, but also a specific wild *place*, a typical or unique

Many people are surprised to learn that bears live in swamps, and in fact locating a swamp bear became a major project for us. But while we searched for the animal, we were also rewarded by the pristine peace of the bayou.

area of that creature's habitat. And it was, we hoped, a way of giving our audience even more to identify with. We wanted people to have the thrill of seeing a program made in their home state, and we also wanted viewers who didn't live in that state to have the chance to feel even closer to an animal by being able to think of it in terms of a particular place. Both whitetails and river otters, for instance, are found in many areas all over the country, but if we tried to show a sampling of them everywhere, I think people would end up with only a vague sense of the actual animal in its environment. They might understand it intellectually, but I don't think they would identify as closely with it, or feel as much for it.

So, within two years of our decision to make the series a consistently balanced overview of animals from all parts of the country, we made four programs set in the East—the ones mentioned earlier, set respectively in Pennsylvania, New York State, and Maine, and "Woodies and Hoodies," also filmed in New York State. The latter is the story of the sometimes wacky interaction between wood ducks and hooded mergansers. We've also researched or filmed programs on "Cottontails," "Doves—Birds of Peace," "Wild Turkey," "Managing Wildlife," and "Shenandoah Springtime," all of which are set, in whole or in part, in the East. It's interesting for me to reflect that it took me five years of producing the series to finally make an entire program about one of the creatures I'd grown up with—the whitetail. When audience response told us that this was one of our most popular programs ever, our enthusiasm was fired even more for filming programs that concentrated on other creatures that I grew up with. Maybe the older we get, the more the grass seems greener closer to home.

Although the "Otters" and "Whitetail" ideas both occurred to me around the same time, it was the river otter program that seemed most attractive, at least initially. These graceful, happy-go-lucky creatures, who make a game out of everything they do, are enormously appealing. I know I've said that if I could be reincarnated as the animal I was *meant* to be, I'd come back as a bighorn. But if I could come back as the animal I'd *want* to be, it would be as an otter. Imagine going through life with the attitude that, hey, if you can't make a game out of it, it's just not worth doing!

Many different animals play, especially the young of most mammals. And even though "play" can be defined as behavior without an obvious goal, consider a lynx kitten tossing a dead mouse, or a baby bighorn cavorting along a cliff ledge, or the rough-and-tumble wrestling of coyote pups. As I've mentioned, all these activities have value as learning experiences, whether by teaching a young animal the smell of its prey, fine-tuning its sense of balance, or by building muscles and social skills. Of course, adult animals play, too. I've watched through my binoculars across a valley as a lone sow bear slid down a snowbank, climbed back up, and slid down again, over and over for almost twenty minutes. She was gaunt and shaggy and looked old enough to have seen everything that a bear could ever see in life, learned all there was to learn, yet there she was in all her dignity, oblivious to my presence, sledding down the slope on her rump.

Otters enjoy this game, too, only they play it with far more vigor and vitality. If the ability to play is a measure of intelligence—and I personally think that it is—then otters must be one of the most intelligent forms of wildlife. Wrestling is another of their favorite games, one which often turns into a group match, with several otters at once biting and pawing and scratching at each other. You'd think it was a serious fight, except that they don't make any noise. When they really do fight, they emit ear-piercing screams. But they don't only play with each other, they're constantly improvising games by themselves. Otters have paws that are capable of picking up objects, and it says a lot about their attitude in general that they use these objects more as toys than as tools. Sea otters use rocks as tools to break open abalone and mussel shells, but a river otter will pick up a pebble from the stream bottom just to bring it to the surface, drop it, and chase it down through the bubbles to the bottom again. Or it will maneuver around underwater with a rock or a freshwater mussel balanced on its head just for fun.

Totally at home in the water, they play at swimming even on land. An otter traveling over snow or ice will lope along on its short legs to build up speed, then dive onto its belly and skid along as far as momentum will carry it. I've also seen them doing this in wet grass and mud. In fact, mud-sliding or snow-sledding is probably their all-time favorite activity. It's usually pursued as a group sport, with an entire family following each other up a riverbank and then down the steep slide. A young, inexperienced otter may at first stiffen its front feet to brake its speed, but before long it streamlines itself into what I call a "what-the-hell" position, folding its front legs back along its side to get the full bobsled effect, and sliding into the water with as big a splash as it can make.

Otters are the only member of the weasel family that have such an advanced sense of play. Their relatives—weasels, ferrets, fishers, mink, skunks, martens, badgers, and wolverines—seem stuffy, huffy, or at least efficiently businesslike, by comparison. But playfulness wasn't the only reason that I wanted to make an otter program. I also liked the opportunity of setting such a film in the Adirondacks. I was astonished to learn that Adirondack State Park, located within a day's drive of the 55 million people inhabiting the northeastern United States and southeastern Canada, is the largest park, state or national, in the United States, and one of the largest in the world—almost *three times* the size of Yellowstone! Anyone

I'd trade places with the playful, endearing river otter in an instant. Whether hunting crayfish, as shown here, or raising its young, the otter makes a game out of everything it does.

who thinks that New York City takes up most of the room in New York State should drive a few hours north. The park's six million acres comprise some of the wildest country I've seen, and one of the most interesting things about it is that it contains not only 2.3 million acres of state-owned forest preserve and wilderness, but also 3.7 million acres of private lands. It encompasses towns and homes and businesses and a population of over a hundred thousand year-round residents —all carefully regulated so as not to intrude upon the area's primary asset of natural beauty. If any place on earth proves that humans and wildlife can coexist, the Adirondack Park is it.

Where does the otter fit in? Well, it would be flippant to answer "almost anywhere," but in an area that contains more than 2,300 lakes and ponds, plus 1,500 miles of rivers fed by over 30,000 miles of brooks and streams, you'd think it wouldn't be too hard to find an otter. And the otter, our oldest land-dwelling carnivore, which we know from fossil records has been cavorting around our continent for at least 30 million years, has long been at home in the Adirondacks. So have beaver, muskrat, wolverines, wolves, moose, elk, lynx, and mountain lions. All were present when the white settlers arrived, but by the end of the eighteenth century most of the large predators had been killed or driven off, and by the end of the nineteenth century nearly all fur-bearing animals, including otters, had been all but exterminated from the region by trappers.

By the early 1900s, effective trapping and hunting regulations were instituted, and by the middle of this century beaver were once again common, and otters had made a strong comeback. But hardly had the situation stabilized before a new threat to wildlife appeared, seemingly out of nowhere. This insidious threat became the third factor in my desire to film the story of "Otters of the Adirondacks."

The East is heavily industrialized, and among the main by-products of many industries are tons of sulfur and nitrogen, which combine with oxygen in the air to form sulfuric and nitric acids. These contaminants, heavier than air, were formerly localized in the damage they could do. But for that very reason, local pollution control ordinances forced the construction of taller smokestacks without demanding that the pollutants they spewed forth be otherwise controlled. So now, though they may remove most poisons from the immediate area, these much taller stacks annually pump more than 70 million *tons* of sulfur and nitrogen into the upper air currents. There, as they drift north and east, they have even more time to react with oxygen before eventually settling to earth as acid rain or snow. The Adirondacks are the first mountains to get in the way of these prevailing air currents, and thus receive a concentrated dose of acid precipitation. Rain and snow in many areas of Adirondack Park has been found to have an acidity equal to pure lemon juice!

So what does this have to do with otters, you might ask, and especially with filming them? Otters are opportunistic carnivores that feed primarily on fish, and also on mussels, crayfish, salamanders, and other creatures whose life cycles depend on water and are extremely sensitive to changes in its acidity. Spring runoff in the Adirondacks carries a shock wave of acidified snow-melt through the soil, where the acid chemically picks up an additional poisonous load of aluminum. Aluminum has the effect of eroding the gills of fish and effectively killing them by suffocation, while increased acidity wipes out much of what the fish eat, and also adversely affects the viability of their eggs. It's estimated that more than 60 percent of the once-pristine lakes above 2,000 feet in the Adirondacks have reached critical levels of acidity. These lakes still look pristine. In fact, they're clearer than they've ever been, since most of them no longer support aquatic life of *any* kind.

How does this affect otters? That, among other things, is what we wanted to find out by going there to film them. Since they eat almost any prey they can find, in the water or out, and are capable of traveling a good ways to find it, I thought it might be intriguing to see if otters remain near fishless lakes, and if they do, what they eat instead of fish. But I wanted to emphasize the carefree, happy-go-lucky side of otter life even more than I wanted to preach against acid rain, bad as that problem is. Though I often waver between idealism and cynicism, I tend to trust the intelligence of our PBS audience. I figure that if we show wild animals in a realistic way, the animals will speak for themselves, and people will care enough about them to do what's necessary to preserve or restore their habitat.

So we loaded up our cameras and headed east for a summer in the Adirondacks. Greg Hensley, my time-lapse specialist, and Steve Kroshel, a new cinematographer I had just hired, had gone on ahead to set up some time-lapse plates in strategic locations to record month-to-month seasonal changes, and also to begin doing time-lapse camera studies of the spectacular sunrises and sunsets that occur over the gentle peaks of the Adirondacks.

He also did a lot of asking around about otters and where we might go to film them. After a number of false leads, Greg finally located a pair of them along a remote stream that was visited by few people other than canoeists. After days of patient stalking, he was also able to find their den, and spent several more days setting up a blind and moving it gradually within filming range of the den entrance. My arrival coincided, happily, with the discovery of two month-old, still blind, baby otters in the den. And it coincided *not* so happily—in fact, miserably—with the onslaught of the blackfly season, the month-long annual plague of the Adirondacks. These relentless little creatures are literally bloodthirsty, squeezing themselves through the tiniest openings in the elaborate protection we wore to keep them away from our bare skin. We donned masks of mosquito netting over our hats and faces, wore long socks and elastic bands around our pants cuffs and wrists, and even tried filming with gloves on, but nothing seemed effective. They work their way through the netting into your ears and eyes, or up your pants leg, or down the back of your neck, until you're a mass of jangled nerve endings that wants to leap screaming into the river with the otters. Unlike most biting flies or mosquitos, their bite isn't really painful until hours later, when it swells up like you've been hit with a ball-peen hammer. Since you can't feel them while they're biting you, you're even deprived of the glee of swatting and squashing them in revenge.

About the only thing that gave any relief was a big jar of army-strength insect repellent donated by a kindly and sympathetic old-timer in the nearest village. This thick, evil-smelling potion made believers out of us, especially when

Greg discovered that it had completely dulled the edge of his steel pocketknife, and was eating away the rim and handle of his plastic drinking cup. Still, the flies managed to get Greg so frustrated that one morning he dropped part of his camera into the water while he was reloading film, and we had to interrupt shooting and ship the camera by floatplane and emergency air freight to the Arriflex people in Blauvelt, Long Island, for repairs. As always, we had more than one camera on hand, so filming didn't completely stop, but for the rest of that month, neither did the flies.

To our complete surprise, the otters' natural curiosity eventually began to amount to a kind of tacit cooperation, which almost made up for the flies. For most of the year, otters are restless wanderers, capable of traveling more than twenty-five miles in a week. But for the first few weeks we were there, the mother was occupied with her babies and didn't roam far. On the other hand, during that early period the father wasn't often to be seen. Otters mate for life, and they stay together during most of the year; but when her litter is born, the protective female banishes the male. Whether she thinks he might eat the young, or carry them off to be used as toys, has not been determined. When the babies are about three months old, their waterproof fur has grown thick enough for swimming lessons to begin, and the father returns to join the fun. In this case, he often took the lead on family forays along the stream banks, and did his part to coax his offspring into the water.

By this time in July, our family of otters had gotten somewhat accustomed to us following them around with our clanking cameras. Perhaps it helped that by then the flies had subsided, and we were no longer wearing our strange, awkward, masked and veiled mosquito net costumes. The otters would let us get quite close to them on land, and even closer, surprisingly enough, when they were in the water, as long as we were in the water with them. When we climbed out on the bank, they moved away again. Perhaps our shadows on the water scared them, or maybe some age-old instinct told them we were bears. Since there were bears in the area, perhaps their caution wasn't so far-fetched.

And speaking of bears, one of the funniest incidents of the summer happened after we discovered that the area where we were filming wasn't quite so remote after all. Or rather, it was, but there was an equally remote backwoods lodge tucked around on the other side of the nearby, almost fishless lake. We discovered the lodge, and met its genial hosts, one day while we were following the otter family on their rounds. Over a period of several days, the otters would move up the stream, off into one or another of its side tributaries, overland to explore some ponds in a protected beaver sanctuary, then back around the lake and downstream to the den area, romping all the way.

We found that we could keep track of the otter family almost as well by spending an occasional night showered and sleeping snugly between clean sheets in a cabin at the lodge as we could by spending every night rolling around in soggy sleeping bags made dank by the heavy humidity or all-too-regular rain. The lodge owners enjoyed wildlife, and to give their guests an opportunity to share this pleasure, they had some floodlights set up outside the picture window of one of the cabins, where they put out food to attract the local foxes, raccoons, deer, and whatever else came along.

It just so happened that one evening while we were staying in that cabin, what came along was a large male black bear. As he trundled into the floodlit area, we could see that he was probably the same feisty bear that we had watched a week earlier, chasing off three other younger, smaller bears. What had attracted him this particular night was a turkey carcass from the lodge kitchen, and as he pawed at it, we decided just for fun to crank up one of our cameras. The fun turned into disbelief as out of the darkness came one of the otters—one of *our* otters—with its bold and sinuous gait, weaving right up under the bear's nose to the turkey carcass. "Oh, no," we thought, "this *can't* be the way our program was meant to end." But I couldn't put the camera down as the male otter started a weird, wriggly dance, bobbling its head back and forth and all but rolling its eyes. At first the bear just stared and drew back its lips a little, but as the otter kept up his strange performance, the bear suddenly turned tail and was gone. Maybe it was the sheer boldness of the otter, or the confusion created by its dance, but in any case, the result was another victory by a playful David over a humorless Goliath.

We had wanted to know what otters eat when they can't eat fish, and we had already filmed them eating crayfish, salamanders, and frogs. But as our male otter slipped smoothly off into the shadows with the turkey carcass, we knew we had a bigger story on our hands than we'd first supposed. Nowhere had I read of an encounter between an otter and a bear, and much less did I suspect that an otter's appetite, combined with its sense of fun, might compel it to confront an animal more than ten times its size.

As the babies grew older, it became increasingly difficult to follow the family as they roamed further and further in their quest for food. After three months of filming, I was as fascinated with otters as I had been when I started planning the program. It was time for me to return to Colorado, but before I left, one more little incident happened that made me feel rewarded for the whole summer of trying to think and act like an otter—a summer spent living out my fantasy of *being* an otter. We were filming the otter family underwater in a bend in the stream, where it was about twenty feet wide and eight feet deep. Swimming with a mask and snorkel, I noticed that one of the two young otters had dived into a hole scooped out by the current under the roots of an ancient white pine. I thought there might be trout in the hole, and trout, now scarce in this particular area and hard for them to catch, were supposed to be an otter's favorite food. So I followed, hoping to film whatever I might see.

It was shadowy under the pine roots, with shafts of bright sun refracted deep underwater. I couldn't see any trout, or any fish at all, and I thought I had lost track of the otter. But just as I was about to turn around, the otter swam out from a shadowed area into the streaks of sunlight, sleek and streamlined. As it undulated toward me I couldn't help but reach out my arm against the current, and as the otter passed, it turned, backpaddling gently, and ever so slightly brushed its nose against my fingers. Just that one touch, from this vibrant, lively, totally *wild* animal, which in its curiosity had recognized my existence, made me want to forget all about filming or even breathing, and just go play, diving and twisting and swimming circles around fish. Otters can hold their breath for four minutes underwater, and for one wonderful, unrealistic moment, I thought somehow I could, too.

266

But pressure from other projects I had committed myself to was beginning to mount, and reluctantly I left the Adirondacks, feeling more like a prosaic beaver than a playful otter. On the way back to Colorado, I drove through Pennsylvania to check on the progress of "Pennsylvania Whitetail." Karen Chamberlain had made a location-scouting trip to Pennsylvania the year before we were ready to begin filming this program. From the information she gathered we were able to develop an extensive "wish list," as we sometimes call our shooting scripts. For instance, since we had gone to great lengths to film a whitetail doe giving birth for "Wild Babies," there was no need to repeat that effort. But on the other hand, we didn't have—and very much wanted—a great sequence of whitetail bucks clashing in a dramatic fight during the rutting season. To go along with that, we also wanted to include a mating scene, in order to show the purpose, or at least the end result, of those antlered battles.

Through various contacts, Karen had learned about an area near the Allegheny Mountains in western Pennsylvania where some unusually big bucks might be found. She had

Mule deer are familiar to those who live in the West. A mule deer buck has antlers that branch, then branch again.

talked to officials at Muddy Run Recreational Area and other places where whitetails had become part-time pests, to farmers who would let us film in their orchards and cornfields, to people who managed deer orphanages, and to game department and utility company people, all of whom were willing to cooperate in telling the whole story of the whitetail in Pennsylvania. Along the way, we wanted some scenes, such as spring softball games, summer swimming and picnics, autumn colors, and hunting season activity, that would depict and celebrate the all-American, down-home lifestyle of people in Pennsylvania.

After this groundwork, we realized that the actual filming would take more than a year, and that I would not have time to do it myself. We were fortunate in hiring the services of a cinematographer whose camerawork I respected, and who could also be given the responsibility of carrying out the project on his own, taking advantage of the contacts we provided and adding to and modifying our story ideas with what he found to be most realistic in the field. Steve Maslowski, of a Cincinnati-based family of wildlife cinematographers, was already well into the project when I passed through Pennsylvania late that summer.

There certainly seemed to be no lack of whitetails in the state. I saw deer in fields, deer crossing the highways, deer dead beside the road. I remembered what a comeback they have made in recent decades, after destruction of their traditional habitat and decimation by market hunters had almost completely destroyed the entire whitetail population in the East by the end of the last century. But the whitetail is one of the most adaptable creatures on earth, and its reproductive habits give it a great advantage once it has established a foothold. Reintroduction of the whitetail in Pennsylvania at the beginning of the century, combined with effective hunting regulations, gave it the chance it needed to thrive even in the face of an expanding industrial society.

Today, a great part of the saga of the whitetail in Pennsylvania and in the East in general is that of management, of keeping this most popular big game animal in the country from multiplying into its own worst enemy, overrunning and overbrowsing forests and croplands. It's a controversial story—

Whitetail deer are more common than ever in our eastern states.
The antlers of a whitetail buck have tines that project from a single
main shaft. This fine "rack buck" was photographed in
Pennsylvania's Allegheny Mountains.

which doesn't make me flinch in the slightest. But since I have
no desire to make programs about biologists ear-tagging and
radio-collaring deer, or standing around talking deer-per-acre
statistics, we decided that we would do what we always try to
do—focus visually on the whitetail itself, on its beauty and
grace and the important events in *its* life, and try to tell the
management story in a softer, more general way. Above all,
we wanted the program to be very positive.

Which means there's a lot we left out.

For one thing, we accepted the given wildlife management
situation as a basis for the program, without considering any
alternatives. Realistically speaking, the point of most wildlife
management practice is to benefit people, not wildlife. Of
course, this attitude assumes that wildlife, or at least the species that we deem important, will be preserved. But after that,
it becomes simply a numbers game. And much as I hate to
say it, America's favorite number is "more." That's where the
controversy begins. In Pennsylvania, the hunters want more
deer to shoot, and the game department people generally
agree because they want to sell more licenses and bring in
more revenue. The farmers and timber companies, on the
other hand, want to sell more crops and more lumber, so
they'd prefer to see fewer deer eating up the margins of their
profits.

As a result, most wildlife is managed as a "harvestable
resource," which means that its numbers are controlled by
hunting, a practice that some people find controversial, or
even offensive. They see that, at worst, this can lead to a
monoculture approach to wildlife management—the "more
deer, more ducks" syndrome that exalts game species at the
expense of non-game species and often leads to the overrun
of the habitat. Fortunately, in recent years wildlife management departments in some states, Pennsylvania included,
are beginning to devote a certain portion of their budgets to
non-game species in the interest of preserving balanced ecosystems. I think that is enlightened and admirable, and would
like to see more of it. And I'm sure most wildlife lovers, both
hunters and nonhunters, would too.

What are the alternatives to regulated hunting as a management technique? Obviously the answer is not *un*regulated

In "Pennsylvania Whitetail" we filmed a whitetail fawn being taught by its mother to lie flat and still in its hiding place—even when approached by humans with cameras—until she signaled that danger had passed.

hunting, since the alternative for wildlife could only be zoos. Without enforced laws, many more creatures would be hunted to extinction than already have been. Think of all the stories about a single hunter blasting away at a cloud of passenger pigeons, bringing down several hundred in a single afternoon, just for "sport." I don't think our mentality has changed much, and if we took the laws away, it wouldn't be long before zoos, which even now get more visitors per year than all spectator sports combined, including football, baseball, hockey, horse racing, everything, would have to begin accepting visitors on a reservations-only basis, because they'd be the only places left to see live "wild" animals.

In one sense, then, wildlife management is a matter of resource management, but in another sense, it's a matter of people management. My choice, if I had one, would be to go one step further, and suggest a solution far more controversial than hunting. I'm glad that many wildlife management people have started to think in terms of balanced ecosystems, and I'd like to see more management of wildlife for its own sake. That means controlling animal populations like deer, antelope, and elk by reintroducing their natural predators into the landscape. Unfortunately, nowhere is it official policy to think in terms of *naturally* balanced ecosystems, since that implies a return to the unthinkable: predators. And after we've just spent two centuries working so hard to get rid of them!

But I'm serious. I would like to see, in places where it's still possible, a management situation which turned over some of the work of controlling deer and antelope and elk populations to their former natural predators. And there *are* places where predator reintroduction is still possible, though perhaps not many of them are in the East. So far it's been out of the question to reintroduce effective populations of wolves into the vast area of Yellowstone Park, where they would compete neither with hunters nor with livestock interests, but *would* help regulate the runaway elk population in a natural manner. So I guess it's just a useless daydream on my part to suppose that predators could be reintroduced anywhere else, especially into the more crowded East. Pennsylvania will probably never again have wolves or mountain lions. For that matter, Colorado will probably never have any significant number of wolves or grizzly bears again either, though it has yet to kill off its last mountain lions. I find this imbalance of natural predators both artificial and unnecessary, at least in areas of the country where they would not impinge on low-density human populations.

But humans are, after all, the top predator. I have nothing against hunters per se—I'd be a hypocrite if I did—but hunting regulations in this country do result in an unnatural effect on most hunted species, an effect totally opposite to that of normal predator–prey relationships. It's the American way that practically any dummy who can find the door handle can drive a car, and anyone above a certain age can plunk down a 20-dollar license fee and go blast away. He or she doesn't have to know anything about wildlife, or even have any sense of sportsmanship.

Most hunters, of course, are knowledgeable and responsible, but most hunters, whether wise or foolish, are after the biggest trophy they can get, whatever species it is. Most want the biggest antlers, or horns, or tusks, and because of their goal, they take animals in the prime of life. And so, whereas the natural evolutionary tendency is for predators to eliminate the weak and perpetuate the strong, humans have the opposite effect. Each year during the last two decades, there have been from 100,000 to 150,000 whitetails harvested each year in Pennsylvania, most of them bucks. One of the overall results of this harvest, studies show, is that there has been a *significant* reduction in the overall size of antlers. Why? Those genes are gone. Those bucks never reproduced. Unless the rules are reversed, or new stock is brought in from outside, deer antlers in Pennsylvania will continue to get smaller.

Perhaps the situation in Pennsylvania, and in the East generally, is the situation of the future. Perhaps a romantic notion that defines wildlife as animals that are independent of human beings and separate from our system no longer applies anywhere. But I think it's important that we realize the absolute and unbelievable power that we exercise over the earth and over what gets to go on living here with us. And it's very important that we take full responsibility for the situation we have created. We have to manage wildlife if for no other reason than to protect it for ourselves, *from* ourselves. In terms of the Pennsylvania whitetail, and the bears, bobcats, foxes, cottontails, wild turkey, and woodcock that still roam our eastern woods, I like to think that however much these animals are managed and manipulated as a species, each individual creature, in using its wits to survive, is still as wild and free as ever.

ELEVEN

WILD WINGS

*The freedom of a bird in flight is exemplified by this streamlined
American egret, its neck and legs tucked smoothly behind to give its
body every aerodynamic advantage.*

To my way of thinking, in all of nature there are no creatures freer, and therefore wilder, than birds. Since primitive humans first stumbled out of a cave and stared up in awe at a soaring ancestor of the eagle, we have dreamed about and craved the power and freedom of flight. I think the inspiration we've received from birds has led us to some of our most spectacular and positive accomplishments as a species—moonwalks and space shuttles, for instance. Closer to earth, from where I live in Colorado, I can watch hang glider pilots float in solitude and silence thousands of feet above the highest peaks, occasionally accompanied by a descendant of that first awe-inspiring eagle.

Lifted free of the land, birds blend with their surroundings as no other living thing can. They are creature and sky joined as one. The power bestowed by the evolutionary adaptation of feathered wings sometimes makes the wildness of ground-dwelling creatures seem limited and vulnerable by comparison. Even the playful abandon of an otter underwater, or the leaping grace of a whitetail in the forest, seem restricted and land-bound compared to the airborne ballet of a pair of scissortailed flycatchers, or the wing-on-wing precision of a squadron of brown pelicans, or the incredibly swift plummet of a peregrine falcon.

Flight confers freedom from the restrictions of time, as well as those of space. Most North American birds migrate, and so are able to escape the seasonal restrictions of diminished food supplies and bitter cold, as they follow the sun north and south in its perpetual path toward summer. In another sense, not only are birds able to *escape* the seasons— they are an integral part of what *creates* the seasons, at least for us humans who live in temperate climates. Winter is the time of few birds, while summer's abundance seems all the richer because of them. We watch them gather in dark flocks and wheel away at the beginning of autumn, and come winging back one by one or in pairs, signaling spring as they delight us with their songs.

Of course, not all birds are graceful in flight, and not all birds can even fly. But that in itself is an indication of the incredible diversity of this group of feathered animals. From the nearly extinct California condor, with its nine-foot wing-span, to the half-ounce Calliope hummingbird hovering above a claret-cup cactus, nature's variations on the theme of wings alone are almost endless. Of course, because of its function, the basic aerodynamic shape of a wing, and even of a flying bird itself, cannot vary greatly. But the more a bird depends on its wings for transportation and especially for food, the more maneuverability it will require and the more its wings must be in harmony with its body shape for swift and efficient flight. All birds, even those that don't fly, have in common certain adaptations that contribute to an airborne lifestyle. Thin-walled hollow bones and the absence of teeth reduce

It might seem from the photo that this male blue grouse is either begging or trying to sniff my hand. But it's not: it's mad. This is courtship season, and it wants to force me out of its territory.

basic body weight, and the possession of a crop and gizzard for digestion means that a bird must feed frequently, but will never be weighed down by a full stomach.

On the other hand, the shapes of other avian appendages seem almost infinite. Think of the bills, legs, and tail feathers of familiar birds, not to mention the sometimes outrageous looking ornamental features of others such as the wild turkey. Flesh-eating birds like hawks and owls have sharply hooked or curved beaks for tearing apart their prey. Seed-eating birds, which include many of our songbirds, have short, thick beaks which enable them to crack open seeds and thin-shelled nuts. Hummingbirds have long, thin, tubular bills for extracting nectar from flowers, while ducks and other dabbling birds have broad, flat bills for gleaning pond weeds and shoots from underwater. Ducks, geese, and other swimmers tend to have short, stubby legs which make them ungainly on land, but very efficient in the water. Wading birds such as flamingos, egrets, and herons have long, elegant legs, and often necks to match, which give them an advantage in finding food as they stalk shallow marshland pools. You can always tell how a bird lives by analyzing its shape in this way.

All these different leg styles remind us that many birds, in addition to being skilled flyers, are also adept swimmers, divers, and even runners: Think of a wedge of Canada geese arrowing in for a water landing, or a merganser duck chasing a trout underwater with the agile tenacity of an otter, or a roadrunner streaking across the desert in pursuit of a collared lizard. Birds have evolved to fill an astonishing variety of ecological niches, nesting on sandy beaches and rocky cliffs, in marshes and deserts, above city streets, and along country roadsides. In addition, they come in a marvelous array of colors, and announce their presence with a wonderful multiplicity of sounds and songs.

It's been said that there is probably no spot on earth that has not been crossed by the shadow of a bird. We think of them as the freest and least earthbound of wild creatures, yet it's amazing to consider that at the same time no other form of wildlife is so accessible and so familiar to most people. Not only can birds be found in every ecological niche, but they often appear in surprising numbers. Perhaps the freedom conveyed by wings is a freedom to live not only in wild and remote places, but also to live in intimate association with people. Birds are often the first forms of wildlife noticed by toddling children, and they are often the last to bring comfort and cheer to the aging.

As a child growing up in Arkansas, I was, like millions of Americans, attracted to the beauty and mystery of birds, and I spent a lot of time just watching them. I hunted them, too, but they weren't as exciting to hunt as they were to watch and try to film. Hunting is literally a one-shot deal, but just try following a bird with a telephoto lens on a camera! It was a real challenge for me then, and it still is. There is no aspect of wildlife cinematography more difficult than trying to pan and focus at the same time while filming a flying bird.

All of which is why, early in the *Wild America* series, I wanted to do a film that celebrated birds, and call it "Wild Wings." After all, almost everyone—from the city dweller feeding sparrows and pigeons in the park, to the arctic Eskimo awaiting the spring return of murres and terns whose eggs feed him—welcomes and appreciates the cheerful difference that these feathered creatures make in our lives.

Though a few birds—mostly imported species like English sparrows and starlings—are considered pests, most are considered good luck: the first robin of spring, the swallow that nests under our eaves, the "bluebird of happiness." Even ravens and owls are considered by many people, including myself, to be good omens rather than bad. Many people take pleasure in attracting birds to their homes with feeders and nest boxes. And many others take pleasure in going out to look for birds, especially the less common varieties. Birders (they used to be called "bird-watchers"), backpackers, and wildlife photographers now outnumber hunters in the United States by a significant margin—which is not to say that many hunters don't also appreciate live birds as much as dead ones.

Although I'm not officially a "birder" myself, "up close and slowed down" is the way I like to watch and film wild animals in general, and birds in particular. Many birds are small, quick, and unpredictable. They can go not only left, right, toward, and away like a mammal, but also up, down, and everywhere in between. And even if they're large, their wings can, and usually do, take them rapidly out of the focal plane. Long lenses and high-speed camerawork are called for, and the longer the lens and the higher the speed, the more difficult it becomes to keep the camera trained smoothly on the action.

Paradoxically, a long lens is what makes a creature look closer, and a high-speed camera actually slows down the action by exposing more than the normal twenty-four frames of film per second. All in all, I'd have to say that, technically and otherwise, filming birds has given me a great deal of satisfaction and an equal amount of frustration. It's true in wildlife cinematography generally, but it's especially true in filming birds, that the uncertainty of what you are going to get keeps you constantly alert and excited. This can be exhilarating when something is happening—but very tiresome when you have to sit and wait.

In filming "Wild Wings" I did a lot of sitting and waiting. Out of it, fortunately, came a good deal of terrific footage, and I'm especially pleased with many of the slow-motion sequences. I caught, for instance, a stunning scene of a brown pelican flapping its wings a few times, then plunging into the sea. In real life this action took five seconds, but slowed down to 400 frames per second, and extended to sixteen times normal speed, the same scene takes about a minute, and you can see what happens to every single feather. This kind of shot is the most breathtaking I can imagine, because it shows every detail of the action and each nuance of beauty in a way that unaided human eyes could never see.

Similarly, I filmed a scene in "Wild Wings" of a trio of scissortailed flycatchers. At 300 frames per second every arc of their wing feathers, every swoop of their long, elegantly forked tails, reflects the tension in their bodies as they change direction in this airborne ballet. And there's another breathtaking slow-motion scene in which tens of thousands of shorebirds are flying wingtip-to-wingtip in unison, as close together as they could possibly be and still have room to beat their wings, and they all fly back and forth past each other so that the whole screen is cross-hatched with wings. Although it's not evident what causes their shifts in direction, the effect is spectacular—like watching the wind made visible.

But not all of the sequences for "Wild Wings" were such fun. In fact, one of them quite literally turned into a nightmare —one of the least favorite projects of my whole career— though I must say that a very unusual sequence did come out of it. It happened while I was filming kingfishers, which are bluish, high-crowned, stubby-tailed birds that feed primarily on minnows and excavate their nest cavities in the bank of a stream. I stumbled across the opening to such a nest early one May morning while on a raft trip near my home with my brother Marshall, and of course I had to reach inside to see if there were any babies. Sure enough, there were, though I couldn't tell exactly how many. Since I didn't have any pressing film projects at that time—and I remember it as the *last* time I didn't—I decided to film a sequence on the kingfishers.

How? Well, first with a shovel. There was no way to film by simply sticking a camera into the entrance hole of the burrow, because that would shut out the only source of light. So I set up a tarp and covered it with grass and branches as a temporary blind to minimize disturbance to the parent birds, and proceeded to carve out the embankment immediately *behind* the nest to expose a cross-section of the burrow. It took me several days of shoveling, and I felt like I had hefted at least a couple of tons of sand and earth, sweating plenty in the process.

When I was through, I had dug a hole just about the size and shape of a grave. It was deep enough to give me a good view into the kingfisher's nest, and wide and long enough to hold me and my camera gear. But the worst part was yet to come. Sitting in that hole, finger on the camera button, waiting for something to happen, was pure torture. It was hot and muggy, the hole was crawling with ants, bugs, and spiders, and most of them were crawling over *me*. There was nothing I could do—either I could stay to film when something happened that was worth filming, or I could pack it up and leave.

I chose to stay, but that wasn't the end of my discomfort. My initial stint in the blind was six full days, from predawn until after dark, using the cover of darkness to enter and leave the blind. For weeks afterwards I would wake up in the middle of the night in my bed at home, frantically trying to brush a horde of bugs and ants off the sheets, or yelling and tossing my spider-covered pillow to the floor. The first couple of times it happened, my wife Diane was really alarmed. But when it kept happening, she realized I'd just been out in the kingfisher blind a little too long that day, and she'd try to reassure me and say, "It's all right, dear, they're all inside your head," before she rolled over and went back to sleep. And then I'd fall back to sleep thinking they really *were* inside my head, and crawling in my ears and eyes, and the whole thing would start all over again. I didn't have this dream every night, but it did recur for several weeks after I had finished filming. I guess this is why I'm not rushing out to do any *Wild America* programs on insects.

The intention behind the kingfisher sequence was to show the babies actually being fed minnows by their mother, and this would have been difficult enough without being bugged by bugs. First I had to get the four baby kingfishers accustomed to me, and to the lights I needed to illuminate the interior of the burrow. Fortunately, the young birds didn't seem bothered by the brightness, but even so I would leave the lights on only for short intervals. At this early stage, though I stayed in the blind all day, I filmed for just a couple of hours so as not to disturb the parent kingfisher's feeding schedule too much. But just to make sure, and partly to make friends, I netted minnows myself and hand-fed them to the babies. Within a day or two, they were receptive to this routine, and would perch on my fingers and tweak my thumb with their sharp pointed beaks, testing to see if it was a fish.

The mother kingfisher, on the other hand, was definitely *not* receptive to this state of affairs—at least not at first. She would bring a minnow to the mouth of the burrow, but not all the way inside, and then try to coax her offspring to the entrance in order to feed them. As soon as I turned on the lights to film, she would quickly back out and fly away, taking the minnow with her. But finally, her maternal instincts won out over her caution—she couldn't have known that I'd been keeping her babies fed—and she brought the minnows inside, and even waited until the baby she gave it to gulped it down before she flew off for more.

This disturbance of a creature's normal routine is one of the gray areas about filmmaking that I'm forever mulling over in my conscience. Many people say things like, "You should never put the welfare of your subject in jeopardy," or "You should never disturb your subject in any way," or even that it's wrong to touch or artificially feed an animal. But, it's virtually impossible to film a sequence that involves birds or animals in their dens or nests—their homes—without causing them some degree of inconvenience. I completely agree that

Digging a grave-sized pit into the back of a riverbank allowed me to film—and feed—young kingfishers in their nest burrow. It also allowed all sorts of insects and spiders easy access to me.

no animal should for any reason be disturbed so that it abandons its home or its young, but I have faith in my own assessment of any particular situation and a little more knowledge than some critics of the resiliency of a wild creature's habits and the strength of its basic instincts.

I was pretty sure, from the time I first reached into the burrow, that the mother kingfisher had been feeding her babies long enough for her instincts toward them to be well-developed, and I figured that if I didn't disturb her with lights for too long at a time, she would keep coming back. I was also prepared to adopt them and feed them to maturity myself if she did abandon them. The tense part was waiting for her to grow accustomed to the change in things. Once she began to behave naturally, it took only a few minutes to obtain the shot I needed, and then I left them in peace. As far as the babies were concerned, they actually seemed to enjoy hopping up on my hand and being fed minnows. *I* certainly enjoyed it, and none of the observations I made later indicated that any harm was done. There is always that certain thrill in touching wild animals, and I think as long as you are very careful and respectful, very sure that you won't harm any part of their life and that they won't harm you, no damage will result.

I had to make another decision about touching animals for a different sequence in "Wild Wings." One spring, some rock climbers I knew found a poorwill, a western relative of the whippoorwill, huddled in a cleft in a boulder. They were wise not to disturb it. Instead, they came and told me about it because they thought it was sick and could use some help. We had been editing a sequence on the arctic tern, which is the champion of all migrating birds, spending summers in the northern Arctic and winters in southern Antarctica, making an annual round trip of more than 22,000 miles. Suddenly, here was a lucky opportunity to film the only bird that escapes the cold not by migrating, but by hibernating.

Even though it was April, the little poorwill was still pretty much asleep. But it was impossible to show this without picking the bird up and very gently petting and stroking it to demonstrate that it was simply lethargic, and not sick or dead. The poorwill wasn't at all frightened. Its whole attitude was more like a child who doesn't want to wake up and have to go to school, and it hardly moved in my hand at all during the few minutes it took to film it. Then I carefully eased the bird back into the rock crevice, and left it to wake up on its own when the time was right.

I'll admit that I do rationalize, and tell myself that my motive in showing other people fascinating things about wild creatures is so that they will learn to care about and help protect them, which justifies my doing things that I probably wouldn't do if I were alone in the woods. If I had come across the poorwill by myself, I might have stroked its head to make sure it was asleep, but I probably wouldn't have picked it up. I do think that it's sometimes necessary to juxtapose a human element in a wildlife scene in order to indicate scale, as when in another film I placed my finger in a hummingbird's nest to show the relatively tiny size of its eggs. But neither the parent hummingbirds nor their eggs were disturbed, which is always my ultimate consideration.

Though most birds migrate to escape the cold, one North American bird actually hibernates. This poorwill was still in a state of torpor when we found it in a rock crevice and filmed it one cold April morning.

Another difficult part of the kingfisher project was trying to catch the exact moment when the mother kingfisher left the branch she was perched on to swoop down for a fish. It makes for bad film technique to capture an action when it's already half over. The point is to have your camera rolling *before* the action begins, so that the viewer can see the animal entering the frame of the picture. But it became almost a matter of sheer luck to have the camera rolling the instant before the kingfisher flew. I couldn't just turn it on and leave it running, because the bird often rested for fifteen or twenty minutes between dives. And shooting in slow motion, at 100 frames a second, the camera exposes film four times faster than normal, so that the finished product will be four times slower. Which means that a ten-minute roll of film would be gone in two-and-a-half minutes, while the kingfisher was still sitting there motionless on the branch. Definitely a good way to waste a lot of film. So, concealed in a second, portable blind across the stream, I would try to sense when there was some irresistible activity from the minnows rippling the surface of the water in the nearby stream pool, and judge when the mother kingfisher would dive. Then I'd just punch the button and hope. This worked a couple of times, and a couple of times was all I needed to complete the sequence.

A camouflaged blind of some sort is almost always necessary in order to film birds without disturbing them. And even if it isn't filled with ants and bugs, sitting for hours in a tiny, hot, darkened enclosure isn't always the easiest thing in the world for me. I have a lot of persistence, but not much patience. I'll follow an animal's tracks for miles, or stay out in a driving snowstorm far longer than I know is healthy, because at those times I can be active. But I really don't like the passivity of sitting and waiting in a closed-in blind. For one thing, in order not to startle the creature you're trying to film, you usually have to be in the blind before dawn, and you stay there until after sunset. You take lunch and water and reading material, but mostly you just sit with at least one eye cocked for whatever might happen. If an animal does show up, I have no trouble staying there for days, watching and filming. But if nothing is happening, not only do I get impatient, I've learned that knowing when to quit and try a new tactic is often the better part of blind-sitting.

I think I most enjoy filming from a blind when it's way up in the air—the higher the better. Many birds nest quite high up in trees, and in order to film activities within their nest, your blind has to be higher than the nest, which usually means climbing a companion tree with a clear view twenty or thirty yards away. I've sat eighty feet up in the air, perched on a tiny platform with camouflage material thrown over me, swaying in the breeze, to film a nest of newly hatched birds being fed by their parents. And I enjoyed it for days on end. Being up that high, rocked by the wind, made me feel more like the birds themselves.

"Wild Wings" was the first program in which my daughter Hannah, then age two, appeared, or rather starred, since she always runs away with the show. We filmed Hannah, Diane, and myself on an eastern beach, with Hannah throwing bread to a flock of seagulls. Of course Hannah loved the whole experience, and her reaction allowed me to make my point—which was to show how accessible and appealing many birds are, and how they can be a child's first introduction to the world of nature. I hope as a result that a lot of people went out with their kids to do some bird-watching.

"Wild Wings" was only one of the two bird films that we did for the second year of the *Wild America* series. The second was perhaps an even stronger film called "Owls—Lords of Darkness," which also drew very positive audience response. I think people liked "Wild Wings" for its lightness, its focus on the glory and beauty of birds in general, and for its family approach. But "Owls," on the other hand, focused on these more mysterious members of the bird world. Not that the program tries to scare people—quite the opposite, since its purpose is to inform and to entertain. But the owl has been mysterious to people for centuries. Though it is by no means the only bird that is active at night, it is the only nocturnal carnivorous bird. And that, along with its haunting, hooting call, its soundless flight, its round glowing eyes and swiveling head, has contributed to the mixture of fear and fascination with which we respond to it.

To many, owls symbolize everything that is dark and frightening about the night. To others, they're a symbol of wisdom. Perhaps it's because they're nocturnal, superbly at home in a nighttime world so alien to humans, that owls are

Owls, with their round glowing eyes and swiveling heads, their mysterious hoots and silent flight, have always aroused fear and fascination in humans. They are the only nocturnal carnivorous birds. This already dramatic-looking great horned owl is still just a chick, and has not developed the feathered "ear tufts" that give it its name.

able to coexist so well with us, living in church steeples, barns, and even attics. Since most of us are asleep during the owl's favorite hours, and as the owl retreats to a safe hiding place to sleep during the day, it's generally a case of "never the twain shall meet."

There are many things about this owl film that please me, not the least of which is that no one had ever before done a solid survey film on the eighteen species of North American owls. At the same time, we were able to obtain a couple of "firsts" in wildlife filmmaking. For one thing, there is a humorous shot of an owl actually taking a bath. And for another, a very clear shot of a great horned owl hooting, so viewers can see how its throat puffs up as the sound rolls out. Many people have heard an owl hooting, but few have seen it, and to my knowledge this behavior had never before been filmed until Steve Maslowski succeeded in capturing it with his camera.

From the contortions we had to go through to get that and the rest of the program's footage, I doubt that anyone else will go to the trouble to do so any time soon, either. Night after night we set up lights in areas that certain nocturnal owls were known to frequent, and with a remote rheostat control we very, very slowly turned the lights up whenever the owl was in the area. We had to be extremely careful not to disturb the birds in any other way, so we used very silent cameras and tried to minimize any other signs of our presence. We burned up a lot of film during those weeks, and still had to throw away about half of the footage that was left, due to underexposure.

But not all of the program was so difficult to make, since much of it focused on the amazing differences there are among the eighteen species. They range in size from the rare great gray owl, with a wingspread of five feet, to the tiny elf owl no bigger than a bluebird. The facial shapes of owls also vary greatly, and all of them, especially the barn owl with its heart-shaped face, are intriguing. Some, like the great horned owl and the common screech owl, have tufts of feathers that look like upright ears, which give them an air of alertness. Others, such as the little saw-whet owl, have no such ear tufts, and they tend to look a little sleepy.

Owls are found everywhere, even where there are no trees. These burrowing owls live underground in abandoned prairie-dog tunnels, and hunt by day as well as by night.

Owls are found from coast to coast, and from the arctic tundra and great north woods to the southern swamps and deserts. Most nest in trees, or in barns or deserted buildings, but some, like the desert burrowing owl, are more comfortable underground, where they keep cool in abandoned prairie dog tunnels. The burrowing owl is one of several that are diurnal, or active during the daytime as well as at night, and these species were naturally easier to film than the more elusive nocturnal owls.

One of the things I wish we could have depicted, although it became clear there was no way to show it on film, is the hunting behavior of the barn owl. All owls have incredibly keen eyesight at very low levels of light, which is their primary advantage as hunters. But it's been proven that the barn owl is perfectly capable of pinpointing the location of its prey using only its *hearing*. The only way to have shown that, of course, would have been to use a blindfolded owl, which has actually been done before by researchers, but that's not exactly what *Wild America* is all about. We did, however, obtain some beautiful slow-motion scenes of owls hunting, and we were able to show how the soft, uneven tips of their wing feathers dampen the flap of their wings, and make possible their soundless, stealthy flight.

One especially notable thing occurred when we were trying to film the introduction to the program. Actually, we were down in coastal Georgia filming "Hog Wild!," and I was running along the beach one morning just before the sun came up. Now, I'm not a jogger, but I guess I was inspired by the spectacular beauty of the early morning seashore. The sunrise was a flare of red and gold, with colors glinting on the wings of the seagulls flying around. It occurred to me then that this would be the way to introduce the owls program, with the image of the sun coming up and moving across the sky, emphasizing that the world of owls is the nighttime world dispelled by the sun. And since we had the script with us for the "Owls" introduction, we decided to film it the very next morning. But the owl spirits of the area must have been casting some kind of a spell, because for the next seven days we never saw the sun. It just rose up gray behind thick clouds of coastal mist and fog, while I and my faithful crew of in-laws—father-

The barn owl, easily recognized by its heart-shaped face, lacks ear tufts but hears extremely well. Experiments have shown that, despite its marvelous eyes, a barn owl needs only its hearing, not its eyesight, to locate and capture prey such as the mouse it's just caught here.

in-law Eric Dale and his son, Kevin—stood there, ready to film, at 5:30 A.M. Of course I don't really believe in spells and hexes, and on the eighth day we did finally get a sunrise. Still . . . it does kind of make you wonder.

After the "Owls" program, I was eager to make another bird film for Year Three of *Wild America*, but this time I wanted it to be about a less familiar subject. So I decided to focus on another group of birds that no one had yet documented on film—the exquisite, bedazzling family of North American hummingbirds. Doing a program in the *Wild America* series on "Feathered Jewels" seemed particularly appropriate, since these birds are exclusively creatures of the New World. Early European explorers to this continent were amazed by the tiny, iridescent shapes they found buzzing through the air, flitting and diving and hovering, and even zipping backwards as well as forwards.

Invisible wings, blurred with speed. Nothing like this had ever been seen in Europe, and for some time there was doubt whether the creatures were birds or insects. But birds they are, of course, and surprisingly enough, hummingbirds comprise the second largest family of birds in the New World. However, only fifteen species nest north of Mexico, and these, especially the males, are the glittering stars of "Feathered Jewels." At first I had my doubts about whether an entire half-hour program on a creature that doesn't sing, doesn't walk, and hardly holds still for a second, could hold the interest of our audience. But I decided to concentrate on how gorgeous the hummingbird's world appears close up, with the flowers it feeds upon filmed in time-lapse by special-effects cinematographer Ken Middleham as they open and close in a slow-motion tapestry of rich reds, violets, yellows, and blues. And to show how some hummingbirds are artists in their own right, bird lover and cinematographer Burdette White filmed the intricate way they construct their delicate nests out of plant down, bound softly together with spider's web, and decorated with bits of colorful orange and green lichen for camouflage.

Above all, though, the hummingbird is the ultimate candidate for slow-motion camerawork. In fact, it would be impossible to do any kind of an effective film on hummingbirds *without* extensive use of this technique. A hummingbird's wings flutter at a rate of eighty or more beats per second—just try tapping *that* out yourself! At a normal camera speed of twenty-four frames per second, the wing beats are a total blur to the unaided eye. But slowed down more than 100 times, to 2,500 frames per second on film, it becomes possible to observe the unique rotating action of the wings—somewhat like a dual helicopter turned on edge—and to distinguish the rapid motion of the tubular tongue darting in and out of blossoms. We slowed these actions down so much that it becomes possible to study in detail every nuance of these miniature marvels of engineering.

"Feathered Jewels" once again proved that bird films are among our most popular, although it seems to me a slow-moving film in comparison to some of our others. But its popularity encouraged us to continue doing at least two bird films a year. Even more important, it was influential in our decision to simply slow down all of our programs. The positive audience response to our bird programs was becoming an important factor in my realization that we didn't have to include close-ups of all the dramatic major events in a creature's life in every program in order to make each show interesting. This in turn encouraged me to keep on making programs that were not only different from anything that had been done before, but different from each other as well.

The following year we made a similar program on woodpeckers, another overlooked family of birds. Here, we didn't try to emphasize the beauty of the birds so much as the unique evolutionary niche they have literally carved out for themselves by their total dependency on wood, and the astonishing way of life they have created, well, by using their heads. It's a survey film that covers most of the twenty-three or so species of woodpeckers that nest in the United States, but it makes a radical departure from all our other films in that it contains no music—an omission for which, incidentally, we've received nothing but praise. Music, we thought, would be superfluous over the rich punctuation of natural sound effects in a forest, and we were glad for the chance to experiment with a suggestion from several *Wild America* fans, to the effect that music could be intrusive or overbearing on a natural setting.

As with the owl and hummingbird films, we again chose a familiar family of birds, representatives of which can be found all over the country, from the acorn woodpecker of California to the favorite red-headed woodpecker of the eastern forests. And once again, it was not an easy film to make. In a sense, I suppose it sounds like this kind of a project should be a piece of cake. Woodpeckers are almost everywhere, even tapping away at the roofs and siding material of people's houses, so why not just take a walk and roll some film. But we wanted to try to film behavior that had never been shown before, such as what happens deep within the nest a downy woodpecker hacks out of a hollow tree.

We set to work to find out, with hammer and nails and saw and blinds. Fortunately, downy woodpeckers, like many others, often return to the same area and use the same nest cavities year after year. So, well ahead of the mating season, cinematographer Bruce Reitherman went about doctoring up a dozen nest holes where downies were known to have lived. He sawed the back part of the tree away and then replaced it carefully so that it could be easily removed again. Then, when a pair of downies did choose to reuse one of the nests he had prepared, we slowly moved a blind closer and closer to the

The aptly named acorn woodpecker will riddle a tree with storage holes all summer, and pack away one acorn per hole during the fall for winter feeding.

The familiar downy woodpecker often nests in the same tree year after year, a habit that enabled us to fit a hollow tree trunk with a removable panel and film the birds inside the nest.

tree. Whenever the male and female were both away, the back section of the tree was then removed to film the baby downies after they'd hatched. Carefully, we accustomed the parent birds to our lights, just as I had the kingfisher mother a couple of years previously, and gradually Bruce was able to film the adult birds entering the nest cavity undisturbed, giving food to their babies.

We included quite a number of scenes of baby birds in the "Woodpeckers" film, and we decided to emphasize this age of bird "childhood" in our next all-bird program, "Woodies and Hoodies." The title refers to two of the world's most beautiful species of ducks—the wood duck and the hooded merganser. Both are native to North America, both seek out wooded waterways for their spring mating rituals, and both compete for large tree-hole nesting sites in the same areas. But there the similarity ends. "Woodies" are brilliantly colored dabbling ducks that feed primarily on plants and weeds near the surface of ponds and streams, while "hoodies," handsomely marked in stark black-and-white patterns, are diving ducks that swim underwater much of the time, hunting fish and other small aquatic animals. The foraging habits of these two species allow them to avoid competition for food— but nesting is another matter.

Competition for nesting sites—including man-made nest boxes—complicated by the difference in feeding habits, often leads to some interesting and amusing mix-ups. We were fortunate in being able to film the story of one of these on location at Iroquois National Refuge in western New York State. Our observant cameraman noticed that a hoody hen had laid at least one of her eggs in the nest box of a woody mother. Sure enough, when the eggs hatched and the woody hen coaxed her offspring to jump out of the nest and take to the water, the last one to leap was—you guessed it: a lone "ugly duckling," a little hoody.

But the little duckling didn't remain ugly—or lag behind— for long. For a while he was content to paddle around in shallow water among the reeds, where the woody mother felt safe with her brood, feeding on pondweed, seeds, and an occasional minnow. But it was when danger threatened, in the form of a swimming garter snake, that the complications began. The little hoody by then had become the leader of his sibling woodies, and his first instinct was to lead them toward deeper open water where *he* could escape by diving. The woodies, on the other hand, had no idea what diving was all about, and were more than eager to follow their mother back into the safety of the reeds. In the program's poignant final moment, the young hoody, torn between inherited instinct and learned loyalty, decides to follow.

Several species of ducks resolve their competition for nesting sites in a similar way, by laying eggs in each other's nests and leaving the care and raising of at least some of the young to another species of duck—or to fate. Yet to my knowledge no one had ever made a film that examined the consequences of this phenomenon. And of course, we didn't know what to expect when we began filming. Even now, I still wonder about what evolutionary survival value this kind of competition might have, or whether it ever occurred before people came along and reduced the number of large standing dead trees available for these ducks to nest in. But what interests me most is the unintentional way in which competition actually becomes cooperation, as the mother wood duck accepts and looks after both her natural and "adopted" offspring with equal concern. Nature's strategies for survival sometimes seem bizarre and indirect to us, but they often work in surprising ways.

One such cooperative strategy that works more directly, and has been fine-tuned over countless generations, is that of the relationship between the ruffed grouse and its age-old predator, the goshawk. Although many wild hunters pursue

Two of America's most beautiful ducks, the hooded merganser (above) and the wood duck, compete for nest sites, though not for food. This can lead to confusion when mixed broods grow up together.

the grouse, none is so superbly equipped to catch it as this short-winged member of the hawk family. On the other hand, no bird is better prepared by nature than the fast-flushing grouse to escape the swift talons of the goshawk. Equally matched, the two birds have evolved in unison, each contributing to the refinement of the other's most successful survival tactics. This was the point that I wanted to make in "The Grouse and the Goshawk"—to show how closely intertwined are the lives of the hunter and the hunted, and how each contributes to the long-term survival of the other.

Another parallel to the relationship between these two birds is the dependency of the ruffed grouse upon aspen trees for an important part of its food supply. In the program, we show three range maps: one for the slender aspen, the most widespread of all our trees; one for the grouse; and one for the goshawk. All three species are found across most of northern North America, and it's interesting to see how closely the three maps coincide with each other. In other words, the ranges are almost the same for each species.

A prime part of this range is in the northern Cascade Mountains of Oregon and Washington, which is where we set this film. Although the grouse does not feed exclusively upon aspens, these trees are especially important in the spring, when their long male flowers, or catkins, provide the major source of protein energy which the grouse need to meet the demands of the coming mating season. Like other types of grouse, the ruffed grouse has developed elaborate courting rituals, centering around the "drumming" rite of the male. In the early spring predawn, the cock takes up a conspicuous position on a log or rock and proceeds to beat its wings in an increasingly rapid staccato that sounds like a fluttering drum. Females are attracted to this display, and when one proves receptive, the result, a few weeks later, is a brood of a dozen or so precocial chicks that quickly learn to follow their mother along the fern-covered forest floor.

The goshawk, a fast, fierce raptor that eats small mammals such as the gray squirrel shown here, also hunts the ruffed grouse, an equally agile and fast-flying bird.

The goshawk, by contrast, usually produces only a pair of eggs, which are incubated by both parents in a nest of sticks high above the ground, often in the limbs of an aspen. The lone chick that we filmed hatching from its egg required the care of both parents for several weeks until it developed the flight feathers it needed to leave the nest. We wanted to show that neither species has an easy time of growing up, and as it turned out, by autumn, when the goshawk fledgling was ready to hunt on its own, half the original brood of grouse chicks we were following with our cameras had already succumbed to other predators, such as foxes and coyotes.

Despite the highly specialized features the juvenile goshawk has inherited for capturing and killing prey, with the onset of winter its life doesn't get any easier. Though its eyesight is among the keenest in the entire animal kingdom, that of the grouse is scarcely inferior. The goshawk's short, rounded wings are ideal for maneuvering swiftly through dense woods—but so are the grouse's. And the grouse has its own specialized abilities, such as burrowing deep into a snowbank to escape detection or pursuit. Move for move, predator and prey are matched like two skilled chess opponents, each bringing out the wiliest traits of the other. This seemed to me an ideal example of the predator-prey relationship, in which the life-or-death moment of predation is the high point for which both contenders have been preparing—not only for all of their individual lives, but for eons of evolutionary time.

Making these bird programs has been a constant challenge, but the rewards, in terms of audience response and my own personal satisfaction, have been consistently high. These shows, on the beauty and glory and freedom of birds, will continue to keep us busy for quite a while. But during the same period that I had begun making and planning these bird programs, I had begun to think about other, odder forms of wildlife as well.

TWELVE

KILLER MICE
AND
OTHER ODDITIES

The wandering shrew shares with the grasshopper mouse a high metabolic rate and a willingness to fight to the death. This encounter between two wandering shrews ended with one killing and eating the other.

As it became clear that *Wild America* was a success and would continue airing on PBS, I realized that I didn't want to film only rare and endangered species, or large and medium-sized mammals, or the familiar birds of our backyards. I wanted to tell the whole story of North America's amazing diversity of wildlife. And to show this variety would mean seeking out the unusual, the bizarre, even the unattractive. If I wanted to give people a better understanding of and appreciation for *all* wildlife, I would have to include lower, lesser-known forms—and I wasn't sure how viewers might react to that. Let's face it: some animals just give people the creeps.

I'm not saying that I'm overwhelmed with personal affection for snakes or spiders or toads myself, though I did usually keep a snake or two around when I was young, just for fun. But personal affection for certain animals is beside the point. What's important is that all of them are essential and indispensable to a healthy planet. I thought that if I could convey a sense of respect and appreciation for those slippery-slimy eels and lizards and frogs, or for those skittery little rodents some people disdainfully call "vermin," then people might better understand how the whole sphere of life is dynamically interconnected, and become that much more aware and tolerant of this complex world we live in.

I'll admit that I do have my own limits. I'm not planning to do a film anytime soon on the secret life of the housefly, or even the deerfly. Their small size requires too much work with a macro lens, and I'm basically interested in animals that relate to other animals in a more visual and active way, or in animals that have some unique feature that helps them fill an evolutionary niche that no other animal can fill. The armadillo, the walrus, the manatee, the musk-ox, the hybrid sharp-tailed/ sage grouse, for instance, all fascinated me, but hadn't fit easily into other shows. The longer I studied these unusual creatures, the more I was convinced that freakish appearance or outlandish behavior often had a distinct survival value. I felt that if I could show this effectively, people might be more inclined to look kindly upon such "Animal Oddities."

What I saw was that each of them were examples of evolution in progress, whether ultimately headed for success or for failure. The armadillo, for example, belongs to the edentate group, an ancient order of primitive, toothless mammals which includes sloths and anteaters. Its long ears and snout, lizardlike skin, and bony-plated shell make it an odd-looking creature indeed. But this armor is the perfect defense against predators, especially when the animal curls up to protect its softer underparts. Armor, however, is only one of its defense techniques; it can also tunnel rapidly into the ground or flee quite quickly to a nearby burrow. Equally peculiar is the fact that it always gives birth to quadruplets, all four of which are the same sex. The survival value of this feature is more difficult to determine than that of its armor, but however unusual these characteristics, they must serve the armadillo well. Despite human incursion into its territory during recent decades, the animal has been steadily expanding its range.

The walrus, the manatee, and the musk-ox are other examples of creatures whose appearance, though a source of amusement or even derision to humans, has a positive survival value. The walrus's scruffy but sensitive whiskers, which give it such a funny face, help it locate clams and other shellfish, which it then scrapes off the ocean floor with its tusks. These huge ivory protrusions are also used in fighting rival males and in defense against other animals. The walrus's great, blubbery form is actually the most streamlined and well-insulated shape possible for efficient locomotion in icy arctic waters. Similarly, the female manatee's conspicuous breastlike appendages evolved not to lure lonesome sailors to their doom (manatees are what some sailors called mermaids), but to provide food for young manatees. The female uses her flippers to cradle her nursing young to her breasts. As another example, the musk-ox's horned head may be homely, but when a band of musk-oxen form a tight, outward-facing circle enclosing their calves, no pack of wolves is going to get past those lowered, hairy heads. And the long, ground-sweeping hair covering the rest of its body makes for an extremely effective blanket.

The only creature we filmed whose adaptations seem to have negative survival value is the hybrid grouse we showed in "Animal Oddities," a result of occasional interbreeding between a sharp-tailed grouse and a sage grouse. It so happens that the males of both these species attract females by performing elaborate, but distinctly different, courtship dances. The birds stomp, run, and leap in the air in frenzied patterns which are nonetheless recognizable by, and appealing to, females of the appropriate species. Unfortunately, hybrid offspring do occur, and a male hybrid of these two birds does not know which dance to perform, while the hybrid female is confused about which to respond to. Hybrids are sterile in any case, but even if they were fertile, this state of affairs would

The walrus certainly qualifies as an "animal oddity," but its ivory tusks and sensitive whiskers are used to obtain food, its tough hide and thick layer of blubber keep it warm, and its powerful flippers propel it gracefully through icy Arctic waters.

hardly be conducive to further reproduction. If it happens with any increase of frequency, both species would seem to be headed toward an evolutionary dead end.

But where evolution is concerned, only time can tell, and nature's long, slow processes have a way of taking some surprising turns. So, too, does the process of filmmaking. My interest in the strange and unusual was certainly a factor when it came to doing another early program, the one we titled "All-American Animals." We omitted the more obvious examples, such as the bison, the bald eagle, and even the wild turkey (which Benjamin Franklin once lobbied to make our national bird), in favor of less predictable ones. The opossum, for example, North America's only marsupial and one of our most ancient "animal success stories," was a fitting nominee.

Some people might not consider this odd, slow-moving animal good for much but the stew pot—not that it's much good for *that*, either. But the lowly opossum, usually nicknamed just plain 'possum, has been expanding its range for the past couple of decades. It is at present found in most parts of the country, and even in many cities, so part of its success lies in its ability to get along with humans.

I was even more fascinated by the unique structure of the reproductive organs of both sexes. The scientific name of the opossum is *Didelphis*, which means "double womb," and refers to the bifurcated, or Y-shaped, female uterus. This type of womb is found in other kinds of mammals, including all marsupials. But in few other American species has the male evolved so intricately to fit the female. The male opossum's penis, like that of all marsupials, forks outward into a matching Y, so that each prong is able to fertilize one branch of the female's uterus.

As a naturalist, I was aware of the 'possum's other unusual qualities, too. I knew that its prehensile tail allowed it to feed without descending from the relative safety of the treetops. Also, that it is one of several creatures that "play dead" by slipping into a state similar to shock and emitting a foul, musky odor repellent to most predators, whose feeding instincts are triggered by the act of killing active prey. Only scavengers would touch an animal that already seemed—and smelled—dead. And I thought that both the opossum's unique reproductive structures, and its method of giving birth to premature young, which later develop for two months in a nippled pouch, were entirely appropriate to this prototypical mammal as specialized means of ensuring the survival of its kind.

There were still plenty of opossums left in my old stomping grounds in the woods of Arkansas, so I returned there to film them. Luck and good timing were on my side, and I was able to get some terrific footage of a pair mating. And with the help of cinematographer Robert Billings, I did some discreet carpentry work on the hollow trunk of a dead tree, inside of which was a 'possum den. Through the opening we created, we were able to film the birth and subsequent precarious migration of the tiny infant opossums through their mother's fur to her pouch. What's so interesting about this is that until as recently as 1954 no one knew how baby opossums were born. For centuries there were only legends as strange as the animals themselves—such as that the male's penis was Y-shaped in order to fertilize the female through her nostrils, and that she subsequently *breathed* her tiny offspring out through her nose into her pouch. More modern speculations, such as that the mother used her mouth to place her babies one by one in her pouch, proved equally false.

I was proud of our never-before-filmed material on how opossums actually mate, and especially of the footage of still-embryonic infant opossums being born and migrating, pink and naked, through their mother's tongue-slicked wet fur to her pouch. This material, I felt, was worth including, even at the expense of leaving some other perfectly deserving "All-American Animals" out of the program. Our aim was to include a sampling of animals and birds that represent some of the "pioneer" qualities that we still admire: the persistence of the 'possum, the toughness of the peccary, the resourcefulness of the pronghorn.

At about the same time we were planning the "All-American" program, we decided to make at least one film each season on cold-blooded creatures, or the "creepy-crawlies," as we affectionately began to call them. The first of these programs was to be on "Fascinating Fishes," because there had never been a good overview program done on North American freshwater fishes. Most fish films have been made

The opossum uses its prehensile tail to hang from branches while feeding, and to carry nesting material to its den. Even more remarkable are its reproductive habits and its ability to play dead.

on game species, where you see two guys in a boat on a Saturday afternoon, talking about how much fun it is to catch bass, showing off their casting skills, and joking about the one that got away. Few of those films ever go underwater, and few show behavior such as mating or egg-laying. Most are told from the perspective of a sportsman or a biologist, never from that of the fish itself.

In "Fascinating Fishes," and later in the three "Cutthroat" programs that grew out of it, we went underwater, right in with the fish, and literally filmed a "fish-eye view" of the important events of their lives. I always try to avoid the sportsman/consumer point of view because of its superficiality, and I usually even steer away from the purely biological approach. Though we're very much concerned with factual accuracy, our purpose is to show how enjoyable wild creatures can be for their *own* sake, and to present them insofar as possible from their own point of view. What do these animals "mean" to themselves, how do they fit into their own natural world, and in what ways can their lives enrich ours?

In "Fascinating Fishes," knowing that we could cover only a small fraction of the more than 700 North American species of fish in a half-hour program, we went for a combination of the common with the odd and unusual. We gave one of the starring roles to the paddlefish, an extremely primitive, monstrously odd-looking, and truly fascinating creature whose history at the hands of human beings epitomizes what has happened to many fish populations in this country. Up until our own century, the rivers of the Mississippi basin teemed with these 200-pound fish, whose spoon-billed appearance, according to fossils, has changed little during the last three or four hundred *million* years. The species was already well-evolved fifty million years *before* the first dinosaurs appeared, and continued to adapt to changing climates and water conditions long after the great reptiles had succumbed.

But now, since people have taken over the rivers and "improved" them by straightening their channels and locking up their flow behind dams, this living fossil that has survived through so many eons may not make it into the next century. That paddlefish have modest but definite requirements for spawning was not discovered until 1960, and by then most of their major upstream spawning areas had already been blocked off by huge dams. Since then, the situation has only gotten worse, until now there are virtually no breeding populations of paddlefish left in the wild.

There are, however, still a lot of paddlefish. This is primarily due to the fact that in the 1930s they became a popular sport fish, taken by snagging them with treble hooks as they gathered for their now-ineffective spring spawning season. When their native numbers began to mysteriously decline, an intensive research program was undertaken at the Blind Pony Hatchery in Missouri to discover a way to artificially hatch and raise them—something that up until that time nobody had been able to do. The efforts of biologist Jerry Hamilton resulted in a program that, by hormonal manipulation of the fish in a laboratory, each year produces several hundred thousand

Huge mouth agape, the primitive paddlefish has been swimming America's inland seas and waterways since before the dinosaur age. Now, because of river control projects, this fascinating creature no longer breeds in the wild.

fingerling-sized paddlefish which are released into the lakes and streams of this creature's ancient habitat.

As long as people are around to maintain this laboratory technology, as long as there are those who care about the fate of the paddlefish, or at least about the revenues from fishing licenses, this species, which swam the warm primeval oceans of our continent long before giant ferns were pressed into coal, will continue to feed, its great mouth agape, in at least a few lakes and rivers. But can a creature that cannot reproduce on its own—simply because it has no place to do so—truly be called "wild"? It's an unanswered question, and one that applies to many other species. All I can say is that I wish the paddlefish well, I wish it a place to recover its wildness, and in hindsight I wish that we had given it a full half-hour program of its own, a program that might have stirred others into helping to make that place a possibility.

While fishes, because of their edibility and appeal to sportsmen, might not be offensive to most people, the real test of audience response came with doing a program on "Remarkable Reptiles." Except for exotic fare like fried rattlesnake fillets or alligator sausage, and except for such dubious events as rattlesnake round-ups or alligator wrestling, reptiles in general are unattractive as food or as objects of sport. In fact, many people consider reptiles in general, with the possible exception of turtles, to have little or no redeeming social value. But ecological value is another thing, and I was counting on the open-mindedness and curiosity of PBS audiences to enable them to revise their prejudice against members of the four groups of North American reptiles—snakes, lizards, turtles, and crocodilians (which include both crocodiles and alligators)—and to recognize the importance of these creatures.

Sure enough, we received so much positive feedback from "Remarkable Reptiles" that we were encouraged to proceed with two other programs that had already grown out of material we had filmed for the reptile program. Originally, for instance, we had wanted to include a couple of minutes on kingsnakes in "Remarkable Reptiles." We had two cinematographers, George and Kathy Dodge, film several North American kingsnakes, a pair of kingsnakes mating, and the subsequent hatching of a clutch of eggs. But when we sat down to look at the work print, there was so much interesting material that we decided we would save it, with the idea of giving the kingsnakes a program of their own.

This show would be another survey program, one that would introduce for the first time on film the diversity of the twelve North American species of this colorful and fascinating reptile. It would show, close up and in slow motion, some of the incredibly odd and intriguing aspects of the kingsnake's behavior. Though gentle and shy with humans, kingsnakes are aggressive constrictors in the wild, immune to rattlesnake venom, and perfectly capable of dispensing with their deadly cousins. Their ability to devour other snakes, combined with their brilliant coloration and regal appearance, made this program's title almost inevitable: "King of Snakes."

The program opens with a sequence that dramatically demonstrates the kingsnake's aggressive nature toward its own kind. Two males cross paths while pursuing a female, and the resulting encounter is a writhing, twisting, wrestling match, with the rivals rolling over and over on the ground, entwined like living corkscrews. The male with the most strength and endurance, of course, wins the female, and a subsequent sequence shows what in my opinion is one of the all-time most sensuous mating sequences I've ever seen in a wildlife film. Slowly and gently, the male rubs his throat along the back of the female, while caressing her with the length of his body, stimulating her to receive his advances. Not only is it a beautiful scene visually, but there is no mistaking the message that techniques of gentle persuasion have at least as much survival value as do those of force and combat.

The resulting brood of young kingsnakes are shown next, hatching from a clutch of leathery white eggs. The baby snakes, while not exactly cute in the way we'd respond to a bunny rabbit, do have the appeal of, say, a baby space creature emerging from its ship for a well-meaning visit to our planet. The young snakes, all hatching at the same time, immediately disperse in separate directions, and grow by feeding

I enjoy making programs not only about the wildlife we love but also about the less appealing species that are just as important and amazing. The Texas rat snake shown here can swallow an egg larger than its head.

primarily on rodents and other snakes. Some become part of the food chain themselves, providing a meal for a hawk, an owl, or a raccoon.

Another amazing sequence shows a kingsnake capturing, constricting, and devouring a rattlesnake longer than itself. Of course, the snake cannot measure the length of its prey in relation to its own body size. Nor, after beginning, can it *stop* eating what it killed, or "save some for later." So its body must have the built-in capacity to stretch lengthwise as well as in diameter to enable it to digest all that it has engorged. The result of being nourished by this meal is also shown, as the kingsnake ultimately outgrows its skin and sheds it, a rarely observed event that is shown scale by iridescent scale in extreme closeup. Snakes are the only reptiles that shed their skins in one piece, and as the kingsnake emerges, it leaves behind a colorless remnant of a newly colorful creature that well deserves its title.

The second program that grew out of "Remarkable Reptiles," "Snake Dance," came about because we had wanted to include in "Reptiles" a phenomenon that I had heard about, but never seen on film. During the spring mating season, and possibly at other times, I had read that male rattlesnakes coming upon each other will sometimes perform a spectacular sort of "combat dance." Neither attacks the other with its

Shy and harmless to humans, the kingsnake is an aggressive constrictor immune to the venom of rattlesnakes, which it devours head first.

fangs (which is interesting enough, considering that rattle-snakes use their poison for defense as well as for securing food). Instead, in this highly ritualized dance, both males rear up with as much as half their body length swaying above the ground, and by deft intertwining, each tries to wrestle the other to the ground.

In theory, it sounded almost normal. Two creatures, lethally equipped by nature, yet restricted by nature to a method of resolving dominance in a way least likely to be detrimental to the species as a whole. Not much different, really, than white-tailed deer bucks using their antlers in ritual combat. Or than humans using conventional weaponry instead of nuclear missiles to settle disputes. But that was theory, and as far as practice was concerned—well, in practice I couldn't find anyone who had ever actually seen this weird phenomenon, much less anyone who thought it could be photographed. Even a researcher in Utah who had spent thirty-five years in the close company of all kinds of rattlesnakes told me that this ritual happened rarely and totally without predictability. He had never seen it, he said, and chances were, nobody ever would while they waited around with a camera in their hands. Very encouraging.

Thanks to a more enthusiastic research contact, however, I later found myself in Oklahoma entering a hibernation den of rattlesnakes that had never read the rules about how rarely and secretively this "combat dance" was supposed to be performed. A relatively short time after we had set up lights and camera, a pair of big male western diamondbacks went at it as if they'd been trained by a professional wrestling coach—weaving and twisting and entwining, each trying to throw the other down, as we rolled film. Stimulated by the musk of sexually receptive females in the cave, they kept at each other for hours. There was nothing to do but sit there and keep the cameras running—until one of the female rattlesnakes tried to investigate *me* a little too closely. But no harm was done,

In an Oklahoma cave, two male western diamondback rattlesnakes sway and wrestle for hours, each trying to pin the other down in a hypnotic combat ritual known as a snake dance.

and we did emerge from the mouth of that hibernation cave with another *Wild America* "first," an extraordinary behavior pattern that had never before been captured on film.

Instead of editing this amazing footage down to a brief minute or two of the "Reptiles" program, I thought it would be interesting to play with another idea I had been thinking about. Most people, carried away by the continuity of action sequences in a half-hour film, don't stop to think that normally it would take weeks, months, or even years to see that much of an animal's life in the wild. Only because of extensive planning, skillful cinematography, and sheer good luck, are we able to record as much as we do of wild behavior on film. And here with "Snake Dance," I thought, was an opportunity to slow down the edited action almost to real time—the real time of the rattlesnake, in a tense and hypnotic trance, sensual and swaying with suspense. I wanted the audience to have the chance to see for themselves what goes on in a given half-hour of an animal's life. Of course, the film reveals other things as well, such as the benefit of caves to certain forms of wildlife, the difficulty of getting into a dark cave past heaps of lethargic but nevertheless large and lethal diamondbacks, and the lore and truth of rattlesnake behavior in general.

So this pursuit of the odd and unusual—the unseen, un-loved, and overlooked—has produced some very satisfying results. And I must admit that one of the most amazing animals I've ever filmed happens to be—yes, a mouse. Now, I had always thought of mice as meek and timid, definitely suited by nature to be a prey species. In fact, my staff jokingly —and not very sensitively—refers to rodents as "Nature's nachos," and we have even considered doing a program on them by that title. But one winter evening while sitting home by the fire, I was researching the kinds of creatures that feed on deer mice, and I was startled to find on the list of predators the name of another mouse: *Onychomys*, the grasshopper mouse.

Immediately I forgot about deer mice for the moment and went off on one of those tangents that sometimes prove more rewarding than the straight lines we set out to follow. I had always been interested in predators, but a predatory *mouse* . . . now, *that* was unusual! And the more I learned, the more

Fiercely carnivorous, the tiny grasshopper mouse stalks crickets, scorpions, and snakes. Upon making a kill, it emits a shrill whistling howl like a miniature wolf.

astonished I became. The grasshopper mouse, I read, is one of the few carnivores in the rodent family, a fierce and fearless hunter whose dietary preferences range from the bizarre to the just plain dangerous. Crickets, cockroaches, stinkbugs, and scorpions are among its favorite prey, and it's also known to relish lizards and snakes, including venomous varieties like the desert-dwelling coral snake. Nocturnal, it stalks its prey with the stealth of a weasel, kills with a swift bite to the neck, and then, to top it all off, throws back its head and lets out a piercing whistle like the howl of a miniature wolf!

It sounded pretty incredible, like the kind of larger-than-life genetic mutation imagined in a Grade "B" science fiction movie. But, weighing in at only about an ounce, this animal is hardly "larger-than-life." Nor is it, as I was to learn, in any sense imaginary. Oddly enough, though, beyond a basic description, information on the real animal and its everyday habits was at first hard to come by. The books in our office library told of two species of *Onychomys*, both native to the western half of our continent. The northern grasshopper mouse ranged from Canada south to Arizona and fed mostly on grasshoppers and other insects. The southern grasshopper mouse, or "scorpion mouse," was found from Arizona and Texas south into Mexico, and was named for its favorite form of prey. Other than that, and a few hints at some of the grasshopper mouse's other, equally un-rodentlike behavior patterns, the books had little to say.

Apparently few people had ever observed these nocturnal mice, and certainly few if any had ever filmed them. I thought that it was only right that *Wild America* should be the first to bring this amazing little North American predator to the attention of wildlife lovers, and from what I'd read, I didn't think it would be too outrageous to call the proposed program "Killer Mice."

But where to start, with so little information available? In planning our programs, our first step is to thoroughly research everything that can be learned about an animal. This means budgeting not only time for reading up on the facts of a creature's life, but also money for making phone calls and writing letters to specialists familiar with that particular animal in the wild. A lot of this work comes easy for me, because of all the reading and footwork and filming I've been doing for years. But in the case of the grasshopper mouse, I had to rely for information on documents dug out of musty university libraries, and track down people who sometimes didn't sound very sure they'd really seen what they said they'd seen.

What I found out, though, convinced me that this was a project worth trying. Predatory behavior in a rodent was interesting and unusual enough, but it also turned out that the grasshopper mouse is one of the few species of rodents, or of any kind of mammal, in which the male shares parental duties with the female. In fact, when more than one litter is born during the season, the older siblings also help care for their younger brothers and sisters. This contrast between ferocious hunting tactics and cooperative family behavior, both of which obviously have survival value, was just one of a number of surprises. The big question was how and where to film these forms of behavior.

We finally narrowed our options down to two choices: filming northern grassshopper mice on the shortgrass plains of eastern Colorado, or filming southern grasshopper mice on the desert grassland fringes of Chiracaua National Monument in southeastern Arizona. It would have been easier to stay in Colorado, but I opted for Arizona because I was excited by the possibility of seeing for myself, and capturing on film, a dramatic encounter between a "scorpion mouse" and the deadly prey for which it's named. And Arizona was the better place to find scorpions. It was also less densely vegetated, which meant that small animals would be more visible.

Once again, I was thankful that I'm not a one-man team. Months before we planned to begin production, Greg Hensley, my staff artist, time-lapse cinematographer, sound man, and jack-of-all-trades, headed south in his van to scout specific sites for filming time-lapses and, hopefully, for filming the mice themselves. This is the kind of indispensable footwork that, with ten programs a year to produce, I no longer have the time to do.

In this case, Greg's talents had to include watching out for his personal safety. The Chiracauas are one of the prime birding areas in the United States, nesting grounds of the rare and colorful, elegant trogon, and of several species of hummingbirds rarely seen north of the Mexican border. But a person can't spend too much time looking up at birds, because this dry spine of mountains is also—and for good reason—known as the rattlesnake capital of the world. The area quite literally crawls with a dozen species of them. Greg reported that the first time he stepped out of his van, he came across three, and heard a fourth, in the space of a half-mile walk. But this time, we weren't out to film rattlesnakes.

Fortunately, Greg also reported that he found many signs of mice in the sparse grasslands that stretch out below the cactus-studded foothills of the Chiracauas. Camping out in his van under bright desert stars, he listened for a piercing, high-pitched "howl"—the faint but unmistakable hunting cry of the grasshopper mouse. During the days, he searched for other tracks and signs. The scorpion mouse has a peculiar fondness for a certain southwestern stinkbug called a pinacate beetle. When molested, this shiny black insect emits a foul-smelling spray from its hind end. Young mice are treated to a dose in the face until they learn to grab a beetle head-on, jam its rear end into the sand, and devour it head-first, like an ice-cream cone. The unpalatable beetle abdomens are left behind, often dozens of them dotting the same pile of sand. Greg came across one of these "burial grounds" (or ice-cream stands, depending on how you look at it), and from there located a nearby burrow. He also located several burrows by following the tiny tracks leading away from the wet mud around streambeds and watering holes and across wind-blown sand hills.

Most mice live out their lives eating seeds and grains in a space of less than an acre. But grasshopper mice, being carnivorous, actively patrol and defend territories of five acres or more. By the time Greg and I headed south together the following May, potential filming problems were already mounting up. Not only would we have to set up electrical-generating equipment to film at night, but I envisioned myself hauling around lights and cameras like some manic modern-day Diogenes with his lantern, struggling to keep up with a creature not much larger than my big toe.

The problems we encountered, however, turned out to be quite different from the ones we expected. Rattlesnakes, for instance, were not a threat, since we made enough commotion setting up our gear to keep even a boa constrictor, if there had been one, at a respectful distance. But strangely enough, the mice themselves, once they became accustomed to our equipment and the lights at night around their burrows, seemed not to pay much attention. In fact, we found them to be exceptionally bold and curious—for mice. They wouldn't quite eat out of our hands, like a pinyon mouse I'd once enticed with chocolate at Lake Powell, Utah. But neither did they avoid us. In fact, we got to know several of them as distinct personalities, and they really told their own story as we filmed them. We called them by wacky names like Stud, Momma, Fat-Boy, and Stubby, though needless to say we omitted such anthropomorphizing from the completed program.

Photographing wildlife at night is always problematic. You must create enough artificial light to properly expose your film, and yet the very reason you're out there filming at such an inconvenient hour in the first place is because wild animals prefer the cover of darkness. How do you get them accustomed to the lights, so they will behave naturally? The answer is, "Slowly." We filmed around several burrow sites, and in each location we set up a 600-watt main, or "key" light, plus a second 600-watt "fill" light. The key light, raised on a pole about twenty feet to one side, provided the look of very bright moonlight. The "fill" light, placed about twenty feet off to the other side and reflected off a silvery umbrella, acts stereoscopically to give more realistic definition to the deep shadows cast by the key light.

Our standard practice in nighttime situations is to use a timer to turn the lights on during the middle of the night, at first for a few minutes, gradually working up to a couple of hours, before we attempt to roll any film. This method allows the animals to accustom their eyes and readjust their natural habits before we introduce the even more radical element of a scuffling person with a quietly whirring camera. In fact, several times at different locations—one in particular near a coulee watering hole—we set up a timer to turn the lights on two hours a night for three full weeks before we even attempted filming. By then, a totally nocturnal family of ringtails in the neighborhood completely ignored the light. In the case of grasshopper mice, since they have such a high rate of metabolism, we weren't surprised that they came out of their burrows to hunt on the very first night despite the lights. They need to eat the equivalent of about half their body weight daily, which means they're probably ravenously hungry most of the time. But what was astonishing was that they didn't immediately run off into the perimeter of darkness surrounding the filming area. Or, when they did, they seemed to do it for other reasons than fear, and they soon returned.

Although we sometimes use battery-powered lights, in this case we ran a generator a hundred yards away from the filming site. Noise is another factor that's hard for wild animals to deal with, so we try to cut down on it as much as possible. By using a long power cord and a small, quiet generator, and by pointing the muffler exhaust in the opposite direction from the filming site, we can resolve most of the problem as far as electrical lighting and noise are concerned. We also use the practically silent Arri HSR camera as much as possible. In the case of "noisy" cameras like the Arri S or the high-speed Photosonics, we muffle the sound of the camera with a padded cover called a "barney," or "blimp," to keep it from bothering the animals, and also to prevent it from being picked up by our sound-recording equipment. For "Killer Mice," just as for our other programs, we wanted to record not only any sounds made by the animals, but also the ambient background tones —what you might call the "atmosphere" of the place itself. The hoot of an owl, the night breezes, the subtle sounds of the desert stillness. . . .

Speaking of owls, at one of the Chiracaua filming sites we enjoyed the company of a burrowing owl that perched in a nearby mesquite bush for several nights, just out of range of the lights. It kept an eye on us, and we kept an eye on it. Obviously, this was the owl's hunting territory, and we suspected that it was probably far more interested in participating in the show as a mouse-eating "co-star" than it was in watching us film. And sure enough, when it finally did choose to swoop down and grab one of the mice scampering around, Greg had his camera rolling, and this event was incorporated in the program to show that grasshopper mice number among the hunted as well as the hunters.

There were also a number of coyotes around, probably hunting mice also. We could hear them yipping, and sometimes we'd see a pair of eyes glowing yellow in the darkness just beyond the lights, but we never did get to film them. Both coyotes and foxes eat other mice, of course, but according to some of our research they regularly avoid grasshopper mice because of their strong musky odor. It would have been a fascinating theory to test on film, but we had no chance to do so. Typically, the "wish list" we start with for any particular project is usually less than half checked off by the time we wrap up filming. But it serves a purpose all the same. In preparing these wish lists, or cinematography outlines, we become aware of what to look for, of what implications an animal's behavior might have. That way, we're aware of the possibilities for filming if an opportune situation should present itself.

We began filming in May and were still at it in August, which is one of two rainy seasons on the Arizona desert. This proved to be an advantage in one way, but a rather scary disadvantage in another. The advantage was that the rain brought out insect hatches, which in turn kept the mice busy at night catching them. The insects also drew other creatures, such as the pallid bats native to the area. These, of course, were impossible to film while they were flitting around up in the dark above our film site, but we were fortunate enough to photograph them when they landed on the ground and hopped around after crickets and grasshoppers. Hopping around on the ground is not the dignified sort of flitting you'd expect from a bat, but those fat crickets no doubt provided an easier meal than darting on the wing after tiny midges.

Another advantage related to the rainy season was that during the days it was easy for Greg to collect insects, too. He kept a menu of beetles, bugs, and all kinds of insect delicacies on ice in the beer cooler we used for storing film. In the evenings, when the mice appeared, cooler temperatures kept these pre-chilled dinner items from becoming immediately active and moving out of camera range too quickly, which in turn helped keep the mice in view.

The big disadvantage of the rainy season was the storms themselves. We weren't in much danger from flash floods, except in one place where we were filming in a narrow arroyo. But have you ever seen an electrical storm on the desert at night? It's like a war zone. Jagged blue flashes and flares constantly zigzagged like white-nerve X-rays, intense crackle and thunder moved closer and closer, gales of wind tried to blow our lights halfway to Nebraska. And there were Greg and I sitting out in the middle of nowhere, with the metal generator and its electric lights beaming an open invitation to disaster, and us with no protection but the flimsy blind we were filming from, which was probably an attraction to the overcharged electricity rather than any kind of protection from it. In a way, it was all pretty exciting, but not the kind of thing you'd want to push your luck with. When the hair on the back of our necks began to stand up and tingle, it was time to forget filming and flatten ourselves to the ground.

Those lightning storms are another example of what I tell people about when they ask me about the dangers of wildlife cinematography. They usually mean, "Aren't you afraid you'll get hurt or killed by a wild animal?" But the fact is, wild creatures present far fewer inherent hazards than the environment itself. Avalanches, blizzards, icy cliffs, sea rocks at high tide—these are the real factors against which you have to measure your degree of preparedness and your skill, luck, and wits. For me, wild creatures are far more predictable and far less whimsical and treacherous than the elements. Long familiarity with grizzly bears, for instance, will teach a person to think like a grizzly and to anticipate what it might do. But who can think like a lightning bolt, or predict when and where it will strike?

Since I had to leave for a week's filming elsewhere, Greg did much of the filming at this time, setting up his mini-tripod with the camera trained on a burrow entrance, lying flat on his stomach behind it with a piece of camouflage material thrown over his head and the camera. When the mice emerged, he'd roll film. If they ran off, he could follow for only a limited distance because of the generator cable. He soon learned that instead of chasing them around, it was easier to film them as they hunted in a nearby patch of prickly pear cactus. They apparently felt more secure hemmed in by the cactus pads, and, intent on hunting, wouldn't run off as easily as they did on the open desert floor.

In this way, and because of their general boldness and aggressiveness, we were able to capture a number of different predation sequences between the months of May and September, including a spectacular fight between a pair of grasshopper mice and a large scorpion. We filmed several encounters between mice and scorpions, but this one was outstanding for several reasons. First, this particular scorpion, a member of Arizona's largest species, was almost as big as the mice. Second, the fight persisted fiercely for almost ten minutes, with the combatants rolling and tumbling and biting and stinging until we thought that neither side could possibly emerge as victor. The poison of most North American scorpions is not lethal to a healthy human, but a tiny grasshopper mouse would presumably be much more susceptible. Repeated stingings, however, failed to daunt the mice. From my observation, it seems reasonable to suppose that some degree of immunity must be involved. In any case, we can speculate quite strongly since the mice *were* stung but did not die.

I say "mice"—the third reason we found this fight so impressive was that it was such an amazing example of cooperative hunting technique. A male and female mouse took turns harassing the scorpion, one attacking the head while the other tried to bite off the stinger, one keeping up the battle while the other rested, until the scorpion was just plain exhausted. The mice in this case didn't actually kill their victim. Instead, the scorpion finally gave up and let itself be eaten. The victorious pair shared a good-sized meal.

This fight was one remarkable example of cooperative family behavior in grasshopper mice, behavior that contrasted so strongly with their merciless hunting methods. We wanted to include other examples in the program. But filming a family of mice getting along together cooperatively inside their nest-burrow proved more difficult than filming any predation or hunting sequence outside of it. As I'd already learned from other projects, filming in burrows is at best a headache, and when Greg got the shovel out of the truck to prepare a burrow for filming, I found myself wishing I had another appointment elsewhere.

We worked at night, waiting until the pair of adult mice had left their burrow to get it ready for filming. Grasshopper mice have several types of burrows—usually single-entrance

ones for storing food and for defecation, and double-entrance ones for nesting. We dug a pit next to what we hoped would turn out to be a nest-burrow, where the female might give birth to a litter. We smoothed off the sides of the burrow's tunnel and nest cavity, closed off the cross-section with a pane of glass, and covered it so that the mice would not feel exposed, if—and it was a big if—they chose to remain there.

In fact, we had to repeat this process several times until we found a pair that continued to use their modified burrow instead of leaving it to dig another one a few yards away. By that time, I did have an appointment in Texas to film for a month or so. Greg also went off to film at other sites, leaving the mice to either adjust to the new conditions and begin raising their young, or to leave and dig another burrow. Luck was on our side this time, and when we returned a couple of weeks later, a pair of mice had not only remained in the burrow, but had produced a litter of three baby mice.

We used a piece of equipment called a "snoot," which funnels a cone of light into a closed area, to illuminate the tunnel and nest cavity of the burrow. In this way, we were able to document the complete story of this family of scorpion mice, including the role of the male parent mouse in caring for its young. Both parents brought food into the nest for the babies, both participated in grooming rituals with the young mice as they developed fur, and when their offspring were ready to begin hunting, both parents often set out from the burrow with them.

Greg and I couldn't follow every movement they made, so we did film other juveniles learning to hunt, as well as other adults, which means that "Killer Mice" is an edited composite, rather than the actual story of a single family of mice. But in this way we were able to show all the important things regarding the behavior of these amazing creatures, about which so little had been previously known. Even more gratifying, through the camera's eye we discovered a few things,

The grasshopper mouse is one of the few mammalian species in which the male actively helps the female raise their offspring. While one hunts, the other guards the burrow—or they may both hunt together.

such as the cooperative hunting tactics of adult pairs, that weren't even mentioned in the literature I had been able to find. Not that I have any delusions of scientific grandeur, but I do feel that adding new dimensions to what is known of wild creatures can be one of the many rewards of wildlife cinematography. We were to have even more success in this way the following summer. If our next subject didn't exactly qualify as an "animal oddity," at least it well served our essential point: that every creature is important to the whole, and that even a cold-blooded animal may have crucial value to an entire ecosystem.

THIRTEEN

CUTTHROAT

The "Cutthroat" underwater film crew—me, David Huie, and John King—ready to dive in our Viking dry suits. Essential in cold water, this awkward gear nonetheless gave me a good case of claustrophobia.

Y ellowstone! Ever since I can remember, that name has made images of wilderness and wildlife dance in my head like no other place on earth. It's the first of our forty-seven national parks, set aside by law in 1872 to protect the beauty and integrity of its unique landscape, and to ensure continuation of the rich diversity of native plants and animals found within its boundaries. It can be considered one of our most successful national parks, too: virtually all the species known to have existed when the park was established are still present today. It's also the largest national park in our lower forty-eight states. Yellowstone's two million acres could easily hold Delaware, Rhode Island, and the District of Columbia, with at least enough room left over for a buffalo wallow or two.

Numbers, however, are meaningless when measuring its unforgettable impact on those who have seen it. Within that territory lies some of the most magnificent wilderness south of Alaska, and some of the most varied. Rims of snow-capped peaks encircle great bowls of stunning landscape. Under bright blue Wyoming skies, cloud shadows float over seemingly endless expanses of lodgepole pine. Forests give way to rich open meadowlands, clear cold lakes, rushing streams, precipitous waterfalls, and colorful sheer-walled canyons. Tucked away in the most unexpected places are boiling thermal springs, bubbling mud pots, and breathtaking giant geysers which regularly spout to the sky.

Yellowstone's "living geology" is evidence that it is also among the most ancient of our parklands. With the exception of the Grand Canyon, nowhere else can you see so much of the earth's ongoing history exposed. For two-and-a-half billion years, gradual evolutionary processes were punctuated by periods of sudden and violent change. Great volcanoes erupted into mountain ranges, mountain ranges were worn down into high plains, the plains were invaded by primeval seas, and the seas were again pushed back by newborn mountains to begin yet another immense cycle.

Here the primal heat of the planet's interior comes closer to the surface than at any other location known. Molten rock lies only a few thousand feet below the mask of topsoil and green vegetation, and the park's thermal pools and geysers are directly connected to, and produced by, this ancient generator. Above ground, solid rock stands exposed along the roadsides, a visible record of vast changes: dark basalt and black obsidian from volcanoes, warm-colored shale and sedimentary formations pressed hard by ancient seas, later sliced by rivers into steep canyons of red-gold and ochre.

Rock Yellow River Land, the Native Americans called it —an appropriately straightforward name for a grand and glorious land. My love affair with this "first lady of our national parks" began when I was only nineteen, and she was pushing forty-nine million years. But we didn't let the age difference bother us. Since our initial meeting, I've returned again and again, drawn by her wealth of wildlife, to film bighorns and grizzlies, moose and elk, grouse and ospreys and eagles.

Remote and serene, Yellowstone's Hayden Valley is a prime example of the park's spectacular landscape, and one of the main reasons I wanted to spend a summer there filming the cutthroat trout.

Marshall, who shares my love of Yellowstone, and I had been thinking about some new program concepts for *Wild America*. And I realized that we were simply looking for an excuse to spend an entire summer filming our favorite park. Still, there had to be a good reason, a solid film concept, behind the trip. Several factors finally helped us decide our program subject. One was that we wanted to show a facet of Yellowstone that hadn't already been seen on film, preferably one that couldn't be viewed from a car or even from a campsite. Also, we had recently been emphasizing smaller, often overlooked creatures, like reptiles and fishes. Fishes! I suddenly recalled all the great times Marshall and I had enjoyed fishing in Yellowstone Lake and adjacent rivers for—cutthroat trout!

Such a program would certainly fulfill our desire to explore and reveal a totally unknown aspect of Yellowstone—the view from underwater. How many of the park's millions of annual visitors had ever considered the whole watery realm of wildlife hidden just beneath the surface of all that magnificent scenery? We would film the program in Yellowstone Lake, where the fish fed, and in the surrounding rivers and streams, where once a year they spawned. And we would shoot as much of it as possible from a fish-eye point of view. Although our intention was to make a film about fishes, rather than fishing, such a program would surely attract the attention of fishermen, as well as nature lovers generally, across the country.

For another thing, the cutthroat trout certainly met our criterion for a "smaller, overlooked creature." Fishermen take some 300,000 of them each summer from Yellowstone Lake alone, so they certainly aren't an undiscovered species, but no one had ever documented the story of the fish themselves. Also, we had just completed "Fascinating Fishes" and had already received some very positive feedback on it, so here was a chance to go into more depth on a single species, a gorgeously marked trout, a member of the salmon family.

I know that many people don't exactly think of fish as "wildlife," but they truly *are* wild creatures—capable of living without human support, adapted and attuned to the requirements of their habitat, and subject to incursions by predators, including—and sometimes primarily—humans. For these reasons, their underwater world is as exciting as the land-bound domain of elk or grizzlies or eagles. In fact, as we were to find out, Yellowstone's aquatic and terrestrial realms are really one interconnected and interdependent ecosystem. This theme became one of the main strengths of "Cutthroat."

The cutthroat is the only native trout in the park and essentially, the most important fish in Yellowstone Lake. In fact, the lake holds the world's largest inland population of these brilliantly colored, scarlet-throated trout. They are also the primary fish in the surrounding rivers and streams. Hence, they are central to the food chain of the entire area. We decided the program would be most interesting if it were planned around this concept of what the trout eat, and what eats them. For instance, they're a food source for animals from grizzlies to otters to other cutthroat, and for birds of prey like the bald eagle that winters in Yellowstone, the white pelican that flies in from the Gulf of Mexico, and the osprey that migrates up from South America every spring. They are also a food source for scavengers like the seagull that flies in from the Pacific coast to spend the summer. All these creatures, to name only a few, subsist and raise their young to a great extent on a diet of trout.

I wanted to show how vital this fish is for so many creatures, and to explore the whole web of life that depends upon this single species in a place where the natural food chain continues unbroken by human intervention. But where to start? I began by sending for the pamphlets and fishing brochures supplied by Yellowstone ranger stations, and by collecting every bit of information I could find on cutthroat in general and on the variety native to Yellowstone in particular. In the process, I learned more about the park itself, and especially about Yellowstone Lake.

In all the times I had traveled to Yellowstone, I had never really become acquainted with this enormous body of fresh water. To me, and I'm sure to most other visitors, the lake was just a big flat shimmering surface, beautifully reflecting the surrounding mountains. As I did my homework, however, I learned that Yellowstone Lake—20 miles long and 14 miles wide, with more than 100 miles of shoreline—is America's largest high-altitude lake, 7,700 feet above sea level. But it's

more than just surface. Its average depth is 137 feet, dipping
down to 320 feet in some places. Over a million acre-feet of
water flow annually from the lake north into Yellowstone
River, which means that all of the water in the lake would be
replaced every ten or eleven years.

Not only is the lake high, wide, and deep, it's also cold.
That's one reason it's such a superb habitat for trout. The
colder a given body of water, the more oxygen is dissolved in
it, and the better it can support the breathing requirements of
an active fish like the trout. The temperature of Yellowstone
Lake averages about 60 degrees Fahrenheit at the surface,
and about 40 degrees only a few feet below—and that's in
July! However, though the lake is a fine environment for cold-
blooded cutthroat, for warm-blooded creatures like cinematographers this vast underwater wilderness was not quite so
inviting.

Or more accurately, it was very inviting, but underwater
filming was somewhat of an unusual dimension for *Wild America*. It required a different kind of mental and physical preparation than even the most strenuous trip to the desert or the
arctic. But let me back up a step. In originally planning the
Wild America series, I had decided that we would focus on
native wildlife of the North American continent, from coast to
coast. And stop there, right on the shoreline. Any sea creatures that depend on the land, as do the seals and sea lions
who come ashore to give birth and to breed (which we filmed
for the program, "Season of the Seals") were within our limits.
But we decided to leave the whole realm of ocean depths and
their inhabitants to the admirable talents of the Cousteau family and others. But while planning the cinematography outline
for "Fascinating Fishes," I realized that in order to do justice
to the concept of North American wildlife, I would occasionally have to go underwater, into streams, rivers, ponds, lakes,
and estuaries, to document the lives of wild creatures that
lived both above and below the surface.

Making the "Cutthroat" program was the first opportunity
I'd had to do this in such a thorough manner, and to do much
of the filming myself. I welcomed the chance. Of course, I
wouldn't be doing it all by myself. For one thing, Marshall
would be there, with his skill at all things technical. And so

would several others with whom I had worked closely on past programs: David Huie and John King would be the additional cameramen, and Greg Hensley would come along to film scenic time-lapses and help handle sound recording. Actually, we were all pretty interchangeable as far as skills went, and everyone got a chance to do a little of everything. Even my brother Mark was able to join us for a few days. And because I don't like to be away from my family for long stretches of time, Diane and Hannah also came to visit for brief periods.

The mental and physical preparation for this trip centered mainly around diving. Like most people, I'm not as at home underwater as I am on land, but I enjoy the technical challenge and the sensation of that strange, totally different world below the surface. I had done some scuba diving in the warm waters of the Mediterranean, the South Seas, and off the coast of South America, but only a little cold-water diving. David and Greg also had quite a bit of scuba experience, and all three of us were certified divers—in warm water, anyway. John King had done some snorkeling, but very little actual scuba diving, so he took it upon himself to arrange for an instructor to give us all refresher lessons. In fact, we opted to take the entire scuba certification course, with an emphasis on cold-water diving and orientation in swift currents.

While we were taking the diving course, we were also lining up other equipment for the trip. Our summer-long "vacation" in Yellowstone would really be a full-fledged working expedition, and we had the good fortune to receive donations for the project from a number of nationally known manufacturers. One of our biggest needs, especially for exploring Yellowstone Lake, would be a boat, and the Boston Whaler Company gave us the use of three of them. Each would serve different but essential purposes. A twenty-five-foot "Frontier" work boat would get us and all our gear to our various base camp destinations; a thirteen-foot outboard runabout would be useful for exploring; and a ten-foot inflatable raft would serve as a mobile diving platform. To power each of the boats, we were loaned four engines from Johnson Outboards; two big ones for the work boat, a medium-sized engine for the runabout, and a small motor to power the raft.

Our diving gear was also donated, most of it from Cressi-

Sub, which gave us everything from signal floats to weight belts and buoyancy compensators. And Viking America helped out with dry suits. Since the lake is so cold, we opted for these dry suits over wet suits for diving. They're much warmer, though hardly as stylish or form-fitting. Big, flappy affairs, they're more like what you'd see old-time sponge divers descending in. They work by trapping body heat in a layer of air between you and the polyethylene suit. To keep even warmer and drier, you wear long underwear—"long johns"—underneath, and the suits have a kind of rubber seal which fits tightly around your neck and wrists, a feature which was to prove very claustrophobic. We accepted the loan of all this gear, from boats to weight belts, with the explicit understanding that we would not advertise for any of the companies during the program, although viewers would occasionally recognize a logo or a company name on equipment we were using. Both the companies and our production benefited by this arrangement.

As usual, a great part of our preparation was research. To this end, we relied a good deal on reports that had been done over a period of many years by various biologists working for the National Park Service, the state of Wyoming, and the U.S. Fish and Wildlife Service. By paying attention to the results of their studies, and by making a number of phone calls to people working on current research projects, we were able to save ourselves a lot of time and headaches when we arrived in Yellowstone. We would have a good idea of the right spots to go to in order to film ospreys on their nests, for instance, or when to be in a certain location to film a hatch of caddisflies.

By the time we loaded up four trucks full of gear and headed for Yellowstone, each of us had our own copy of a neatly typed shooting script that our associate producer, Paula Smith, had researched and written. It told us when the trout did this or that, where we could find and film them doing it, when various populations of insects hatched, all about the depths and temperature range of the lake, where we could and couldn't take our power boat, what islands of nesting birds were off-limits, and what predatory species might lend themselves to specific sequences. But after we arrived at the park, the actual production schedule, as is so often the case, departed quite radically from our script. Little did we suspect that we'd find so much *else* to film, so many more concepts that related to the trout. After the first week or so, the shooting script ended up as kindling for our campfire. Not that it was a waste of time—it wasn't—but by then we had memorized most of the important details and had already begun to explore possibilities we couldn't have known about beforehand. Basic research is important, but the real story usually unfolds according to unforeseeable circumstances. And so we picked up the boats, which had already been delivered to the park, and set out from Bridge Bay Marina across Yellowstone Lake.

Our exploration began on the southeast arm of the lake, in a remote area of the park that included some of the wildest wilderness left outside Alaska. One thing that we wanted to show was the way in which Yellowstone Lake is "backwards." That is, in most warmer lakes, the smaller fish of any species, usually called fingerlings, keep to the shallows along shore, where they are safe from predation by larger fish. The adult fish, on the other hand, stay in deeper water near the middle of the lake, where the water is cooler and their gills can take in more oxygen, and where they wait for fingerlings to stray within feeding range. In Yellowstone, the situation is opposite. In the first place, the water temperature is cold enough for larger fish even in the quiet shallows. And for another, crustaceans such as freshwater shrimp and forage fish such as redside shiners—both of which the adult trout prey on—are limited to the shallower water near shore. So that's where the mature trout spend most of their time. They are rarely found at depths greater than forty feet.

The small trout find what they need to feed on, mainly plankton (small, floating animal and plant life) out in the open, deeper parts of the lake. Here they are protected from being preyed upon by the larger trout, because each age group tends to live in different parts and depths of the lake. Of course, if there were other species of predatory fish in the lake, it might be a different story, but it was amazing how the cutthroat, as a typically cannibalistic piscine species, has evolved to protect itself from itself. Not only that, but there is another interaction that incidentally helps the young fish survive. Redside shiners, which were introduced into the lake from other park waters by fishermen using them for bait, eat many of the same food items that young trout feed upon, but spend time in shallower water where they are preyed upon by the larger trout, so competition with young trout never really becomes a factor.

After spending our first night camped fifty miles from the nearest road, we were in the water before the sun cleared the horizon the next morning. Diving was no simple process, what with putting on seventy-five pounds of dry suits, weight belts, buoyancy compensators, and compression instruments, and gathering up another fifty pounds of camera gear, batteries, and lights. I recall one morning watching a pair of mergansers —superb diving ducks that feed on smaller trout—as they floated near our boat, and wondering if those natural divers could possibly be looking down their fish-eating bills at all our paraphernalia. "Plan your dive and dive your plan!" had been our instructor's favorite motto, but when we got forty feet down, encumbered with all that gear, there were times when it was hard enough just to remember to breathe.

Meanwhile, Marshall, the technician of our crew, was circling around in the little runabout, setting out diving buoys. In that remote part of the lake it was unlikely that any other boats would come close enough to bother us, but the buoys were one of many regulations we were required by park officials to comply with. It was a crowded summer in Yellowstone, and the buoys would act as a warning to any passing power craft to steer clear. If anything on the surface went wrong, Marshall would be there to correct it. David Huie made himself responsible for preparing and checking out the diving gear. Because of the lake's high altitude and frigid temperatures, extra precautions were required with our scuba tanks and their gauges.

When we were finally ready, in we went, headfirst and backwards, with a splash.

Because of the clarity of the water, the place where we were diving, off Plover Point, looked deceptively shallow. The bottom there is about forty feet deep, composed of obsidian sand, boulders, fine clay, and silt. By sea level standards, Yellowstone Lake is relatively barren. It lacks any large crustaceans such as crayfish, but abounds in smaller versions of that same family, especially two types of very small freshwater shrimp that feed along the bottom on microscopic organic matter. These in turn are fed upon by trout. Keratin from these shrimp and from the shells of insects is responsible for turning the flesh of the trout its characteristic salmon-red color.

Low nutrient concentrations and cold temperatures limit the life forms in the lake, but a number of plants have adapted to survive along the lake bottom. On one of our first mornings underwater, we made a strange discovery: in some places the entire lake bottom was carpeted with tiny "balls," varying in size from a BB shot to a marble, and on up to about an inch-and-a-half in diameter. And they were all colors—red, green, yellow, purple, and orange—covering the bottom like a layer of tiny Easter eggs, a foot deep in some places. One gentle wave of the hand along the bottom would lift them by the thousands, and they would swirl up to engulf us, floating and whirling magically. Some seemed to be attached to each other, but most floated free. Some were hollow, others were dense and solid, like grapes. Later we learned that they are called nostoc, and are a form of blue-green algae that grows only in pristine waters. Each ball is actually a complete colony of tiny single-celled organisms.

In filming these balls I learned something significant about the bottom of Yellowstone Lake. Even though the water was only 300 feet deep or so, the actual bottom of this 600,000-year-old volcanic lake bed is more like 1,500 feet deep. Years ago, when park rangers measured the depth of the lake with a weighted plumb line, they found that its waters rested not on a solid bottom of sand, but on an incredibly deep layer of fine silt. We knew from experience just how pervasive this layer was, since every time we would try to stir up the balls and film them dancing in the water, up would swirl the silt, clouding the water and blinding our film attempts. Only by swimming very slowly just above them, letting our flippers raise the balls, could we film them without the silt.

During one of these attempts to film nostoc, I had the closest call of the summer. First of all, I must admit that I wasn't really all that happy with the claustrophobic feeling the tight-collared dry suit and all that entangling camera gear gave me. My problem stems from a time when I was down in Belize in Central America, diving with some old rental equipment from a poorly run dive shop in one of the little villages. I was seventy-five feet underwater when the regulator hose blew off and I was forced to make it to the surface with what little air was in my lungs. I had to exhale slowly the whole way up, so that my lungs wouldn't explode. Although I tried to keep calm, I was stricken by the thought that I was "wasting" air that I just might need before I reached the surface. There are probably few things more nightmarish than the feeling of being underwater and out of breath. That last ten or twenty feet feels like miles, and until that final, miraculous moment when you take a life-granting breath of air, it's just agony. And that first bad experience was in the warm-water tropics, with nothing to encumber me but the lightest of diving gear! In Yellowstone, the many pounds of heavy, dangling, tangling equipment emphasized my claustrophobia, and the thought of blown regulator hoses was foremost on my mind whenever we dove. One day, we were pushing ourselves a bit hard, finishing up a two-hour session of filming nostoc balls underwater. David and John had already used up their air, surfaced, and were just floating around near the shore waiting for me. We had been working together, one person on lights and one on camera. I had made the mistake of staying behind and trying to do both myself. When I started coming up, lights in one hand and camera in the other, both my legs suddenly seized up in spasmed cramps. I couldn't move them, couldn't use them to kick myself up to the surface. Instead, like dead weights, my legs and all the extra weight in my hands were pulling me back down. And with both my hands full of equipment, I couldn't grab and inflate my buoyancy compensator, either, which would have helped me to surface.

I could have dropped the camera or the lights, but $40,000 worth of equipment would have plummeted into the silt, and I would never have found them again. I still don't know how I made it, but I finally broke the surface gasping for breath and weakly signalled to John and David, who quickly swam out to help me in.

It took us a couple of weeks to get our bearings in the lake, to work out the bugs in our underwater filming methods, and to film all we could of the cutthroat's story there. We shot footage of adult cutthroats feeding in the shallows, immature ones in deeper water, and got close-ups of many of the items in their diet. Although their impact on the trout is not yet fully understood, we also documented the presence of several other species, such as the bottom-feeding long-nosed sucker and the redside shiner, that had been accidentally introduced into the lake from Yellowstone River and other nearby waters. We even filmed some freshwater leeches, which attach themselves to the trout for occasional meals, though in this wide-open aquatic environment they pose no serious parasitic threat either to individual fish or to the cutthroat population as a whole. Since there are plenty of trout, a leech simply fastens on long enough to take its small fill of the trout's body fluids, then drops off and drifts until it needs to find another trout. In an undisturbed ecosytem, there's plenty for everybody.

We had planned to explore and film more of the above-water portions of Yellowstone Lake, but the mature cutthroat were already moving out of the lake and up into their spawning streams, and we wanted to follow them. Like their cousins the salmon, cutthroat return to the headwaters of the same stream

High, wide, and cold, Yellowstone Lake supports few species of fish other than the cutthroat trout. This long-nosed sucker is a scavenger accidentally introduced into the lake from Yellowstone River.

in which they themselves were spawned, braving massive waterfalls, trickling shallows, and other obstacles to get there. The spawning season begins in May, peaks in late June, then continues through July and even into August. Males mature at three years and females at four years, and by the time they are ready to reproduce both sexes are at least one foot long. With brilliant scarlet slashes under their throats, the trout seem almost "dressed for the occasion" during this season. The males glow most brilliantly, flashing reds and golds to attract the female.

The spawning fish also attract the attention of visitors to the park. In fact, watching the fish is now as popular as catching them. Hundreds of people gather each day at Fishing Bridge to watch the cutthroat as they gather near the mouth of Yellowstone River to spawn. The Bridge was closed to fishing in 1973, after decades of unregulated fishing caused the collapse of the cutthroat population in the 1960s. At the beginning of the century, trout of enormous size were common, but for many years there was no limit on the size or number of fish that could be taken.

Now the cutthroat have recovered, and although no fish have been taken recently that come close to the old records, angling for cutthroat in Yellowstone's waters provides what many consider the best fishing experience in North America. The best thing about it for me is that, although in some streams fish of any size can be kept, and others are catch-and-release or closed entirely, in Yellowstone Lake and its tributaries only trout *under* thirteen inches are allowed to be caught. Such commendably wise management procedures leave the larger, older fish to produce more offspring, and ensure that a certain percentage of the cutthroat will be reserved as food for the park's original inhabitants.

Our first destination on Yellowstone River was LeHardy Rapids, seven miles above the place where the river flows north out of the Lake at Fishing Bridge. Although most trout leave the Lake to spawn in smaller streams, some which already live in the river actually return to its mouth in the Lake itself and do their spawning in full view of the spectators on the Bridge. But filming those trout would not only have been too easy, it would not have shown the most dramatic spawning behavior, which includes migrating upstream against the full force of rapids.

For us and for *Wild America*'s viewers, LeHardy Rapids promised to be an exciting and rewarding filming experience. Here we would film the fish as they grouped tightly together in large numbers, gathering strength for a run at these tremendous rapids, where the water velocity averages five feet per *second*. At LeHardy, from anyplace along the shore we could see cutthroat lined up by the dozens, row on row in the frothing pools at the bottom of the rapids. They were so tightly packed that, leaning out from some boulders along shore, I could scoop up slippery fish in my bare hands. It made me feel like one of those early nineteenth-century explorers who reported being able to catch fistfuls of fish without using so much as a line or net. But I let the fish go immediately, realizing that it needed every last bit of its strength for conquering the rapids above.

From among the rows of gathered fish, first one would leap, then another, then another, according to some mysterious impulse. Though most of the trout seemed to require two or three attempts, a few would make it up the falls on their first jump. That moment—when a cutthroat leapt in a living arc straight up out of the water—was one shot that we wanted very much to get because of its stunning power and beauty. But that moment was completely unpredictable, and lasted less than a second. Because we really wanted to see and savor the graceful arc of the leaping trout against the dramatic backdrop of the bubbling waterfall, we chose to film it in extreme slow motion, at 400 frames a second, with the action slowed down sixteen times normal speed. At 400 frames a second, it takes only about thirty seconds to expose a ten-minute roll of film. If nothing happens while film is rolling and the camera is trained on a spot where the fish didn't leap, then—presto!—you've just wasted one roll of film.

We wasted many. We waited along with the fish at LeHardy Rapids for three separate afternoons, while the sun was just right, low in the west, and the fish would be lit with the prettiest light—and each of those three times, we shot six rolls of film. Out of eighteen rolls of film, we threw away fourteen without even sending them in for processing, since we knew no fish had leaped and saw no need to pay for developing footage of nothing but tons of falling whitewater. We did end up with some great fish jumps, but they were expensive to get!

The suspense of waiting for a fish to jump, and then glimpsing that bright slash of color curve its way up against the tumbling whitewater, was thrilling, kind of like watching a fireworks display, but far more satisfying. Even with all the expended film, I never did get impatient. But I was eager to film them from underwater, as well. The trout made holding their places against the current at the bottom of the rapids look easy, but for us, one wrong step and we'd be swept downstream. What the water lacked in depth, it more than made up for by being fast and rough, and the slick black boulders strewn about the riverbed made footing extremely treacherous. Several times apiece, one or the other of us would slip and go shooting off downstream, bobbling under the current, and disappear around the bend. Then the unlucky one would have to struggle ashore in an eddy, crawl out, and waddle several hundred yards back upstream in his diving suit to our filming location.

A cutthroat leaps LeHardy Rapids, a major obstacle in its spawning journey up Yellowstone River. During the spawning season, fish gathered below the rapids preparing to jump become so tightly packed that they can be scooped up by hand.

Finally we found a hole behind a large boulder where the current split and swirled in one place and the footing was better, and there we went underwater. It was then that we began to discover that cutthroat were anything but the stupid, scaly, cold-blooded creatures that fit some people's standard image of a fish. For one thing, life in the wild has taught them what to approach and what to avoid, and we observed over and over what appeared to be a learned survival behavior. When we were underwater with them, swimming in a horizontal "fish position," they showed no fear of us and would come quite close. But the moment one of us stood up and loomed partially above the water, the fish would dart quickly away, at which point we had to stop filming until they relaxed and returned. But as long as we stayed underwater with the trout, even our cameras and lights seemed not to bother them.

In fact, one of the most exciting moments of the entire summer was discovering that the trout would actually accept their natural food, such as stonefly nymphs, right out of my hand. I'd catch the nymphs underwater by overturning small rocks and plucking them off the undersurface of the rock. Then, grabbing a boulder with one hand to brace and hold myself against the current, I'd slowly reach out the other hand with the nymph in it. Sure enough, several fish would turn and show interest, and then one would flip past my fingers, open its mouth, and take the nymph. With the river pounding all around me, the sensation of feeding the wild trout was a bit different than that of having a bighorn lick salt from my hand, but nonetheless it was an exciting experience, and one that John was fortunately able to capture on film.

Beyond feeding the trout, the nymphs themselves opened up a whole new filming opportunity. A good deal of the cutthroat trout's success in Yellowstone depends on a series of superbly timed "super-hatches" of various insects in and along the river, which supply much-needed protein for the fish during the arduous season of spawning. Millions of immature caddisflies, stoneflies, and mayflies rise to the water's surface to shed their last nymphal skin before starting life as adult winged insects. They pause at the surface for a short time, adjusting to the new medium of air, before flying off to nearby rocks and plants, and as they hesitate, the trout feed furiously upon them.

Underwater, some of those little larvae are just amazing, and they definitely opened my eyes to the wonder of "bugs." At this immature stage, several species carry their temporary homes around with them. If you turn over rocks in a stream, you may find caddisfly larvae looking like tiny bits of sticks with sand and debris stuck to them. Each species has its own characteristic construction and appearance. The secreted stick-home of the caddisfly acts as both camouflage and hard-cased protection until the nymph is ready to shed it in the process of being transformed into an adult—the stage at which it is most vulnerable to being consumed by a trout.

The large stonefly, or salmonfly, is one of the most important insects in the life of the Yellowstone trout, and is eaten both as a nymph and as an adult. Relics of an ancient past, these insects colonized the continent during the ice ages. We filmed the nymphs underwater and as they crawled ashore to molt out of their shells. The newly emerged adults stay hidden near the particular shore where their metamorphosis took place for most of their short two- to three-week lifespans. Most cannot feed at all during this time, but they can mate. And so they do, day and night, writhing frantically in a sort of insect orgy. It's not uncommon to find several dozen clustered together, copulating in the shade of a leaf. The males even try to mate with females of other species, but with little success, since their copulatory organs are compatible only with female salmonflies.

It's while they're mating that the salmonflies provide a wealth of food for several animals in addition to the cutthroat. Near the ground they're snapped up by leopard frogs and salamanders. In the air, they become a feast for gulls and other birds. And near the surface of the water, of course, they become a tasty mouthful for the trout. But many survive, and we were able to film a typical female, with a ball of fertilized eggs stuck to the tip of her abdomen, leaving the land and returning to the river to deposit her egg-laden burden. Her tiny contribution to the ecosystem offers the promise of preservation not only to future generations of salmonflies, but to cutthroat as well, and it stands as one small symbol of the fertility of that world where land and water meet.

Another important food source is the caddisfly, a mothlike

insect in its adult form. In its larval form, however, the cad-disworm is a strange little caterpillarlike creature that moves around with its home surrounding it. We encountered a number of these larvae with a variety of bristly homes stuck together from pine needles, gravel, or tiny bits of plants. The bristly projections probably work two ways, by trapping food particles and by discouraging predators. We also examined underwater mayfly nymphs, with gill-like structures that look like tiny leaves fluttering along their abdomens. They, too, provide important trout nourishment in both their immature and adult form. And we filmed midges hovering in the air above the stream, or swarming in thick clouds above the tree-tops, moving up and down in unison. You've probably seen them, looking like wisps of smoke in the shadows, or like a bright mist of raindrops as they dance in the sunlight.

Fascinating as these creatures were, it was time to move upstream with the cutthroat. The trout eat along the way, but

Almost as interesting as the cutthroat itself are the insect nymphs and larvae it eats. Here the film crew waits and watches as a salmonfly emerges from its larval shell as an adult.

stop for nothing until they have reached what instinct tells them is their destination. And as they moved farther up Yellowstone River and into some of the most narrow and shallow streams, we followed—all the way to a tiny tributary of the Yellowstone called Grizzly Creek. The fish were searching by instinct for the right conditions: six to ten inches of water flowing over a three- to six-inch-deep gravel bed, and a water temperature of 40 to 60 degrees Fahrenheit. A trout's breathing rate varies with the amount of oxygen dissolved in the water; the colder its temperature and the faster it moves, the more oxygen it holds. In the bubbling, oxygen-rich river, the fish breathe very little. In the lake, they breathe a bit faster, and in the shallow, sun-warmed headwater streams their breathing rate jumps to a rapid level.

First the brilliant red-gold males arrived at Grizzly Creek, then the slightly less colorful females. While we donned camouflage nets so as not to scare the fish, and set up our cameras along a six-foot-wide stretch of the creek, the water was thrashed by male cutthroats fighting among themselves for females. Their fights sometimes continued up to the very moment of egg-laying. The female, meanwhile, used her tail and body motions to dig out a nest, or "redd," in the gravel, about two or four inches deep and up to a foot across. Finally, poised side-by-side over the redd, a pair would complete their ancient mating ritual, the female emitting her eggs simultaneously as the male, with a shudder, released his sperm. Mating between the same male and female would be repeated several more times until the female had exhausted her supply of approximately 1,000 eggs. Then, again using her tail, she would cover up the redd with gravel, and both trout would swim away downstream. Many of them were destined never to return to the Lake—an average of 15 percent of the adults die from the rigors of the spawning season—but by then they have left behind their legacy.

As for the eggs, only 200 to 300 of the original 1,000 will survive to hatch about a month later. By summer's end, no more than a half dozen or so tiny trout, one to two inches in length, will have survived to make their way downstream. Most of the offspring perish due to changing water temperatures, fluctuating stream flows, and a whole gamut of predators large and small. But the remaining survivors are by that time well along their way into the deeper waters of Yellowstone Lake, where they stand a better chance of making it to adulthood.

In order to tell the complete story of the cutthroat, we, too, had to return to the lake. We'd documented not only the journey of the cutthroat to its spawning grounds, but the life stories of many of the fascinating little creatures it fed on along the way. Now we wanted to film some of the animals for which the trout were a significant means of survival. While we were traveling up the Yellowstone River to Grizzly Creek, we managed to get some footage of a family of otters, and also some on grizzly bears, both of which enjoy trout over any other carnivorous items in their omnivorous diets. But along with those two mammals, the most voracious consumers of trout are some of the park's larger species of birds. And our research had indicated that the best place to film birds would be in specific locations on Yellowstone Lake.

Surprisingly, the major predator of the cutthroat in Yellow-

Of the approximately one thousand eggs deposited by a female trout, only two or three hundred will hatch and develop into "sac fry." Of these, no more than a half-dozen or so will survive the journey downstream to Yellowstone Lake.

stone is the white pelican. In fact, the plentiful supply of trout is what draws the pelican, which we normally think of as a seashore bird, inland as far as the northern Rockies to nest. These great-billed birds fly into Wyoming in graceful squadrons from the Gulf Coast in early spring, when ice and snow still cover some areas of the park, and settle into their traditional breeding colony on the Molly Islands in the southeast arm of the lake. This particular rookery is the last such pelican nesting area in Wyoming, the only one within the borders of a national park, and one of only fifteen now remaining in the world.

Of the four kinds of waterbirds that nest in Yellowstone, the pelican alone has been persecuted. In the early 1900s, it was blamed for depleting the trout population. Of course, no one bothered to take into account the fact that the Bureau of Fisheries was at that time removing upwards of 187 million trout eggs a year from the park for restocking elsewhere. And the second strike against the pelican was its role as primary host for a species of tapeworm that infests the trout. Consequently, the pelican's eggs were destroyed and the babies as well as the adults were killed. Today, trout eggs are no longer removed, the tapeworm is now known not to be a serious threat to trout populations, and the pelican has come to be appreciated for what it is—a unique and interesting creature that presents no threat to the cutthroat, and no serious competition to humans for the fish. In fact, the pelican is not even in competition with the osprey, for whom trout are the major portion of its diet, since the pelicans take larger adult fish in the shallows, while ospreys dive primarily for the smaller immature ones out in deeper water.

Although we had had no trouble getting close to the cutthroat underwater, getting close to the pelicans and other nesting birds was not so simple. For one thing, in the area around the Molly Islands, powerboats are prohibited in order to protect the nesting birds. To get any footage of the colony itself, we had to row in with our equipment. Even then, we had to content ourselves with photographing from the less-than-stable raft before moving on to Frank Island, a favorite habitat for another fish-eater, a scavenger from California— the California gull.

Like the pelican, the gull is drawn to Yellowstone's abundance of trout. About half its diet consists of that fish, found washed up dead on shore or scavenged from fishermen and other predators. On Frank Island, we got much closer to the birds, and filmed a flock of screaming gulls as they haggled over a scavenged fish. We couldn't have asked for better timing when, almost as if on cue, into the scene floated a big pelican, which glided back and forth a couple of times along the shore, almost as if patrolling a gang of raucous juveniles. Then, just as the gulls were rising and squawking at each other loudly over the fish, the pelican suddenly flapped its huge wings and flew in low to steal the pecked-over trout.

We were a little surprised to see that the proud pelican is not above scavenging from the scavengers themselves, although with its enormous bill (which can hold about three gallons of fish and water) and its unique habit of generally diving in a group to surround the fish in a circle of submerged bills, it seemed to us that this individual act of thievery was almost a kind of joke. I was also surprised to learn that, although the pelican's bill is exceptionally useful for scooping fish out of the water, it is not used for carrying them. Instead, the prey is partially swallowed and held in the bird's gullet or esophagus for transportation back to the nest, where it is regurgitated into the throats of its young.

The bald eagle is another fish-hunter with even fewer reservations about scavenging. In fact, it seems to prefer stealing food from ospreys and other birds to catching its own. Unlike the pelican, the eagle has no oversized bill for scooping fish, and so must depend on the accuracy of its eye-foot coordination and the sharpness of its talons to get a meal. It's a master hunter, but in Yellowstone, unlike most other places, the eagle seems to prefer birds to trout. Fishes figure significantly in its menu—about 25 percent—but of those only about half are trout. Waterfowl are the mainstay of the eagle's diet. (By contrast, in other places fish may provide 95 percent of a bald eagle's meals.) No one has been able to offer a satisfactory answer for why the situation might be different in Yellowstone, but since such a high proportion of the fish it does eat are *not* cutthroat, and since cutthroat are by far the most numerous fish in the area, perhaps it could be speculated that

*The white pelican catches cutthroat in its cavernous bill, but does not carry
them there. Instead, fish are partially swallowed, transported to the nest, then
regurgitated for offspring, as shown here.*

in some way, comptetition from its smaller cousin, the osprey,
influences the eagle's choice of food.

The osprey, a major consumer of trout, comes each year
to Yellowstone from as far south as Costa Rica to raise its
young on the wealth of cutthroat, which make up over 90
percent of its diet. The osprey, however, is not a scavenger.
Instead, it specializes in catching smaller fish from the deeper
waters of the lake. Its powerful wings and sharp talons make
it a superior fisherman, and in the air it can often outmaneuver
a large eagle attempting to steal its catch. This is fortunate;

since it fishes far out in the lake and has farther to fly back to its nest, it therefore runs a greater risk of having its food "hijacked" along the way.

Although an individual osprey can usually hold its own against the bald eagle, unfortunately the species is not holding its own against the encroachments of civilization, even within the park, where less than 2 percent of the land area is affected by people. The decline in osprey numbers is thought to be due to human disturbance, and/or to pesticide residues in waters where ospreys fish along their migration paths. Such chemicals are ingested by fish and absorbed by the ospreys when the fish are eaten. Pesticide poisons can cause the birds' eggs to be overly thin-shelled and brittle, and to break before the young ones hatch. It's another reminder of how fragile and interconnected all the lifeways on our planet are, and that even a great refuge like Yellowstone can do little to protect the future of species that must migrate in order to reach park boundaries.

Filming the osprey provided us with some of the most difficult conditions we encountered all summer. Because of the vulnerable status of the osprey, its major nesting areas, like those of the white pelican, were also off-limits to motorboats. Our solution was to go in as far as we could, and drop David Huie off in the inflatable raft with a Photosonics high-speed camera and a 600-mm telephoto lens. He rowed in to one of the islands, then located a nest and climbed more than 100 feet up into a nearby live spruce. He chose the spruce because it not only overlooked a great view of the lake, but also an osprey nest in the top of a bare snag about seventy-five feet away. On that first trip, he carried with him a "high hat" (a short, tripod-mounted piece of equipment), which he roped to a limb. Then he lashed some big sheets of camouflage material over the high hat and left them in the tree, fairly well hidden by branches and needles.

On his first visit, he stayed only about an hour, just long enough to get some of the equipment in place. He let the ospreys grow accustomed to that for several days. Then we dropped him off from the boat again, and with the aid of a flashlight, he climbed the tall tree in predawn darkness, wrapped himself up in the camouflage material, and was able to film the ospreys without disturbing them. David stuck to this schedule for three days' worth of filming, coming down from his perch and rowing back across the lake in semidarkness, arriving at our camp in time to share a meal around the campfire.

Over those several days of filming, we observed that the family group of mother, father, and two unfledged young ate only one fish among them per day. This surprised us, since some of the scientific reports we had read said that ospreys eat more fish than that. For that matter, having seen a much smaller kingfisher eat a dozen proportionately sized minnows in one morning, I would have thought that ospreys would eat more fish than that. Although we saw the parent birds miss more often than they catch fish, that's normal; yet the fact that they ate so few trout certainly didn't mean that there were few fish to eat. We could find no completely satisfying explanation.

We also got quite a bit of footage of the ospreys out on the lake, filming right from the bow of our largest boat as one or another of these fish hawks flew in front of or alongside it, and occasionally dived in feet first to snag a trout. It took the birds a few hours to get used to our boat trailing along, but with a long lens we managed to stay back about 100 yards, and soon the birds proceeded to fish in an undisturbed manner. The lake was rarely smooth, but even when going 30 to 35 miles per hour in the boat, the viewer never senses that the cameraman is bouncing along on the bow of a boat. On the other hand, I was reminded of it for several days afterwards by my black-and-blue camera eye, the socket bruised by the eyepiece when we smacked into the waves.

Perhaps the most amusing—and thought-provoking—incident of the whole summer happened while we were filming ospreys. One day David Huie had rowed to the island to film the osprey family at their nest. John King was also out of camp —in fact, he was about fifty feet below the lake's surface, filming some underwater plants. Greg Hensley had hiked half

The osprey, a smaller cousin of the bald eagle, comes from as far south as Central America each summer to raise its young on the wealth of cutthroat to be found in Yellowstone Park.

a mile off to check on a time-lapse camera, and my brother Marshall was away down the shore filming seagulls from a camouflaged canvas blind. Which left me alone in camp. Camp at the moment consisted of our large boat tied up to an old plank dock, and a tent set up on land next to a small firepit. Our equipment was piled every which way inside the foul-weather cabin of the boat, and draped outside all over the deck and rails was a motley array of jeans, socks, boots, and assorted diving gear hung out in the sun to dry. It looked less like a fishing boat and more like a gypsy jamboree. I had my camera set up on the makeshift dock in front of a small aquarium full of lake water, and was trying to focus my macro-lens on some tiny freshwater shrimp suspended in the water, when along came a park ranger in his boat. He pulled up alongside, tied his boat to the little dock, and stepped onto it, right next to me.

"What are you filming?" he asked casually.

"We're doing a little story on the cutthroat trout," I told him from down on my knees, still trying to focus on the almost microscopic shrimp.

"Oh?" he said. "Where?"

I glanced up at him, a little puzzled by his question. Then I realized that he couldn't see the almost microscopic shrimp that I was trying to film in what to him must have looked like an aquarium full of nothing but clear water.

Brought back to human reality by his presence looming over me, I looked around. As I haltingly started to point toward this person or that person, I realized that there were no other humans in sight.

"Where?" I repeated, gesturing lamely in the directions where everyone had gone. "Well, everywhere!"

He stared at me, studying the camera and the "empty" aquarium, while I gazed up over his head at the crystal-blue sky, and listened to a pair of ravens croaking in the distance. I became aware of the gently creaking dock, the quietly lapping water, my stiff legs and sore knees, and a small salty drop of sweat in the corner of my eyepiece eye. I began to feel very uncomfortable.

Finally the ranger asked, "Do you have any cutthroat trout in your possession?"

We were in a catch-and-release area of the park, which meant that the trout could be fished for, but if caught, they had to be released back into the water if they were over thirteen inches in length.

"No," I said.

"And you say you're filming the story of the cutthroat trout?"

"Yes . . . everywhere," I answered, relieved that somehow he seemed to be beginning to understand what I couldn't explain or show him.

He looked down again at the camera, the aquarium, and me, still on my knees on the wooden plank dock.

"Could I see some identification?"

I realized with a shock that this man thought I was crazy! He was examining me in the same cautious way that a city cop might look at a stumbling drunk on the street. It suddenly struck me that I *was*, after all, dressed only in my underwear, having just undressed from the dive I'd made to gather the tiny shrimp, and I was all alone thirty miles from nowhere, and I was down on my knees filming an "empty" aquarium.

As the absurdity of the situation became apparent, I shook my head and started to laugh. Not just a little chuckle, but a full belly-roar. The ranger stepped back a few paces, then a few more, and almost tripped over the gunwhale of his boat. The more stunned and confused he looked, the louder I laughed. By then he certainly must have been completely convinced that I was nuts, if he hadn't been before. Facing me, he carefully backed off the dock onto his own boat, untied the lines, started the engine, and slowly idled away.

Later that week, when we had wrapped up that part of our filming and were pulling into the dock at Bridge Bay Marina for a few days, I happened to see that same ranger. But he quickly averted his eyes and strode briskly away. I never did have the chance to explain to him just what was going on.

What *was* going on, when I look back on it, was one of the best summers I've ever spent. We exposed enough wonderful footage to edit into *three* fascinating half-hour programs: "Cutthroat—Part 1: Yellowstone Lake," "Cutthroat—Part 2: Yellowstone River," and "Cutthroat—Part 3: Grizzly Creek." We were able to tell the complete story, not only of a single species, but of an entire ecosystem. We were able to make the point that the once-diminished trout population has recovered—due in large part to careful planning and management on the part of the Park Service—enough to resume its ancient, important role in feeding otters, bears, eagles, ospreys, pelicans, and seagulls, as well as human fishermen. Best of all, we had fun doing it.

Yet the experience on the dock, strange as it might have seemed to the ranger, gave me a chance to reflect back on fifteen years of filming, and to understand something very important for myself. It's this: the programs we make may be based on real life, but they are definitely *not* real in the sense that the viewer is watching what really happened during a half-hour in the wild. Even we cameramen often don't see what we're filming at the time we film it, and many discoveries are made in the editing room. What *is* real, and very satisfyingly so, is the *whole process*, from conceiving a story to getting out in the wild to film it to viewing the finished program. This process in all its complexity and interdependency is a kind of marvelous ecosystem in itself. And its illusory qualities, combined with the way it does reflect the reality of life in the wild, makes it a whole interconnected way of life.

A LIFE WITH WILDLIFE: THE MAGIC OF FILM

What I love most about producing the Wild America *series is getting out in the wild to film. No matter how difficult or uncomfortable the conditions, I always find the contact with wildlife exciting.*

To me, the most interesting aspect of filmmaking is that it's a way of capturing the present and preserving it for the future. Even as a child, I thought this process was magical, and I still do. What makes it even more exciting is that today, the boundaries of what we call the present have been greatly expanded. Not too many years ago, a picture of an animal standing in the middle of a meadow chewing its cud was a good enough scene for a wildlife film—so long as it was not too shaky, too dark or too light, and just so you got the ears and tail of the animal in the frame. Since then, photographic techniques have advanced by leaps and bounds until there's almost no place we can't go with our cameras. Almost any geographical location on earth is accessible, as is the inside of the most secluded den or nest, or even the inside of an animal's body. Cameras, with the help of highly specialized lenses, microscopes, and fiber optics (and who knows what else that's being invented this very moment), can see more than the human eye, and often reveal more than the human mind can comprehend without assistance.

From my early teens on, I wanted to learn to use the camera as an extension of my eye and as a way to record what my memory could recall only imperfectly. I wanted to use the camera's special properties to slow down time and collapse space so that I could see beyond the ordinary appearance of things and discover the secrets of wild creatures and their ways. And I wanted to share my discoveries with others. I've always loved showing people things that they couldn't otherwise see on their own: an oak tree sprouting from an acorn in time-lapse, or a flower opening from bud to full blossom; baby woodpeckers hidden in a hollow tree nest, or baby kingfishers in the dark of a riverbank cave; cutthroat trout in the spasm of mating, or merganser ducks diving underwater in a silver slipstream of bubbles. I love the surprising and even the freakish, but I also love the ordinary, especially when I discover, by filming it, the things that make it extraordinary. And especially when I can share what I've found with others.

This fascination with the possibilities of film is what has led me along what's become my path in life, at the center of which is my dedication to wildlife. Just as illusion and reality are united in filmmaking, I'm always amazed at the extent to which the world of film and the world of wild creatures have combined to make my whole life an interconnected web. Together, these two worlds have touched every part of my experience and continue to link past with present, personal with professional, in a very special way that makes me feel like one of the luckiest people alive.

Looking back, I see that my first big adventure, filming Alaskan wildlife, led to my second, traveling on safari in Africa. My dismay at the death I saw in Africa brought me back to America, to film the life and vitality of bighorn sheep. Filming bighorn set me on the road of recording the plight of our disappearing native species. Documenting endangered creatures made me realize that the most persecuted of all are the predators. My interest in restoring predators to their rightful habitat resulted in the two years spent with Griz. Raising Griz opened me up to the very special world of animal childhood, and filming "Wild Babies" made me even more aware of the incredible diversity of our native wildlife heritage. At that point the opportunity to do the *Wild America* series came along, and I was able, suddenly, to make programs about every aspect of that heritage.

None of that, though, could have been possible for me without the interested support of those closest to me. My family has always been very important to me, and very much involved in my filmmaking pursuits. As I've said, not only did my mother nurture my interest in wildlife and my father encourage me in mechanical and technical pursuits like photography, but both parents totally supported my decision to follow a career in wildlife photography at a time when most of my friends were being admonished to sign up with a corporation or join the army. And my parents not only encouraged me verbally, but backed me all the way with material support as well. They stood by me when things got difficult, and they took as many risks as I did. Best of all, their backing was never perfunctory—"my kid right or wrong"—but stemmed from a genuine interest in what I was doing. My mother even edited a number of sequences for my African film, so she could send me messages in Botswana about what scenes had been filmed successfully and what I still needed to try for.

They did the same for my brothers and sister, and their reinforcement helped us to grow individually, and also kept us close as a family. My brother Mark and I worked together on many projects, some that I originated, some that were his idea, and some that we worked so closely on that I doubt if it matters which was whose. We invented time-lapse techniques, developed a quick-release, camera-carrying backpack, and in general had a lot of fun being serious about what we were doing. Now that he has his own film production company, we're both too busy to do much together, but we're always interested in each other's latest projects.

Marshall, too, has gone on to other things, though we still see each other frequently, and take camping trips together in Yellowstone. And for many years Marshall's assistance as camera and sound man, reliable technical expert and master "fixer"—not to mention good company—has been invaluable in camps we shared from Arkansas to Montana. While my sister, Mari, hasn't been part of our productions, she's always interested in and supportive of what each of us is doing.

Film as a way of life not only includes the family I grew up in, but the one that's growing up around me. Even back when we were engaged, Diane accompanied me on several filming trips, and occasionally did some of the filming herself. Diane has appeared in a number of *Wild America* programs, and some of the fan mail we get comes addressed to her. More important, she's been my sounding board, financial advisor, and emotional guide ever since we met, and has always had a beneficial influence on the direction of our programs. Though now she has little to do with the day-to-day making of the programs, she stays informed about what's happening as far as television trends go. "Don't try to be corny on-camera," she'll warn me, or "that program has two minutes too much music," or "people want to see the pretty, gentle side of nature as well as the dramatic, predatory one." It helps.

My daughter Hannah has been part of the series since before she was old enough to walk. She's a natural actress and loves to be on-camera even though she's smart enough to pay no attention to the camera itself. With her debut in "Wild

Wings," she illustrated a central point we wished to make about how fascinating and accessible birds are for people of all ages. She had a major part in "Tracking Wildlife," co-starred in "Fishers in the Family," and ran away with the show in "Growing Up Wild," which was a program I made in her honor, in a way. While some of it was about baby animals growing up, its main theme was how rewarding it is for baby humans to grow up with wild animals in their lives. I'm sure Hannah would agree, and I'm bracing myself for the day when she asks me if she can borrow not my car, but my camera!

Friends are another important element in my life, and in this case too, filming wildlife has for the most part enhanced the ties of friendship. I've received invaluable help and support, as well as insight into human nature, from friends like David Huie and C. C. Lockwood, whom I've known since childhood. How many people can say they've spent months camping and hiking around in the wilderness with their best friends, and ended up making a living from doing so? David and C.C. have been my travel partners in many filming adventures, and have each remained in related fields: C.C. as a wildlife still photographer, David as a cinematographer and sound recordist.

And I've been influenced by others as well, some of whom I may not have known as long or as well, but whose work and attitude I also respect. Most of them have something to do with wildlife: naturalists and biologists, veterinarians and lumberjacks, hunters and trappers, park rangers and outdoor people of all types, and a number of indoor types as well. In fact, if I weren't doing what I'm doing, I'd probably be doing what one or another of *them* is doing: keeping track of grizzlies or elk in Yellowstone, guiding fishermen or fighting forest fires in Alaska, studying the reproductive habits of elephant seals or—who knows, feeding elephants at the Washington Zoo.

In fact, I know that if I weren't making films about wild animals, I'd be involved with them in some other way. On the other hand—and this seems even more interesting to me—I *wouldn't* be making films about other things. Though both aspects of my life give me a great deal of satisfaction, and now seem inseparable, animals came into my life before cameras, and they still come first.

Combined, however, the two provide me with the most

fulfilling work experience I can imagine. And although I usually spend fourteen or more hours a day on the job, I don't think of it as real work; it's just an extension of interests I'd be pursuing anyway. As a means of earning a living, producing the *Wild America* series offers me more variety, challenge, and creative opportunity than any ten jobs I can think of. Making films for public television, with all the inherent deadlines and responsibilities, requires a strong business sense as much as a creative sense. Fortunately, that aspect is seldom a problem, since my staff is a competent, highly motivated team that works well together and whose members are willing to take responsibility. They do the important details of picture and sound editing, research and writing, bookkeeping and promotion, plus some of the filming and sound recording and even composing music. This frees me to handle things no one else can take care of, such as planning each year's programs. The planning process is one of the more satisfying aspects of producing *Wild America*, since it gives me an excuse to do massive amounts of reading, and I'm always learning something new about wildlife.

And to create these programs, I often get to do what is still my favorite aspect of being a wildlife film producer: getting out in the wild to film. I love every moment of being out in the woods, the mountains, the swamps, even the tundra or desert. No matter how much hard work, ugly weather, nasty terrain, and just plain drudgery is involved, at least I'm out where the animals are, filming sights that I hope others will find as exciting as I do. That always gives me an exhilarating sense of freedom, and however bad the working conditions get, I always figure they're no worse for me than they are for the creatures I'm filming.

Though I also act as host and narrator for the programs I produce, I still think of myself first and foremost as a cinematographer. It's hard to put my finger on any one reason why hauling around seventy-five pounds of camera gear can result in such satisfaction. Perhaps part of the thrill for me lies in bringing all of my senses, my intuition, manual dexterity, physical coordination, alertness, and timing into play during those intense moments of rolling film. I probably feel much like a predator does when it pounces: I lose the sense of what

I'm doing, and become totally absorbed in my quarry's behavior. Camerawork becomes second nature. Much of my success in filming comes out of the skills I learned hunting. But in filming, I *feel* more like a wild predator than like a hunter. I'm concentrating on more than just that one spot where I'm going to put the bullet—I'm focused on the whole animal and every move it makes.

On the other hand, since I'm not out to kill the animal, but to capture its spirit, in a sense I'm also like Stone Age hunters, who, as some believe, drew bison and elk on cave walls not to make art, but to bring success in hunting those wild animals. They tried to capture an animal's spirit in the drawing as part of the process of capturing the animal with their spears. In that way, in making films of wild animals, I sometimes feel like a prehistoric hunter set down in the twentieth century, capturing an animal's true spirit rather than adhering to any academic notion of making "art." A major part of film magic to me is being able to capture the spirit and essence of a

If I weren't making films about wild animals, I'd be involved with them in some other way—wildlife is my number one interest. On the other hand, I know I wouldn't be making films on any other subject. Here I join Griz in her number one sport—sliding down a snowbank.

creature, and I think that when primitive people refuse to be photographed because they fear the camera may seize their soul, they may be intuitively right.

But I'd be fooling myself if I didn't admit that in some ways filming wild animals is for me a substitute for hunting them. I enjoy the same ancient patterns in this contemporary form of the chase—the age-old excitement of tracking, stalking, sighting, and capturing prey. Other similarities between hunting and filming can be seen in matters of technique: you sight down the barrel (or lens) and focus your prey (or subject) in the cross-hairs. You squeeze, rather than jab, the camera button—just the way you would squeeze the trigger of a rifle. My early years of wandering around the woods of Arkansas with a gun made me a better cameraman in that, like any good hunter, human or animal, I can sense what an animal's going to do next—whether it's going to run, freeze in its tracks, or just sniff around.

Filmmaking also satisfies my attraction to the mechanical and technical. I grew up around racing cars and engines as well as guns and cameras, and thanks to my father, I've always appreciated the workings of precision machinery. I'm always reading the latest camera and equipment magazines, I take pleasure in talking shop with other cinematographers about equipment and techniques, and though I don't spend budget money on every latest gadget, I do enjoy using the best available camera and sound-recording equipment and pride myself on keeping it in top condition.

Other technical aspects of film production—editing machines, computers, electronic synthesizers, and so on—also enhance my enjoyment of this creative process. I'm always fascinated, when we do our final post-production mixes and transfers at Western Cine film lab and Wickerworks video studios in Denver, by the space-age technology available to us. Thirty-foot banks of electronic dials, levers, buttons, and

Filmmaking satisfies my interest in things mechanical and technical. Shooting with two cameras at once, as I am here, doubles the challenge of correctly matching focus, speed, and aperture settings, but allows me to use two different lenses to follow a subject.

glowing lights enable us to make the most minute or complex adjustments in sound or color balance, to generate multistage range maps, and to combine taped elements with film transfers in creating the finalized programs.

My life with wildlife and film together means that I'm always learning and I'm always creating. What better combination could there be? And what better goal could there be than to unite all of these aspects—technical, organizational, financial, cinematographic, human, and artistic—to serve a single purpose, which perhaps can be wrapped up in a simple word: storytelling. It may sound odd to some people that I don't start with a loftier goal, like saving the universe, or at least saving habitat for wildlife. But all through history, our most important and lasting messages have been handed down by songsters and storytellers. For me, these have always been special people who can combine wisdom with childlike wonder and come up with meaningful tales that satisfy our need to know about the world and our place in it.

Human beings are communicators. It's innate, as essential to our success on earth as the wings of a bird are to its success. And to communicate, we tell stories. As children, my brothers and I demanded a bedtime story before we went to sleep, and my daughter Hannah does the same thing now. "Tell me a story, Daddy." We like to be entertained, but even more, I suspect, we want to make order out of the seeming chaos around us. Stories show us how the puzzle pieces fit together, how to make sense out of the grand mystery of nature and out of the greatest mystery of all—ourselves. So I like to think of myself as a storyteller beckoning to the audience and saying, "Come here, look at this. Isn't it wonderful!"

Breath, life, and soul were called *anima* in Latin, from which comes our word "animal." I can't help but think this derivation implies our incredible sense of identity with other creatures who share this world. For most of our time on earth, our relationship to wild animals has been as hunter to prey, and we've shown great respect not only for the animals that fed us, but for our fellow predators. Even today, this admiration is reflected in the way we nickname ourselves after wild animals. Our sports teams are called Bears and Lions and Wildcats. We get together at Elk and Moose lodges, and Boy Scouts earn Wolf and Eagle badges. We like to compare ourselves with, or to strive for, the strength, freedom, grace, and seeming ease of accomplishment that we see in wild animals.

Primitive people admired the creatures they hunted, but watching wildlife wasn't weekend recreation, and it most certainly wasn't done in the warmth and comfort of a living room. Watching wild animals, and watching them closely, was a daily matter of life and death. The slightest raising of hair, ruffling of feathers, twitching of ears, or narrowing of eyes were powerful signals that could mean feast or famine for the hunter. But we don't depend on wild animals in such a crucial and life-giving way now—or do we?

I think we do. Wild animals may no longer provide our daily meals, but they refresh us and renew our spirits. They're important as symbols of what once was and what may yet be. Nature's wild and free creatures are able to tell us about life's complexity in a simple and wonderful way, by just being themselves in all their beauty and wonder. We cherish the idea that if we could find a way to live in balance and harmony with what wildlife is left, we'd have found the lost piece of an eternal puzzle that enables us to rest at peace with our ancestral home, planet earth, the only paradise we can ever know for sure.

The trouble is, not much is left. The woods that I roamed as a kid are gone, and the lake where we went swimming and fishing is now an immense parking lot surrounding another shopping center. The sad part is that I'm not the only one who doesn't recognize the place where they grew up, or who's lost that connection with a personal past. Part of the reason that I love Yellowstone and return to it whenever I can is that it's always the same. I know whenever I go there that I'll see the same peaks rising above the same forests and lakes, the same meadows lining the same rivers—sometimes even the same animals. Maybe they'll be doing different things at different times of year, but I certainly won't go there one summer and find a shopping mall where Old Faithful used to spout, or snowshoe out to Hayden Valley some winter and find a paved-over parking lot.

Part of our attraction to wild animals, I think, is that they provide a similar sense of continuity with our past and with our own deepest feelings. Wild creatures have always roamed the earth and always should, or so we think. Yet relatively few people have direct, daily contact with wildlife. At the beginning of the twentieth century, 75 percent of the population lived in rural areas. We weren't strangers to nature or to the outdoors then. By contrast, today 75 percent of us live in cities with populations greater than 50,000. And of course, it's not that we have gone to the cities, but rather that the cities have come to us, expanding and engulfing natural areas and making us strangers to each other, to the land, and especially to the creatures that once shared it with us.

Perhaps that's what makes it even more important to us to get out into what's left of nature, to seek out the wildlife that remains. Fully half our population, according to a recent national survey, takes part in some kind of wildlife-related activity. Although there are proportionately fewer hunters today than fifty years ago, their actual numbers are higher—according to recent figures, nearly 20 million hunting licenses and more than 40 million fishing licenses were sold. Many of those licenses, some researchers contend, represent an excuse to get out in the woods, rather than any burning desire to bag a trophy or fill a creel. More and more people are realizing the truth of something Thoreau once noted, to the effect that "most people who fish their whole lives never realize it's not the fish they're after." Records show there are more than 70 million visits annually to our national parks, and backpacking, kayaking, cross-country skiing, hiking, and mountain climbing draw record numbers of city dwellers back to the land and the animals. People who watch birds outnumber people who hunt them—and in fact outnumber hunters of all kinds. And we're "capturing" wildlife in yet another way: a recent survey estimated that there are as many as 18 million amateur nature photographers in this country. Perhaps this shows the more separated we become from nature, the more important it becomes to us to stay in touch with its rhythms.

The other way that we're becoming increasingly involved with wildlife is in gathering around our "electronic campfires" —our television sets—watching any number of wildlife or nature programs. Those programs help us by showing how animals, like us, must cooperate with each other and must also fully and watchfully participate in an often dangerous world. We often learn more about ourselves by learning about animals. Through them, we have a chance to reestablish our nourishing connection with nature, and to look for the underlying priniciples, meaning, and beauty that we've almost lost to a world of mortgage payments, time clocks, and computer printouts. Wildlife programs feed our desire to discover a pattern and meaning in life's processes, a rare freedom and wildness in our increasingly plasticized world, an ancient magic and mystery to sustain us in these stressful times.

Just as wild creatures can help us understand the pattern of life, so too they can help us comprehend the puzzle of death. They can help us to look beyond ourselves, to see that the survival of a species is more important than the life of an individual, that the health of the ecosystem or planet depends on a great diversity of thriving species, and that in any healthy system, some animals kill and feed upon others. Death is such an inevitable occurrence that nature makes provision for it. For example, as many as 70 percent of certain wild youngsters, both predator and prey, die in their first few months of life. Nature overproduces, and her surplus is the bounty that feeds us all.

But the death of a wild animal, especially a baby or a prey species, reminds us of our own frailness, our own mortality. It makes us angry because we can't do anything about it, and we rage against its inevitability. To the sensitive, nature sometimes seems too red of tooth and claw, too violent altogether. Of course, this is not the case, but just as we don't want to face death in our society, so we turn away from it in the wild. In doing so, we miss one of the most important, dramatic, and essential manifestations of nature.

The only time I object to death on camera is when it's gratuitous, when it has nothing to do with these natural processes. What we don't need more of is the "Hollywood" kind of storytelling—wolves attacking pioneer families, killer whales sinking boats, grizzlies mauling trappers, and a whole crew of "villain" animals doing in "innocent," usually soft and furry, "victims." Those kinds of distortions are destructive

371

because they get people thinking of wild animals as deliberate monsters instead of the curious or hungry creatures they usually are. Of course, they aren't tame, and they can be dangerous, but most of all they just want to mind their own business.

Several eye-opening studies have been done by Dr. Stephen Kellert of the School of Forestry and Environmental Studies at Yale University on our attitudes toward animals in general and wildlife in particular. His results clearly demonstrated considerable public interest in and affection for animals, and above all a willingness to support wildlife conservation in this country. Forty-four percent of those he interviewed had fished, 35 percent had read a book about wildlife, 25 percent had birded, and 14 percent had hunted. More than three-fourths of his population sample said they had watched wildlife programs on television. These statistics point to the potential power television can exert as a force for changing our attitudes about animals and about the wilderness.

I think some of our attitudes towards wildlife and wildlife management are stale, outdated, even destructive, and need to be changed. Good wildlife films are helping to accomplish this. Their very popularity is proof of their influence. Even though major networks have shied away from more challenging wildlife programming, PBS and some of the cable channels have filled in the gap. Ironically, the networks' loss is Public Television's gain: of the twenty-five most popular programs ever shown on PBS, sixteen have been about wildlife.

Most of these programs do their utmost to raise the level of consciousness and understanding of their viewers. Some of them, I think, get a little too earnest, with sequence after sequence showing biologists with tranquilizers, ear tags, and radio-collars manipulating animals and altering habitat with their studies. It's not that their work isn't important; it's vital and essential and I wish them great success. But sometimes so much emphasis and attention is given to an abstract problem that the wild animals themselves—the reasons *why* anyone would care to solve the problem in the first place—are neglected.

With the *Wild America* programs, we don't ignore the problems, but we do try to sweeten them by showing *why* we should care about what happens to these animals. The "why" is that they're beautiful, intelligent, fascinating, funny, and just plain important. And we try to demonstrate this importance by showing how they fit into the ecosystem, how they interact with other creatures, how they reproduce and raise their young, how and what their babies learn, how they escape from their enemies, and even how they die. And sometimes we're even able to show the eerie, familiar ways in which they can be like you and me.

In the classic definition, beauty is seen as a harmony both *within* an object and *between* that object and ourselves. From our human point of view, I think that's the kind of beauty we look for when we seek out wild animals, either in their natural habitat or through the transformation of film. We're looking for that harmony both within ourselves and with the outside world that wild creatures possess and express with such grace and ease. In connecting with nature, we find a way toward the harmony of our own bodies, minds, and spirits.

At least this is what I feel my own very fortunate existence has been about. Making wildlife films is a magical way of life for me, and I hope to continue doing it for as long as I can strap on my showshoes. I've so many plans and ideas for new films and new stories that I feel I could spend three lifetimes producing them and hardly begin to scratch the surface.

There's yet another sense in which I could compare making wildlife films to ancient people's way of hunting. They drew pictographs of bison and caribou not only to capture the spirit of an individual animal and to assure success in hunting it, but also as a way of pacifying the gods who could see to it that game continued to be plentiful, season after season. Unlike us, primitive people weren't interested in having "more" each year. "Enough" would do. As long as the herds of game did not migrate elsewhere, were not wiped out by disease or natural catastrophe, or were not killed off by other tribes, they and their children would have enough to eat, and it probably never occurred to them to ask for more.

In the same way, making wildlife films is to me a way of asking—insisting would be more like it—that the herds survive, along with the predators that keep them healthy and the myriads of other creatures, each of which have an essential role in maintaining a stable and inhabitable environment for us as well as for themselves. Of course, since we've now destroyed so much of our wildlife, I would like to see "more," but if what I do simply helps to maintain the status quo against all the powerful forces still working to diminish wildlife, I'll feel that I've at least accomplished something worthwhile.

To paraphrase a very wise and perceptive man named Gandhi, if animals could speak, what they'd say would make a very sad case against humankind. Since they can't, I'll take it upon myself to be their voice—the voice of my alter ego, the bighorn sheep, of my all-time favorite, the lynx, and of the animal I'd most like to be in another lifetime, the river otter. And of the overlooked, the misunderstood, the loners, the unattractive critters that nobody notices. Just as they speak to me in all their magic and mystery, with all their wisdom and wildness, so I will speak for them, and for a forever wild America.

*I have so many plans and ideas for new wildlife films that I could
spend three lifetimes making films and hardly scratch the surface.
So, until next time, enjoy our Wild America!*

BLACK-AND-WHITE PHOTO ACKNOWLEDGMENTS

page 4: Animals Animals/Marty Stouffer Productions **5:** Marty Stouffer Productions/C.C. Lockwood photo **7, 10 and 20:** Agnes and Martin Stouffer Sr. **9:** Animals Animals/ Marty Stouffer Productions **69:** Animals Animals/C.C. Lockwood **71:** Animals Animals/ Marty Stouffer Productions **75:** Marty Stouffer Productions/C.C. Lockwood photo **85:** Animals Animals/C.C. Lockwood **86:** Animals Animals/Marty Stouffer Productions **97:** Animals Animals/Lynn Stone **100 (top):** Marty Stouffer Productions/Mark Stouffer **107:** C.C. Lockwood **109:** Stouffer Enterprises/John King photo **113:** C.C. Lockwood **118:** Animals Animals/Marty Stouffer Productions **120:** Animals Animals/Marty Stouffer Productions **122 (top):** Animals Animals/Marty Stouffer Productions **122 (bottom):** Marty Stouffer Productions/John King photo **125:** Marty Stouffer Productions/Mark and Marty Stouffer **127:** Marty Stouffer Productions/David Huie photo **131:** C.C. Lockwood **133, 135, 145, 148, 149, 150, 153, 156, 159:** Marty Stouffer Productions/Mark Stouffer photo **167:** Animals Animals/L.L. Rue III **168:** C.C. Lockwood **170:** Animals Animals/Michael Habicht **171:** Animals Animals/Breck Kent **173:** Animals Animals/Oxford Scientific Films **183:** Animals Animals/Marty Stouffer Productions **189:** Marty Stouffer Productions/John King photo **191:** Marty Stouffer Productions/David Huie photo **193:** Animals Animals/L.L. Rue III **195:** Animals Animals/L.L. Rue III **197:** Animals Animals/Irene Vandermolen **198:** Animals Animals/C.C. Lockwood **210–11 (filmstrip):** Marty Stouffer Productions/David Huie **215:** Marty Stouffer Productions/ David Huie photo **226:** Animals Animals/Joe McDonald **228:** Animals Animals/C.C. Lockwood **241:** Marty Stouffer Productions/John King photo **243:** Marty Stouffer Productions/C.C. Lockwood photo **247:** Marty Stouffer Productions/John King photo **251:** Animals Animals/Mark Wilson **255:** C.C. Lockwood **257:** Animals Animals/C.C. Lockwood **269, 271:** Marty Stouffer Productions/Steve Maslowski **275:** Animals Animals/ R.F. Head **277:** Marty Stouffer Productions/C.C. Lockwood photo **283:** Marty Stouffer Productions/David Huie photo **285:** Marty Stouffer Productions/Michelle Brandt-Morton photo **288:** Animals Animals/Charles Palek **289:** Animals Animals/John Gerlach **291:** Animals Animals/Zig Leszczynski **294:** Animals Animals/George Bryce **295:** Animals Animals/L.L. Rue III **299:** Animals Animals/Mark Wilson **301:** Marty Stouffer Productions/Mark Stouffer photo **304:** Marty Stouffer Productions/Jim Balog photo **312:** C.C. Lockwood **313:** Animals Animals/Breck Kent **326, 329:** Marty Stouffer Productions/ Greg Hensley photo **331:** Earth Scenes/Lynn Stone **341:** Marty Stouffer Productions/ David Huie photo **347:** Marty Stouffer Productions/Marshall Stouffer photo **352:** Animals Animals/Harry Engels **355:** Animals Animals/L.L. Rue III **359:** Marty Stouffer Productions/John King photo **365:** Marty Stouffer Productions/Mark Stouffer photo **367:** Marty Stouffer Productions/Diane Stouffer photo **375:** Marty Stouffer Productions/John King photo
All other photographs by Marty Stouffer Productions/Copyright MSP Ltd.

COLOR PHOTO ACKNOWLEDGMENTS

page C-1: Sequential of sow grizzly and caribou (seven images). Velma Harris photos **C-3:** *(both images)* C.C. Lockwood photos **C-4:** *(sequential)* Marty Stouffer Productions/ Greg Hayes photos **C-5:** *(goshawk)* Marty Stouffer Productions/Greg Hayes photo *(shrew)* Mark Stouffer *(raccoon)* C.C. Lockwood **C-6:** *(grizzly and cubs)* Mark Stouffer **C-7:** *(barred owls)* C.C. Lockwood **C-8:** *(both images)* C.C. Lockwood **C-9:** *(hummingbird nest)* Marty Stouffer Productions/John King photo **C-11:** *(cottonmouth rattlesnake)* C.C. Lockwood **C-12, C-13:** *(all photos)* Mark and Marty Stouffer
All other color photographs by Marty Stouffer Productions/Copyright MSP Ltd.

INDEX